Through Time

An Unauthorised and Unofficial History
of *Doctor Who*

THROUGH TIME

An Unauthorised and Unofficial History
of *Doctor Who*

ANDREW CARTMEL

continuum

NEW YORK • LONDON

2005

The Continuum International Publishing Group Inc
15 East 26 Street, New York, NY 10010

The Continuum International Publishing Group Ltd
The Tower Building, 11 York Road, London SE1 7NX

www.continuumbooks.com

Printed and bound in Great Britain by MPG Books Ltd, Bodmin, Cornwall

Library of Congress Cataloging-in-Publication Data
Cartmel, Andrew.
  Through time : an unauthorised and unofficial history of Doctor Who / by
Andrew Cartmel.
     p.   cm.
  Includes bibliographical references and index.
  ISBN-13: 978–0-8264–1734–3 (hardcover : alk. paper)
  ISBN-10: 0–8264–1734–5 (hardcover : alk. paper)
  ISBN-13: 978–0-8264–1732–9 (pbk. : alk. paper)
  ISBN-10: 0–8264–1732–9 (pbk. : alk. paper)
  1. Doctor Who (Television program)   2. Doctor Who (Television program)
I. Title.
PN1992.77.D6273C37   2005
791.45'72—dc22
                                                        2005028900

For Ben Aaronovitch,
without whom the story of Doctor Who
would be much less interesting

Contents

Acknowledgements

Special thanks are due to the following:

Jim Martens, who set the ball rolling.

David Barker and Gabriella Page-Fort for unfailing courtesy and patience in the face of overwhelming authorial provocation.

David J. Howe and Marc Platt and Marcus Hearn for sharing their expertise in all things Doctor Who.

Ben Aaronovitch for reading the manuscript and laughing in the right places.

And the BBC for giving new life to a great television classic.

Introduction

Another Book about *Doctor Who*

On 14 March 2005, I was ushered into the insulated hush of a BBC Radio recording booth in Broadcasting House near Oxford Circus, in central London.

I was given a pair of headphones, shown which microphone to use—one with a foam shield of a bright glaring green, so no problem remembering that. I was then left to my own devices as the enormously heavy door drifted silently shut behind me. In a minute or so, I would be on the air. I sat in the small quiet room. Voices came alive in my headphones. My producer, in Edinburgh, and my host, in Glasgow, said hello to me, warming me up for tonight's interview on the *Arts Show* for BBC Scotland.

I was being interviewed about my book *Script Doctor*, a candid account of what it had been like to be on the firing line as the script editor of *Doctor Who* for three of its most turbulent years. In those years, I had chosen the writers and shaped the show and now, over a decade later, the publication of my memoirs was cunningly timed to exploit the wave of publicity accompanying the return of *Doctor Who* to our screens.

It was a major cultural event. A new series of *Doctor Who* had been made by the BBC, the first since 1989. Interest in the show was rising steadily, and by the time the first episode aired in late March 2005 the media had been whipped into a positive frenzy.

In the weeks following my radio interview, the show debuted to much fanfare and settled down to a weekly terrestrial audience of over eight million viewers. It was a hit. At this point, I received a recording of my interview from Radio Scotland.

I listened to it, and I was just complacently concluding that I came over rather well. You'd never suspect my interviewer and I were sitting hundreds of miles apart, had never met each other, and couldn't see each other. Then I realised, with growing alarm, that I had committed the cardinal gaffe of referring to the Doctor's home planet as Skaro.

Of course, everyone knows this is the home planet of the Doctor's arch foes—the Daleks. The correct name for the Doctor's planet was Gallifrey.

On reflection, I was a little relieved. No fan would have made such a slip. But I was no fan. I had loved the show purely from the standpoint of someone working on it, labouring in the engine room.

Literally hundreds of books have been written about *Doctor Who*, mostly retellings of the Doctor's on-screen adventures. There have also been numerous works of exegesis. Many are scholarly and highly accurate works taking full account of the difference between Skaro and Gallifrey. Exhaustive and complete works.

I'm aiming at something rather different here. We won't be considering every *Doctor Who* story ever made; instead, we'll be taking a tour through what I regard as the best or most interesting or most characteristic ones.

Hopefully, this book is a little like Kingsley Amis's *The James Bond Dossier*, an affectionate, personal insider's account of a cultural phenomenon. A very British phenomenon. The most quirky science fiction drama ever made by the BBC. Or anywhere else.

❊   ❊   ❊

I first became aware of *Doctor Who* watching a few fragmentary episodes on our old black and white television in the basement of 208 Kings Drive, overlooking the muddy curves of the Red River in Manitoba. It certainly made an impression on me, a scary story about a sinister old scientist who was taking young people through space in a strange vehicle—a telephone box. The young people met some very scary monsters on their travels—including those evil and sinister robots called the Daleks. In fact, they turned out not to be robots; if you cracked open the metal casing of the Daleks then the slithering creature within was revealed. A sinister jellylike thing which looked spectacularly menacing despite—or perhaps because of—the crudity and limitation of our primitive black and white set.

That thing just came squirming out.

One crucial fact escaped me watching those key episodes there in my white two-story prairie house in the flood zone. The Doctor wasn't just a space traveller. He was also a *time* traveller. In a way, this book is going to be an exercise in time travel. In the following chapters we will become acquainted with the Doctors of the past and their adventures.

I should make clear that this is a book written from the point of view of a script editor on the show, which is not a bad point of view to have. It is, after all, this point of view that oversees the creation of the stories which power the show and give the show its identity. Important creative contributors such as the producers, actors, designers, composers, and directors are all given their due. But above all, we'll be looking here at the writers, script editors, and storytelling.

chapter 1

The First Doctor

Doctor Who comes from a tradition of British fantasy that flows from the general direction of *Alice in Wonderland* and Sherlock Holmes and comes by way of H. G. Wells and Nigel Kneale. It also embraces Troy Kennedy Martin and Dennis Potter en route.

In case any of these writers' names are unfamiliar, here's a sampling of their work. Wells, of course, was a novelist and wrote such late nineteenth century science fiction masterpieces as *The Time Machine, The Invisible Man,* and *War of the Worlds.* The other three are all screenwriters.

Nigel Kneale was a remarkable British writer who throughout the 1950s made science fiction not only respectable but astonishingly successful. The pubs emptied on nights when one of his *Quatermass* stories was on the television. Depending on whether you are cynical or not, this makes it all the more remarkable that his *Quatermass* scripts were so rich in character and depth and so intelligent. Other key works from Kneale were his BBC adaptation of George Orwell's *1984,* and his original (highly original) BBC television plays *The Creature* (later made into the feature film *The Abominable Snowman*), *The Road, The Year of the Sex Olympics,* and *The Stone Tape.*

Troy Kennedy Martin created the seminal police series *Z Cars* for the BBC before writing the classic heist movies *The Italian Job* and *Kelly's Heroes.* He would return to the BBC to write the astonishing quasi-science fiction thriller *Edge of Darkness.*

The late Dennis Potter is best known for *The Singing Detective* and *Pennies from Heaven,* serials that reinvented television drama.

While none of these luminaries ever wrote for *Doctor Who,* they influenced the show—and quite possibly vice versa.

The creator of *Doctor Who* was a Canadian named Sydney Newman who had made a name for himself as a producer at the CBC before immigrating to England. When *Doctor Who* debuted in 1963, Newman was the newly appointed Head of Drama at the BBC, having recently moved from a senior post at the British channel ABC, part of ITV, Independent Television.

Sydney Newman arrived at the BBC fresh from helping to create another British television classic, *The Avengers* at ABC. Sharing some key writers (including Terry Nation, creator of the Daleks), *Doctor Who* and *The Avengers* are both iconic 1960s shows which have demonstrated remarkable longevity. *Doctor Who* also strangely resembles *The Avengers* in that the true potential of the show only emerged after the first season.

And, as with *The Avengers*, it was the departure of the lead actor that led to a dramatic reinvention of the show's basic formula for *Doctor Who*.

In the case of *Doctor Who*, this reinvention hinged on the fact that the Doctor was an alien. He might *look* human, but he came from an advanced civilisation on a far off planet (as yet unspecified). Not just an enigmatic time traveller then, but one who wasn't even human. This alien being, it was decided, might well have the power to *regenerate*— that is, to cast off his old physical form and assume a new one. In other words, a new actor could start playing the same character.

This was shameless retrofitting, of course, something any good script editor might be called upon to come up with in a moment of crisis. To some it smacks of desperation; to others it is clearly a stroke of genius.

And it has certainly guaranteed the longevity of the show. At the moment, there is a theoretical upper limit on what might be the maximum number of regenerations for the Doctor. It's twelve. Or, wait a minute, is it thirteen?

In any case, this piece of holy writ is in itself no cause for alarm. No doubt when the crunch comes, some additional clever retrofitting will save the day.

The first actor to play the role, the man who might be said to have originated it, was William Hartnell. Hartnell was in his mid-fifties, though he could and did look considerably older in the role of the Doctor. He was an actor with a preference for playing comedy, but he was often cast as an unlikable character.

On 19 September 1963 the cameras rolled, and Hartnell found himself blinking in the glare of the lights at Ealing Studios as shooting began on the first ever episode of *Doctor Who*.

"An Unearthly Child"/"100,000 BC"
by Anthony Coburn

The first series of *Doctor Who* was produced by an ambitious young female producer, Verity Lambert, and the script editor was David Whitaker. This first story, a four-parter, was written by Anthony Coburn and directed by Waris Hussein. At this stage *Doctor Who* didn't feature official titles for complete stories (only for individual episodes), and the first adventure is variously referred to as "An Unearthly Child" (after the first episode), "The Tribe of Gum," or "100,000 BC." For the sake of convenience and clarity, and because I think "The Tribe of Gum" is a terrible title, we'll stick with "An Unearthly Child" for the opener and "100,000 BC" for the remaining three episodes.

At the time he first appeared on the screen as the Doctor, William Hartnell was only fifty-five years old, though to the astonished and pleasantly terrified children who comprised the bulk of his audience he looked vastly, unimaginably older. He was a crotchety, irascible (sometimes to the point of tedium), white-haired enigma. Indeed, it would turn out that the Doctor *was* vastly, unimaginably older. Centuries older, in fact. (His current declared age is something over 900 years.)

Hartnell's experience as an actor in films such as *Brighton Rock* and television sitcoms like *The Army Game* had done nothing to prepare him for the phenomenon that was to become *Doctor Who*. He was about to write his name in the pages of history.

"An Unearthly Child" begins with a London police constable patrolling in the mist, past some gates that are emblazoned with the faded words Foreman's Scrap Merchant. The cop wanders off and doesn't notice the gates open—spookily, as if of their own volition—and the camera probes inside the junkyard. At this point we could easily be watching one of the more conventional British television series of the period, a cosy police drama like *Dixon of Dock Green*, say, or the hit comedy with a junkyard setting, *Steptoe and Son*. Then we see the police telephone box standing in the middle of the yard, a kind of visual non sequitur, and we hear a faint eerie pulsing vibration. We begin to realise that we're entering uncharted territory.

Looking at it today, even with all its technical crudities, this first effort remains a rather compelling and atmospheric piece of work. All of Sydney Newman's basic concepts are in place. It's an engrossing science fiction serial, complete with cliff-hanger endings, about a mysterious stranger in the shape of an ill-tempered old man who turns out to be a voyager through space and time. His ship has the mind-bending quality of being larger inside than it is outside. It also has the ability to blend into its surroundings by imitating the appearance of an everyday object in its environment.

In the case of London in 1963, the everyday object chosen (apparently by writer Anthony Coburn) was a blue police telephone box. British TV was in black and white at the time, but people knew what colour it was supposed to be because everyone knew what a police call box looked like. Once a commonplace, these boxes now seem exotic. They were designed to allow communication between the cop on the beat and his home station as well as providing members of the public with a direct line to the police, and they were a reassuring and familiar sight on English streets at the time.

The police call box was just the first shape that the Doctor's chameleonlike ship was supposed to assume. For reasons of continuity and budget—or perhaps because people knew a good thing when they saw it—the Doctor's vehicle has remained stuck in this guise on most of its ensuing adventures, making for an entertainingly incongruous sight when it turned up among, say, the entourage of King Richard the Lionheart in the twelfth century Palestine. In fact, it looks splendidly incongruous even on the streets of London now, in the twenty-first century. Such telephone boxes largely vanished from the capital in the late 1960s, having been replaced by police radios. The blue police box is now iconic and almost uniquely identified with *Doctor Who*. Indeed the BBC had the savvy to purchase the copyright in the design.

The Doctor's vehicle, incidentally, is called the Tardis, an acronym for Time And Relative Dimensions in Space, although originally it was Dimension—as with Keith Richard's surname, the terminal "s" came and went. It's a name which, on reflection, makes very little sense; nevertheless, it remains memorable and impressive. Again, this imaginative contribution is credited to Anthony Coburn.

From the junkyard in "An Unearthly Child," the story takes us straight into Coal Hill School (a location we'll revisit twenty-five years later in "Remembrance of the Daleks"), a busy London comprehensive school where we meet the young teachers Ian Chesterton and Barbara Wright (William Russell and Jacqueline Hill). There is the lukewarm suggestion of an ongoing romance between Ian and Barbara, but as they stand chatting in the chemistry lab, the chief subject of their attention is a student called Susan Foreman. (Later in the story, when he is addressed as "Dr Foreman," the Doctor's blank incomprehension suggests that Susan adopted the name from the junkyard rather than the other way around.)

Susan is a fifteen-year-old problem child. But it's a peculiar sort of problem that she presents. "She knows more about science than I'll ever know," concedes Ian. Barbara has a similar problem with Susan's history lessons, but her main concern is that this talented student is falling behind and has refused an offer for Barbara to give her personal tuition at home. In fact, the whole issue of home seems to be a sensitive one. Susan has stated that her grandfather doesn't like strangers. The assertion that Susan is the Doctor's granddaughter will take some explaining later on, as the mystery and mythology of Doctor Who began to accrete around its central character.

Yet again, the man responsible for this key decision was evidently writer Anthony Coburn. In the book *Doctor Who: The Sixties*, David J. Howe, Mark Stammers, and Stephen James Walker describe how Susan was originally conceived as simply a young woman who travelled with the Doctor (exactly like Rose in the current series). Reportedly it was Coburn's worry that this relationship might be construed as sexual, and with an unwholesome age disparity (just for the record, at the time of making the first episode, Carole Ann Ford was twenty-three, making William Hartnell some thirty-two years her senior). This led to Coburn suggesting that Susan be changed in the story to the Doctor's granddaughter.

This might have temporarily held back the tide of prurient speculation, but even today, there are those who feel that there must be *something* in the Doctor's association with his travelling companions. This is perhaps because the Doctor has generally been cast as a strange and mysterious older man, while his companions are generally attractive young women. Some incarnations of the Doctor have also been dashing younger men. That only causes the speculation to heat up.

Coburn was an Australian writer who, like script editor David Whitaker, was on BBC staff when *Doctor Who* was in development. Having made his considerable mark on the show with this first story, Coburn would never write for *Doctor Who* again. He would go on to become a successful writer and producer elsewhere, but after his second attempt at a *Doctor Who* story was rejected, he didn't have anything more to do with the show.

In any case, in Coburn's seminal first episode, Susan's domestic situation arouses Barbara's curiosity, and she goes snooping around Susan's home address only to discover that there is no house there, just the junkyard we saw in the opening shots.

Accompanied by Ian, Barbara decides to confront Susan as school ends for the day. The teachers find her with a transistor radio pressed to her ear and doing the hand jive as she listens to a twangy guitar combo led by the uninspiringly named "John Smith" (sort of watered down John Barry Seven style protorock). Susan is the very picture of 1963 teenage normality here, except that she declines a lift home from her teachers, saying she likes walking in the dark. She thinks the dark is *mysterious*.

Here, as elsewhere, Anthony Coburn's writing is adept and concise, conjuring mood and character and atmosphere.

The teachers accept the rebuff and leave Susan with the book Barbara wanted to lend her. It's about the French Revolution and the cheapjack prop, hilariously, consists of a book with the words *The French Revolution* on its cover and nothing else. Susan leafs through it and frowns. "That's not right," she says, with the air of one who *knows*.

Meanwhile Ian and Barbara, the world's two most nosy teachers, decide to stake out 76 Totters Lane, Susan's home address. They park in Ian's car in the foggy street outside the junkyard and wait for her to turn up. As they watch, they continue to compare notes about Susan's strange behaviour. Barbara doesn't know how to account for a teenage girl who doesn't know how many shillings are in a pound. We then see a flashback to her history class. This is a brilliant little scene where the uncomfortable Susan looks like a rabbit in the headlights while her classmates laugh at her. "Of course," says the perturbed Susan, "the decimal system hasn't started yet."

This vignette cleverly establishes the alien nature of this "unearthly child" while also being a neat piece of social prophecy—in 1963 the decimalization of England's unwieldy currency was still nearly a decade away.

Not to be outdone, Ian also has a flashback, to his science class. Susan doesn't perform so impressively here though, spouting some gibberish about space being the fifth dimension, as if she wasn't aware that it's actually the first three. There is, however, some admirably eerie background music over these scenes, by Norman Kay.

Then Susan appears and enters the junkyard. Ian and Barbara follow, but Susan is nowhere to be seen. As they explore, Ian drops his flashlight, which provides an excuse for the continuing eeriness as they find the Tardis, which gives off a faint vibration. "It's alive," says Ian, meaning in an electrical sense—but he's right in more ways than he knows.

*   *   *

Then the Doctor appears, looking suitably dapper in his black hat and scarf (the costume design is by Maureen Heneghan). He wields a sleek miniature flashlight that looks passably futuristic even today, aiming it at the lock of the Tardis as he searches for his keys. Then he senses the presence of Ian and Barbara and points the flashlight at them.

The teachers ask where Susan is and the Doctor plays dumb, refusing to open the door of the police box. Then Susan gets impatient waiting for her grandfather, and opens the door of the police box from within.

Barbara goes straight inside, and Ian and the Doctor are compelled to follow.

This is a pivotal moment, and a landmark in British television history. From the dark muddle of the junkyard, Ian and Barbara step into the baffling contrast of the bright white futuristic interior of the Tardis (the excellent design is by Peter Brachacki).

Susan stands waiting in an interior vastly too large to be housed in the closet-sized police box. Barbara doesn't seem to register the extraordinary event that has just taken place. Instead, she's more concerned with quizzing Susan about her living arrangements. It's left to Ian to question the spatial anomaly—and his sanity.

"The point is not whether you understand," says the Doctor, who is at his most sinister now, "but what is going to happen to you." He looks at Susan and adds, "They'll tell everybody about the ship."

Susan tries to placate her teachers with an explanation. She breaks down the acronym for them. Time and relative dimension (singular, just this once) in space. She says it's a name she coined herself. The explanation doesn't seem to help. The Doctor smiles and draws a parallel between Ian and Barbara and a Native American who first glimpses a steam train invading his land. "His savage mind thought it an illusion too," says the Doctor.

It's intriguing to see how self-assured, vividly realized and convincingly alien the character of the Doctor is even at this, the earliest stage in his long career. Such a moment suggests considerable skill on the part of the writer Anthony Coburn, although it's entirely possible that the script editor David Whitaker or the producer Verity Lambert—or even Head of Drama Sydney Newman—had a hand in shaping these crucial scenes.

The Doctor explains that he and his granddaughter are exiles. Susan pleads with him to let her teachers go, strengthening our suspicions that Ian and Barbara have tumbled down a rabbit hole and might not like what is waiting for them there.

The duplicitous Doctor offers to open the door, but instead he sends the ship travelling, and for the first time we hear the unforgettable noise of the Tardis in action, a small piece of genius from the BBC Radiophonic workshop that sounds like a mechanical dinosaur clearing its throat. We see the rooftops of London dwindling, followed by the same striking feedback effects—rippling black and white swirls—a kind of low budget monochrome forerunner of the "Beyond Infinity" hyperspace trip in *2001: A Space Odyssey*. Superimposed on these visuals (which subsequently became the show's title sequence) are the faces of the Doctor and Susan, accompanied by some impressive sound effects.

We then fade to a barren desert landscape, as glimpsed through the viewing ("scanner") screen in the Tardis. Ian and Barbara lie on the ship's floor, rendered unconscious by the trauma of travelling through time and space (a convention that would be quietly dropped hereafter). Outside we see the Tardis standing crookedly among sand dunes and scrub vegetation. An ominous shadow approaches, and the title superimposes on the image: "Next Episode—The Cave of Skulls."

"100,000 BC" by Anthony Coburn

That highly effective opening episode, with its terrific ending, promised great things. Unfortunately, it's pretty much all downhill for the remaining three parts of the first story. Episode two begins with the (rather sensitive) face of a caveman who is staring at the Tardis, which looks suitably bizarre sitting in this primitive landscape, with the light flashing on its roof. Soon, however, we're back in a cave amongst his tribe and everyone is wearing furs and talking in hokey and unconvincing Palaeolithic platitudes. The story that emerges, such as it is, concerns the fact that the tribe has lost the secret of how to make fire.

They ask where the fire has gone, as they ineffectually try to conjure flames by rubbing on a bone. It doesn't help that the characters have names like Za, Hur, and Horg (played by Derek Newark, Aletha Charlton, and Howard Lang). The considerable interest generated by the accomplished first episode begins to drain away rapidly, despite admirable work by designer Barry Newbery on the cave and other sets.

Director Waris Hussein does his best with the material here, but the story is slow and tedious and there is precious little plot material. There is much talk and the only sources of drama are the conflict between the Doctor's crew and the cave tribe, and the interior conflicts within each group, for example the Doctor and Ian bickering.

Occasional moments of quality shine through, though. Someone on the production team, no doubt Barry Newbery, has done proper research and we get to glimpse an authentic looking hand axe (a leaf shaped flint with a cutting blade) which is referred to, not unreasonably, as a knife. It is used by one of the tribespeople to cut the prisoners' bonds and set them free (the aforementioned internal conflict within the tribe having come to a head).

The Doctor and his companions escape, are recaptured, and dragged back to the Cave of Skulls again. "This place is evil," says the Doctor. "Tiresome" might be a more apt adjective.

Finally, the Doctor and his companions manage to make fire, thereby saving themselves from becoming sacrificial victims. They don't win their freedom, however. There's still an arid expanse of plot to be navigated. Luckily, however, the best sequence in the three stone age episodes is coming up. A fight to the death ensues between two tribesmen in the flickering firelight of the Skull Cave, surrounded by skeletons and intercut with close-ups of the faces of the Doctor and his companions as they watch. This is an extremely well photographed and choreographed sequence (the film cameraman is Robert Sleigh, the studio lighting is by Geoff Shaw, and the fight arranger is Derek Ware). Waris Hussein also deserves full marks for this set piece, which is surprisingly brutal and violent.

After this highlight, the story subsides into a static pattern of waiting once again before Susan playfully places one of the hollow skulls on a burning torch, creating a majestically spectral artefact with flaming eyes. Using a clutch of these to create a diversion (the tribespeople stare at them in superstitious awe), the Doctor and his companions finally escape. The cave dwellers overcome their fear swiftly and there ensues a well-handled chase through the forest which is shot largely in close-up, with the actors jogging on the spot to simulate running—but none the less effective for that.

Back at the Tardis, the Doctor and the others fling themselves inside with the tribesmen close on their heels. We hear the now familiar roaring noise and the police box disappears just as the pursuers throw their spears . . . at what is now empty space.

Far from taking the harassed schoolteachers back to London, the Tardis next appears in a sepulchral forest of bone-white petrified trees. "It could be anywhere," says the Doctor helpfully. But it is Skaro, the planet of the Daleks, a subject to be examined in detail in the next chapter.

*   *   *

If you look at the world from a *Doctor Who* point of view, the years 1963 to 1966 are the William Hartnell Years.

A more balanced view of things, though, might also take into account some of the following historical events. The assassination of John F. Kennedy took place the day before the transmission of the first episode of *Doctor Who*, which was broadcast on Saturday 23 November 1963.

Also in 1963, Cosmonaut Valentina Tereshkova became the first woman in space, and Ken Kesey's *One Flew Over the Cuckoo's Nest* was published. On 27 February 1964, Cassius Clay (later to be known as Muhammad Ali) defeated Sonny Liston, and the US became involved in Vietnam in an "advisory capacity."

In 1965 Malcolm X was murdered, Martin Luther King led a civil rights march on Montgomery, the capital of Alabama, and the war in Vietnam began to heat up with the US shelling the North Vietnamese coast from its warships. Meanwhile on 26 October 1965 the Beatles receive the OBE from the Queen for services to music. In 1966 *What's New Pussycat?* premiered in Leicester Square, Hugh Hefner arrived in London to visit the Playboy Club, and rioting broke outside the US Embassy in London to protest the Vietnam war.

"The Aztecs" by John Lucarotti

Season 1 of *Doctor Who* ran until 12 September 1964. It consisted of forty-two episodes comprising eight stories, and it was a huge hit with the public, thanks in no small part to the sinister appearance of the Daleks (to be discussed in the next chapter). Even in this first season, certain clear patterns for the show were beginning to emerge.

The three main strands of stories were the science fictional (involving outer space, monsters, or the far future—on the Earth or elsewhere), historical or Earth-past (set on Earth in the past and involving fictionalised history lessons), and Earth-present in which the time and place are reassuringly familiar but some kind of exotic or alien threat intrudes to perturb normality.

A classic example of the historical story is John Lucarotti's "The Aztecs," which was broadcast as the sixth story in the first season (its first episode transmitting on 23 May 1964).

One of the chief virtues of "The Aztecs" is simply that it still exists fully intact and has been lovingly restored by the BBC on DVD. Watching it today one is struck by the effectiveness of the sound design of the show. Whenever the Tardis disappears, it is accompanied by that strikingly eerie sound, masterfully created by the BBC Radiophonics Workshop. It's a reminder that whatever the weaknesses of the visuals, resourceful sound effects could make a drama work.

This was hardly a new lesson. Nigel Kneale's brilliant science fiction scripts for the BBC during the 1950s made imaginative use of sound (presumably to compensate for the potentially dodgy visuals), notably in *The Creature*, which is available on DVD in the Hammer Films version, highly effectively despite the sensational title *The Abominable Snowman*.

At the very beginning of "The Aztecs," sound is similarly put to good use with the hoarse trademark noise of the Tardis marking the vanishing of a (laughably obvious miniature) Tardis and its arrival elsewhere. In this case, elsewhere proves to be an Aztec tomb, circa AD 1400.

When *Doctor Who* was first discussed, Sydney Newman and the other program makers were keenly aware that nobody would want to watch a show about an old man, even an old man with a police box that travelled through time and space. It was always the intention to give the Doctor a group of (more or less) everyday companions. Throughout the first series the occupants of the Tardis accompanying the Doctor—his *companions*, in *Doctor Who* parlance—remained as the teachers Ian and Barbara and the teenage Susan.

Emerging from the Tardis, Barbara and Susan are surprisingly casual in their reactions to an Aztec tomb, but by now, they've seen a hell of a lot, including cavemen, Daleks, and Marco Polo. It goes a little beyond casual, however, for Barbara to promptly rob a corpse of its jewellery and don it herself. Of course, this turns out to be a plot point, with the jewellery prompting the High Priest of Knowledge to identify Barbara as a reincarnation of the goddess in classic white-gods-from-the-sky fashion.

Never mind the wrath of the spirits descending on tomb robbers, when the time travellers emerge into the light of day (which is to say, the lights of the television studio), the true curse of Doctor Who manifests itself.

They stare out at what the dialogue describes as an "extraordinary city," but what the viewer instantly sees as a manifestly phoney back-cloth whose painting of the Aztec cityscape is drooping and wrinkled.

Doctor Who was often marked by scripts of vast imagination that were calamitously let down by unsympathetic or compromised design. In the case of "The Aztecs" the designer was a vastly talented man and anything but unsympathetic. In an interview featured on the DVD Barry Newbery explains just what went wrong. To anyone who's ever worked on the show, his account provides the sort of painful sense of déjà vu that leaves you uncertain whether to laugh or cry.

For a start, no designer was ever chosen for *Doctor Who* because their talents were seen to be a good fit for the show. As Newbery says, "We weren't picked for our skill—we were just chosen because we happened to be free." This sort of Russian Roulette policy could be guaranteed to occasionally throw up a designer who hated the show and whose work would reflect this. I would discover this to my own cost some twenty-five years later when, after months of hard work perfecting the scripts for the show, I sat down in a press screening beside a lady journalist and had to listen to her gag with repressed hilarity when she got her first glimpse of just how bad the monster makeup was.

But during the first season of *Doctor Who*, the show had the astonishing good fortune to fall into the hands of two highly talented designers who did extravagantly good work. Barry Newbery worked on the historical stories while Raymond Cusick undertook the futuristic or science fictional ones, including the epochal design for the Daleks that is discussed in chapter two.

On "The Aztecs" Barry Newbery's chief problem was that the show was being recorded in the small "D" studio at Lime Grove so that there wasn't sufficient space for the background cloth. It was also unsympathetically lit, hence the obvious wrinkles in what is supposed to be the "extraordinary" city vista. There was also the small matter of half the sets being accidentally junked and *destroyed* before the shoot was complete—an example of what I like to refer to as the Curse of Doctor Who.

Factors like this, all fairly standard *Doctor Who* debacles, worked against the excellent design on Aztecs, but evidence of quality still survives. Summing up, Barry Newbery says, that the trouble with designing for Doctor Who was perpetual compromise. The show was treated as if it was an ordinary half hour drama. In other words, designers like Newbery were given the same resources to make a story set in the Aztec empire that they would be given to make a story set in an accountancy office overlooking Leicester Square.

But the costumes and props in "The Aztecs" were scrupulously researched and of an obviously high standard (the costume design was by Daphne Dare and Tony Pearce, while the props were Newbery's work). The show also benefits from a music score by the composer Richard Rodney Bennett (who would go on to great success with the film *Murder on the Orient Express* and would still be providing outstanding sound tracks for BBC drama forty years later with *Gormenghast*). There were also some convincing performances from good actors who help distract the viewers from the fact that the ancient Aztecs are all speaking modern English. (Doctor Who desperately needed an equivalent of the Babel fish as used in *The Hitchhiker's Guide to the Galaxy*, which you stuck in your ear and it translated any alien language for you.)

The plot of "The Aztecs" follows a predictable pattern, with the Tardis swiftly being rendered inaccessible, locked away in a tomb. With the first season not even over, this had already become a standard and wearying trope of the show: depriving the characters of such an extravagantly easy means of escape from jeopardy.

While fully understanding the utility of such clichés, I fought long and hard to avoid them when I was script editing the show (although, in all fairness, it's a lot easier to avoid these story devices when you're making fourteen episodes a year instead of forty-two).

Another standard *Doctor Who* trick was to separate the Doctor and the companions, so the writer could run several parallel strands of (usually uninspired) plot. Here again I put my foot down when I was working on the show. It was my edict that the Doctor and the companion had to be kept together as much as possible. I was lucky in only having one companion to juggle. Keeping three or four of them with the Doctor at all times would have made for a very cumbersome ensemble piece.

"The Aztecs" is rather slow moving, which is unusual since it is only a four-part story (for some really laggard plotting, *Doctor Who* could offer seven-, eight-, or even ten-parters). The subplots gradually lumber into life, with the Doctor scheming to meet the temple's architect (and thereby work out how to get back to the Tardis). Barbara in her role as reincarnated goddess wants to reform the Aztecs' bloody behaviour ("You can't rewrite history," says the Doctor. "Not one line."). Meanwhile Ian dazzles the Aztec warriors with a knowledge of martial arts, which is unusual in an inner London chemistry teacher. Three companions is a lot to come up with plot for, so Susan is pretty much sidelined. This is somewhat unforgivable in that the story also features long exposition sequences where the dialogue is by minor characters and our regulars are left with nothing to do. Rule number one of series drama is to give as much as possible of the best material to your stars and save the scraps for the guest cast. For fairness sake though, I should mention that the Carole Ann Ford, who played Susan, took a holiday during the shoot, which may account for her low profile in the story.

But "The Aztecs" offers good music, good lighting, outstanding (if compromised) design, and moody black and white photography that adds substantially to the impact of the piece. The executioner's make-up is striking, and the sequence of the rain sacrifice is decidedly effective. Also, despite fluffing the odd line, William Hartnell is impressive here as the Doctor. He's great visually. With his long hair and nineteenth century jacket and trousers, he looks like some kind of sinister Mississippi riverboat gambler.

The DVD release of "The Aztecs" also provides a documentary about restoring the ageing and worn footage of the show. The admirable and painstaking efforts of individuals like Steve Roberts and the composer Mark Ayres have led to remarkable results in the restored version. However, there is a moodiness to the damaged original that is somehow more spooky and evocative. You just can't win.

David Whitaker was the script editor throughout the first season and on the second season until "The Dalek Invasion of Earth," episode 6 "Flashpoint." The story after that was written by Whitaker, with Dennis Spooner taking over as the script editor. Spooner, who script edited the show up to and including the final episode of "The Chase," near the end of Season 2, was another *Avengers* stalwart. He was also involved in creating such cult television classics as *The Champions* and *Randall and Hopkirk (Deceased)*, both shows with paranormal or supernatural leanings.

Thereafter the new script editor was Donald Tosh, who came from Granada Television where he had been instrumental in setting up *Coronation Street*, Britain's most successful and longest running television soap opera. By all accounts, Tosh was an extremely intelligent proto-hippie, wearing floral shirts as a kind of provocation to the BBC establishment. (He eventually left television to become caretaker of a castle in Cornwall.) Donald Tosh script edited the show from the start of "The Time Meddler," which Dennis Spooner wrote, until the middle of Season 3, at which point Gerry Davis took over. Davis was another veteran of the Canadian Broadcasting Corporation who went on to create the classic BBC eco-drama *Doomwatch* with Kit Pedler, as well as co-creating the classic *Doctor Who* villains, the Cybermen. When Davis assumed script editing duties on *Doctor Who*, Donald Tosh switched over to become a writer on the show.

This rather bewildering pattern of shifting names—the dance of script editors and writers—makes perfect sense on reflection: David Whitaker is script editor on the show until Dennis Spooner takes over. At this point Whitaker promptly begins writing for the show. Spooner script edits until Donald Tosh takes over and then Spooner in turn starts writing. In due course Gerry Davis becomes script editor, allowing Tosh to sign on as a writer.

The point is, contractually, the BBC couldn't employ someone as a script editor at the same time they're writing for the program. Since it's the script editor's job to hire the writers, it's bad form to let them hire themselves. On the other hand it makes perfect sense for a script editor, who knows and understands the show perhaps better than anyone else, to write for it. Hence the pattern of script editors handing over to a newcomer and leaving to write. Then the newcomer leaves the post to do the same.

Another device to allow an incumbent script editor to write episodes was for him notionally to do the writing while he was on leave. John Nathan-Turner, who was producer of the show in 1986, explained all this to me when I joined. "We'll have to get you writing the scripts," he said, but I virtuously refrained from doing any writing on the show. There were very limited slots at that time; fourteen episodes a year, divided up into four stories, so only four writers could be hired each season. I felt passionately that we should encourage fresh talent, and give new writers a chance. Having just got through the door my-self, I was eager to invite others in. I also felt that commissioning myself was vaguely immoral and unsporting, like shooting a fish in a barrel.

Of course, today I'd probably want to write every episode.

"Planet of the Giants" by Louis Marks

The second season of *Doctor Who* debuted auspiciously on Halloween 1964 with an Earth-present story called "Planet of the Giants" written by Louis Marks. Louis Marks is an intriguing figure. He started writ-ing for television with *The Adventures of Robin Hood* and would go on to become a BBC script editor in the 1970s. Marks commissioned Nigel Kneale's masterful reinvention of the ghost story, *The Stone Tape*, in which paranormal phenomena turns out to be a form of re-cording, preserved in the stones of a house—but none the less terrify-ing or destructive for all that. *The Stone Tape* is available on DVD for anyone interested in tracing the family tree of British television sci-ence fiction beyond the line of *Doctor Who*.

"Planet of the Giants" was a three-parter that had originally been shot as four episodes and was subsequently cut down in an attempt to condense incident and increase pace and drama. Given the fairly slow development of the plot, even in its three-episode form, this seems to have been a sound decision. One reason for turbocharging "Planet of the Giants" was that it had originally been intended as the penultimate serial in the first season, but now it had to serve as the curtain-raiser for the new season, so it needed to have as much impact as possible. In fact, it wasn't at all a bad choice.

The story, as the title suggests, involves the crew of the Tardis dis-covering that they're in a world where they are tiny by comparison with the native inhabitants. According to David J. Howe and Stephen James Walker's invaluable *The Television Companion*, there had been two previous attempts to mount a story of this kind. Indeed the first *Doctor Who* adventure ever was originally intended to be "The Giants," written by C. E. Webber, a script that was evidently deemed inappropriate. A further attempt at similar material had been made by another writer Robert Gould. With Louis Marks's script, the third time proved lucky.

The persistence with which the production team pursued this particular plot suggests that someone understood the potential of putting
actors among sets and props that represented familiar objects on a
giant scale. It's a simple and effective story device and one that has
plenty of mileage. (I wrote a similar script myself for the sword and
sorcery series *Dark Knight* in 2001.) The appeal of such stories is simple enough: one can achieve drama and a sense of wonder with the
minimum of effort through a straightforward story device. It's pretty
much foolproof, providing you have even vaguely competent design.

The design for "Planet of the Giants" was much more than competent. At times, it was positively inspired. That's hardly surprising,
since it was in the hands of Raymond Cusick, the man responsible for
designing the appearance of the Daleks in the first series. Cusick's
work here is frequently excellent, particularly in the case of the giant
sink, the telephone, and some of the insects.

The story begins with the Doctor, Ian, Barbara, and Susan in the
Tardis. The Doctor is rather dashingly dressed in a cape, a holdover
from the previous story, "The Reign of Terror," with its French Revolution setting. One of the plot devices of the first series was that the
Doctor was not in full control of the Tardis, so he couldn't simply
return Barbara and Ian to the time and place (London, 1963) where
they belonged. Much was made of the Doctor's various bungled attempts to do so, and here again he tries to send his ship to contemporary London. This time he gets it right—with one slight complication.
The Tardis malfunctions on arrival.

The Doctor barks orders at Susan, who seems quite *au fait* with the
alien technology of the ship, but clearly something is wrong. When
the four eventually emerge from the ship, after some lengthy preliminaries about what has gone wrong with the landing (the door opened
prematurely), and why the Doctor looks around and says, "What a
strange rock formation." Soon they have discovered a (dead) ant about
the size of a German Shepherd and, more tellingly, a giant seed
packet—the evocatively named Night Scented Stock ("Hardy annual.
Sow in the open.") and a giant matchbox which Ian clambers inside.
It turns out that the "Planet of the Giants" is actually Earth in 1964,
one of the most clever features of this script.

"We have been reduced to roughly the size of an inch," declares the
Doctor, promptly cueing a shot of a crude model of Tardis, approximately one inch high. This develops into an impressive shot revealing
that the "strange rock formation" surrounding the vessel and its crew

is actually a crack in the crazy paving of a footpath leading up to a normal suburban house. The juxtaposition of the familiar and comforting with the menacing and alien has seldom been so economically and deftly achieved.

No sooner has the story laid out its basic premise than the first giant (or normal sized) human turns up, initially shot in such a way that we can't see his face—like the maid in an old *Tom and Jerry* cartoon. Later the giant greets a cat sunning itself on the lawn, and as soon as we see the feline we begin to suspect what the Doctor and his friends are in for.

Of course, none of this was groundbreaking, even in 1964. Similar stories go back to Jonathan Swift, and seven years before this *Doctor Who* version, the feature film *The Incredible Shrinking Man* (adapted by Richard Matheson, from his brilliant novel) had thoroughly and imaginatively explored similar situations on a considerably more generous budget. Four years later, in 1968, Irwin Allen's American TV series *Land of the Giants* would appear on screen. Reportedly, originality was not the strongest feature of Irwin Allen's science fiction TV work. *Lost in Space*, which appeared in September 1965, bears quite an emphatic resemblance to *Space Family Robinson*, a Gold Key comic written by Del Connell and drawn by Dan Spiegle, which first appeared in December 1962.

Given this kind of pedigree for Irwin Allen shows, it's interesting to speculate whether "Planet of the Giants," with its oddly similar title, might have provided some inspiration for *Land of the Giants*.

The special effects in the Allen show, which was shot in colour, were unsurprisingly of a higher standard than much of the work in the *Doctor Who* story. In fact, it isn't long before a majestically phoney-looking (dead) giant bee drops from the sky in front of the Doctor, Barbara, and Susan. We soon learn why all the insects they're encountering are dead. The giant we first saw is a civil servant called Farrow (Frank Crawshaw) who has come to tell an evil industrialist (Alan Tilvern) to stop work on an insecticide called DN6. The substance is too deadly, even by lax 1960s standards, to be allowed into the environment. It is described as an "everlasting pesticide" and "more deadly than radiation." But the evil industrialist, called Forester, responds to this suggestion by promptly shooting the hapless civil servant dead, providing a thunderous noise of gunfire which baffles the inch-high Doctor and his friends.

On the one hand, this subplot for the story is perfunctory, predictable, and lacking in any real science fictional depth. On the other hand, with its worthy opposition to pesticides and its defence of the ecosphere, it seems oddly modern and plays quite well even today. The paranoia inspired by such chemical hijinks ("No eating or drinking," warns the Doctor) certainly hasn't dated.

Ian finds the dead body of Farrow and stands gazing at it, a tiny figure confronted by a giant face. Then, as expected, the cat discovers the tiny humans. The Doctor and the companions stand absolutely still on his advice. He also advises against making eye contact, a warning that would make a lot more sense if they were nearer to the size of the cat. Then, disappointingly, the cat gives up rather easily. *The Incredible Shrinking Man* this is not.

Next, in a classic example of splitting up the protagonists, Ian and Barbara are transported into the house through the inventive device of taking refuge in a briefcase that was left on the lawn. They find themselves on a giant laboratory bench. The Doctor and Susan set off after them, getting access to the house through a giant drainpipe, which is another effective set. Similarly convincing giant props are discovered in the laboratory by Barbara and Ian, including some giant grains of wheat, covered with a suspicious sticky substance. Barbara foolishly touches these and spends the remaining episodes terrified that she has poisoned herself with insecticide. Which indeed she has. Much is made of the rather implausible suspense device of her not telling the others about her plight. When the Doctor finally learns about it, he makes the sensible, and scientifically convincing, suggestion that she must return to her full size, thereby reducing the toxicity of the insecticide to a sublethal dose.

Luckily, "Planet of the Giants" is not one of those stories where the Tardis is routinely rendered inaccessible to its crew. However, before they return to their ship, the Doctor and his friends must resolve the subplot about the murderous tycoon. Along the way, they encounter a truly first-rate special effect in the shape of a giant fly that terrifies Barbara. The fly is already succumbing to the effect of DN6 and its movements are restrained and sluggish—allowing the effects team to do a splendid job. Brief as it is, this is one of the most successful such sequences in *Doctor Who*. A healthy fly in full flight would no doubt have defeated their resources in 1964, but oddly when the fly is discovered dead later, and utterly motionless, it looks patently fake again. This is in contrast to the dead ant at the beginning, which was relatively convincing.

Another suspenseful set piece takes place in the giant laboratory sink, a brilliant piece of design. Barbara and Ian begin to climb down the chain attached to the plug to rejoin the Doctor and Susan, who have emerged via the waste pipe from the drain in the sink. Just then the giant scientist Smithers (Reginald Barratt) appears, and the tiny humans hide. The Doctor and Barbara go back down the drain, which proves to be a mistake when the scientist starts to fill the sink with water . . .

The climax of the adventure comes when the Doctor and friends use a giant match to ignite a flow of gas from a giant tap on the laboratory bench and thereby ignite a flammable can of the pesticide—an oddly reckless thing to do, given all the discussion of the extreme toxicity of such substances. However, this is the occasion for some diverting and genuinely Doctor-ish dialogue. "It will be just like that air raid Grandfather, do you remember?" "Yes, very well," says the Doctor, "What infernal machines those zeppelins were."

It's a shame that the wonder of time travel is only invoked through a scrap of throwaway dialogue in this story. "Planet of the Giants" still succeeds, by and large, with a strong central conceit, some memorable design work by Raymond Cusick, and effective music by Dudley Simpson (beginning what would be a fifteen year association with the show). There is also the satisfaction of seeing the evil industrialist blinded (temporarily) by an exploding can of his own pesticide, just before the police cart him off.

"The Web Planet" by Bill Strutton

An example of the third style of *Doctor Who* story, the science fictional or alien one, is an adventure from the middle of the second series, "The Web Planet." They don't get much more alien than this—all the guest characters in the story, are aliens. Of course the Doctor is an alien, too. But these guest characters were all out-and-out bug-eyed monsters of one kind or another. "The Web Planet" is written by Bill Strutton, an Australian whose long lists of credits as a television writer (including *The Saint* and *Ivanhoe*) do nothing to explain the extraordinary story he contrived for *Doctor Who*. Indeed "The Web Planet" is reminiscent of such weird creature extravaganzas as David Lindsay's

Voyage to Arcturus, William Hope Hodgson's *Nightland*, or Stanley Weinbaum's *Martian Odyssey*. Also, and perhaps more appositely, it brings to mind the comic strips of Basil Wolverton.

The story begins traditionally enough in the Tardis with the Doctor in Roman robes, a holdover from his previous adventure called, predictably enough, "The Romans," while Barbara is wearing a bracelet she got from Nero. Also onboard the Tardis is Ian and since, as we'll see, Susan left the crew during a Dalek adventure, a new companion, Vicki. (The anodyne quality of the companions' names would, fortunately, improve. Over the years, more memorable and vivid cognomens such as Ace, Leela, Romana, Zoe, K9, and Brigadier Lethbridge-Stewart would start to creep in.)

Vicki is played by Maureen O'Brien, who steps in when Carole Ann Ford decides to leave the series. With Ford's departure Susan is written out, along with any notion of the Doctor having family (although this problematic notion would surface again in 1996, with the McGann Doctor reminiscing about halcyon days spent with his father).

Vicki is an Earth girl of the future rescued from a crashed spaceship by the Doctor and his companions (in the story "The Rescue"). After the visit to ancient Rome, "The Web Planet" represents Vicki's second adventure with the Doctor.

The planet where the Tardis materialises is clearly a set, but also clearly a good one. Peering out at it from the Tardis control room through the viewing screen Barbara says, "It's like a cemetery. It's so quiet." This is intended to inspire us with foreboding, but instead it inspires us with puzzlement. Since the viewing screen provides only a picture and no sound, it's bound to be quiet.

What we actually see is a desolate landscape with some sparse rock formations and a black sky, the latter a backdrop of alien planets and stars that is quite well achieved. This sky remains black throughout the story, suggesting either a lack of atmosphere on the planet or a lengthy night cycle. Scientific explanations are irrelevant. The black sky adds immeasurably to the mood of the story, contributing a strong sense of place, and an extraterrestrial place at that.

The first thing that happens, of course, is that the travellers are split up. In later *Doctor Who* adventures such formulaic separations could be avoided by reducing the number of companions in the Tardis and by encouraging writers to employ more ambitious and less clichéd structures for their narratives—both situations that prevailed when I was editing stories for the show.

In what was already becoming a standard plot ploy, some strange force is draining the power of the Tardis. Ian and the Doctor leave to investigate while Barbara and Vicki stay onboard. Outside on the planet's surface the Doctor chuckles like a tedious old fool (or someone asked to play a tedious old fool) muttering, "Fascinating . . . mica" as he investigates the local mineral deposits. He does, however, have a very natty hat (the costume design, again by Daphne Dare, is ambitious and admirable throughout). Soon the Doctor and Ian have discovered some rather dramatic mineral formations, in the shape of a very impressive pyramid with a crystalline base. The pyramid, like the rest of the forbidding planet-scape, is the work of designer John Wood who provides an effective and impressively alien environment for the story.

The use of filters on the camera lenses give a smeared, blurry appearance to the shots of the landscape that add to their otherworldly aspect, although this proves a less than ideal stratagem in the scene where the star of the show crouches down and his face vanishes in the blur.

The Doctor stops Ian from dipping his hands into a pool of black liquid. He asks Ian for his necktie, which Ian is wearing as a belt. "I hope my pants stay up," says Ian. "That's your affair, not mine," says the Doctor, dipping the tie into the inky pool, where it proceeds to smoke and dissolve as if being eaten by acid. Ian is chagrined by the destruction of his Coal Hill School tie. The Doctor responds that they almost had a dissolved Coal Hill School teacher instead of a Coal Hill School tie, which shuts Ian up.

Back at the Tardis, Vicki isn't doing much except snoozing on Bauhaus furniture. Barbara is having a more interesting time, getting spooked because her limbs are suddenly moving out of her control, and later by the onset of strange phenomena like poltergeist activity. The Tardis doors open of their own volition (revealing a certain amount of damage suffered by the prop in Riverside Studio 1) and the same strange force that is draining the Tardis's power, or perhaps a different strange force, drags her out like a sleepwalker.

Barbara isn't wearing even the minimal breathing apparatus cursorily employed by Ian and the Doctor on their wanderings. That's the least of her worries as she is dragged across the planet's surface, towards pools of acid and close encounters with alien life forms.

The first aliens to appear are giant (man-sized) ants called Zarbi who walk on their hind legs in a semi-upright fashion. As *Doctor Who* monsters go, they're quite admirable. The humans in the costumes are well concealed and their odd method of movement, which must have been very uncomfortable for the actors, adds to their alien quality. Accompanying the Zarbi are some long slung scurrying trilobite creatures who look comically unconvincing. These are the Larvae Guns, so called because of the proboscis they possess that can be fired like a weapon.

The third set of aliens on this densely populated planet are the Menoptra. Variously described as looking like giant moths or butterflies, they actually bear a striking resemblance to the Bumble Bee Man on *The Simpsons*, another example of this satirical cartoon show retrospectively undermining old *Doctor Who* adventures. The colour scheme of the Menoptra costumes even consisted (though you can't tell from the monochrome footage) of black and yellow stripes.

The question of who got the job designing the creatures on *Doctor Who* was always a complex one. In some cases the costumes were clearly "costumes" and went to the costume departments. Other times, as with the Daleks, the costumes were more like a piece of technological hardware and were designed by the designer, in this case Raymond Cusick.

Making a convincing alien could even, arguably, be the responsibility of the make-up department, as I discovered years later on the story "The Happiness Patrol" (1988) where the task of designing the sinister inhuman Kandy Man went to makeup designer Dorka Nieradzik, who did an exceptional job.

In the case of "The Web Planet," the Zarbi and the Larvae Guns were designed by John Wood, and the Menoptra were the work of Daphne Dare and the costume department. The masks on the Menoptra costumes are actually rather good. It's the full length shots, which allow one to see what are obviously humans dressed up in bulging and rather amusing costumes, that tend to sink the enterprise. One reason the antlike Zarbi work is because they have a sinister attenuated, slender look whereas the Menoptra are rather chubby and cuddly looking. Cuddly monsters are a contradiction in terms, as I would learn to my cost with the Cheetah People in *Survival* (1989).

However, one thing the Menoptra do well is *move*. When one of these bumblebee men leads the sleepwalking Barbara to join his companions, they glide around the woman in a slow, eerie dance and for a moment the viewer is spellbound. According to Howe and Walker it was Roslyn de Winter, an actress playing one of the Menoptra, who was responsible for devising and coordinating these balletic movements. The sense of watching a macabre and engrossing ballet recurs throughout "The Web Planet." It's particularly strong in the wonderful moment when one of the Menoptra, pursued by the Zarbi, flees to the top of a plateau and suddenly takes flight into the dark sky. It's a *coup de théâtre*. A later sequence of swooping back down from the darkness is equally arresting. As with the black sky background and the set of the desolate planet, we're aware that what we're seeing isn't real, or even realistic, yet it works in the way a symbolic but well conceived stage set can work. We suspend our disbelief and become absorbed in the mood of the narrative.

It comes as no surprise to learn that the flying sequences were accomplished by a team who specialised in providing similar effects for ballets. However, just as we are being beguiled by the strange, gliding, dancelike movements of the Menoptra, one of them speaks in a plummy, posh female English accent and the spell is broken. It's curious how such things can make or break a special effect. Later in the story we will encounter another alien life form, the Optera, limbless upright worms that jump around. The costumes for the Optera are probably the worst in "The Web Planet," never looking like anything other than costumes and silly ones at that. Yet when one of these creatures *talks,* the performer is so compelling and so convincingly alien that one forgets their ludicrous appearance and begins to be won over. A similar effect was evident in the 2005 series, when some underwhelming monsters called the Slitheen suddenly began to speak and were transformed into a convincing menace.

In a series of adventures, confrontations, and escapes, the Doctor and his companions gradually piece together what is happening. The planet, called Vortis, is under attack from an intelligence called the Animus, a kind of cosmic yeast infection that is in the process of enshrouding this world with a living web structure called the Carsenome. When we eventually meet the Animus it turns out to be less like a spider at the centre of a web than a jellyfish at the centre of one. Bill Strutton's script seems strangely modern in terms of its science fiction ideas, with the biotechnology of the Larvae Guns and the Carsenome's living defences. As the Doctor says, "Remarkable. Most interesting."

Elsewhere there is the odd infelicity and inconsistency. When Vicki is left alone in the Tardis she stumbles against the control panel and seems to activate the mechanism. The Doctor comes back to find that the Tardis is no longer where he left it—and he is utterly bereft. It is one of Hartnell's most effective moments of acting, and all he says is "My ship. My Tardis . . ."; yet he conveys worlds of loss.

However, it's unclear in the story whether Vicki's actions caused the Tardis to move or whether it was merely dragged off by the inhabitants of the planet. It hardly matters. When one of the Zarbis blunders through the open doors of the Tardis, a sinister shiny black antlike creature in this sterile white interior, it feels like a genuine intrusion. A violation. The Doctor certainly seems to feel that way when he finds out.

More disturbing still is the scene where Vicki and the Doctor are shrouded in a web by the Zarbi. The effect is impressive and the result genuinely unsettling. Soon enough the Doctor and his beloved craft are reunited. It turns out that when Vicki stumbled against the control panel she realigned the fluid link, which is deemed to be a good thing. "Fluid Links" would later become the (rather alarming) title of a column in *Doctor Who* magazine.

The Animus is defeated, thanks to the Doctor and his trio of companions, and peace restored to the planet. "We've managed to come out of this unscathed," concludes the Doctor. "Except for my old school tie," says Ian.

Overcomplicated and perhaps overambitious, "The Web Planet" has moments of oddly compelling power that are swamped by moments of inadequacy or absurdity. "The Web Planet" evidently, and not surprisingly, went considerably overbudget so presumably original music was considered a luxury that couldn't be afforded. The fact that the incidental music is therefore just stock library cues serves to weaken the story (though in later years, stock music would be used to astonishingly good effect, as in "Inferno" in 1970).

The sets, props, and costumes are all occasionally brilliant and the concept of a world where everything is organic or mineral—not manufactured—makes for a successful and original look.

The story remains interesting, and quite brave, for its attempt to conjure an utterly alien environment occupied by similarly alien characters—although they all do speak English.

*   *   *

Obviously the episodes discussed here can only give a flavour of what *Doctor Who* was like during the tenure of William Hartnell as the first Doctor, rather than an exhaustive and comprehensive overview. But then such a thing isn't possible.

Because, unlike say *Star Trek*, *Doctor Who* has suffered the astonishing indignity of having some of its episodes destroyed, a situation which we will discuss in some detail, after an encounter with the Doctor's most fearsome enemies, the Daleks.

chapter 2

And the Daleks

Although the Daleks are allegedly the Doctor's most ferocious enemies, utterly dedicated to his destruction, one could argue that actually instead they have saved him from oblivion. He wouldn't exist without them.

This is because the ratings for the first *Doctor Who* adventure were modest and it was by no means certain that the show would survive its first season without cancellation, let alone be renewed for a second one. It was only with the second story—and the advent of everybody's favourite alien killing machines—that the show became solidly established and even something of a hit. Following the Daleks' debut, the audience figures for the third story nearly doubled those of the first adventure (from just under six million to over ten million) and *Doctor Who* was here to stay.

But the Doctor's existence remains a symbiotic one, precariously intertwined with that of the Daleks. It seems he needs these enemies to keep him alive . . .

The Daleks were a huge pop cultural phenomenon in Britain in the 1960s. Someone even coined the word "Dalekmania" to convey an impression of the impact of these alien villains, equating them with the (admittedly somewhat greater) impact of the Beatles. Nonetheless, these metallic monsters were undeniably emblematic of 1960s England, like an Austin Mini car or a Mary Quant miniskirt.

They made their debut in the 1963 story that was the Doctor's second adventure, the same episode that scared the pants off a certain younger incarnation of the author. Sitting in my prairie basement I watched in disgust and astonishment as that thing slithered out of its metal carapace . . .

The Daleks are soft creatures who glide around in armoured machines. Quoted in Howe and Walker's *The Television Companion*, *Doctor Who* fan writer Trevor Wayne makes the interesting point that such aliens were introduced in English literature almost a century ear-

lier in 1898 in H. G. Wells's *War of the Worlds*. It also notes that the
first Dalek adventure bears certain strong points of similarity to
Wells's *The Time Machine*—as we'll see, "The Daleks" featured twin
races: peaceful, physically beautiful surface-dwellers coexisting with
grotesque and dangerous underground creatures.

But perhaps the most striking and memorable feature of the Daleks
is simply the way they look. On paper, as described by their creator
Terry Nation, they might have been any one of a wide range of legless,
gliding robotic entities. (His original script reads thus: *hideous ma-
chine-like creatures. They are legless, moving on a round base . . . A
lens on a flexible shaft acts as an eye. Arms with mechanical grips for
hands . . .*) What arguably makes the Daleks so unique and memorable
is their specific design. When Terry Nation's script was prepped for
production in 1963, featuring the first appearance of these things
called Daleks, someone had to be given the job of turning a work of
the imagination into physical objects that a camera could shoot. This
would be the work of a BBC staff designer.

It was very nearly the work of a staff designer called Ridley Scott,
who would make his own not inconsiderable contribution to science
fiction iconography with *Alien* and *Blade Runner*. It is intriguing to
think what would have happened had Scott taken the Daleks job. He's
undeniably a man with a great visual flair.

But speculate as we may about this fascinating crossroads in pop
culture, the fact is that Ridley Scott sidestepped this particular assign-
ment, and the job went to another designer touched with genius, Raymond P. Cusick.

Cusick's contributions to *Doctor Who* in general, and the Daleks in
particular, is immeasurable. As good as Nation's writing is, had it been
clumsily or laughably given visual reality by some mediocre talent, the
Daleks could have been swiftly consigned to the dustbin of history.

But fate was kind. Cusick got the job, and the ideas in Terry Nation's script were allowed to come to vivid, unforgettable life. Doctor
Who and the Daleks were woven into the fabric of the public imagination. By June 1965 a spin-off feature film was showing in English cine-
mas, Milton Subotsky's *Dr. Who and the Daleks*. This title does seem
to sum up the situation. In the public imagination, it wasn't just one
or the other, it has always been *Doctor Who* and the Daleks. Even in
2005, in the week of a general election, it wasn't the candidates for
prime minister who were appearing on the cover of the *Radio Times*
(the BBC's somewhat perversely titled official TV listings magazine),

it was the Daleks. Their return to our screens was bigger news than any election.

There is an apocryphal story that Cusick's design for these metal fascists was inspired by a pepper shaker he saw on a table in a BBC canteen, and it's certainly true that they would frequently be referred to disparagingly as pepper pots in years to come. (Terry Nation himself offers the insult "motorised dustbins," in "The Dalek Invasion of Earth.") But rather than emulating a pepper shaker, Howe and Walker describe how Cusick actually based his design on the shape of a person sitting in a chair. This was a simple, elegant, and highly intelligent solution to the problem. After all, the Daleks would have to contain people to operate them in the studio, and a seated operator would not only be more comfortable than an upright one, they would also provide an unusual low silhouette for the prop.

This helped to disguise the fact that a human operator was inside the Dalek and removed any suggestion of the obvious man-in-the-suit effect that is so frequently the bane of science fiction effects.

This strategy was so effective that many viewers believed that the Daleks were somehow operated by remote control.

Cusick also considered putting tricycles inside the fibreglass shells for the operators to use when moving the Daleks. In the event, castors were employed instead but the tricycles would be installed in the Daleks for the second adventure, "The Dalek Invasion of Earth."

Legend has it that when producer Verity Lambert first glimpsed the Daleks that Cusick had built she was outraged. But the legend also goes on to relate how Lambert was won over immediately when the things began to *move*, gliding eerily around. Somehow the sinister nature of the Daleks doesn't come across as strongly when they are stationary.

"The Daleks" by Terry Nation

Beginning its transmission on 21 December 1963, the Daleks' first adventure was known to the production team as "The Mutants," but in the years since the first transmission it has become unshakeably retitled after the creatures it introduced, and it would be exceedingly pedantic to go against the flow and now call it anything other than "The Daleks." A seven-part adventure, it began on 21 December 1963 with an episode entitled "The Dead Planet." In this episode the Tardis lands on the planet Skaro and after a perfunctory check on the local radiation levels, the Doctor and his companions set off outside.

Naturally, the moment their backs are turned, the needle on the radiation meter swings into the danger zone and a warning light begins to flash, unheeded.

The Doctor, Ian, Barbara, and Susan emerge into a ghostly mist-shrouded forest (initially shot in negative to add to the uncanny effect). Already in these scenes the strength of Raymond Cusick's designs are apparent. Investigation of the brittle, lifeless plants and trees reveal it to be a petrified forest (or jungle, as the Doctor calls it). It's only Ian and Barbara's second outing with the Doctor and they're still settling into the routine. At this early stage, Barbara is pretty consistently drippy and morose, while Ian is drippy and supportive. Neither seems especially fond of the Doctor. When Barbara intimates that she wouldn't mind seeing some harm befall the old man, a broken leg perhaps, Ian chuckles indulgently.

The first monster to be encountered in this episode is a small reptilian creature made of metal and called a Magneton. Again Cusick's design scores strongly. The Magneton is dead, petrified like the forest, and Barbara's startled gasp seems to us an overreaction. In any case, she should be saving her breath for the really big scream she'll need at the end of the episode.

Then Ian discovers the vista of a distant city and things begin to pick up. The city consists of futuristic buildings clustered in a valley with a mountain behind it. It's just a model shot but it's notably well executed, and benefits from some judicious use of low-lying mist.

The Doctor immediately wants to investigate, but Ian won't let him. The Doctor isn't pleased. After all, it is his Tardis, a fact that is hammered home when they try to leave the planet and discover they can't. A vital component, the fluid link, has been accidentally drained and needs to be refilled with mercury before they can go anywhere. The Doctor declares there's no mercury on board, so it's off to the city after all, to search for the stuff. He shrugs and asks what else can be done, with a foxy gleam in his eye. The emptying of the fluid link is, of course, a subterfuge so he can get his own way.

The petrified forest our heroes travel through is impressive enough, but the city, seen up close, is first-rate. As soon as they arrive in this angular, futurist environment, Ian suggests that they separate and go different ways. This is almost an Ur text for ensuing *Doctor Who* adventures in which the main plot engine (sometimes the only plot engine) is the separation of the characters and their struggle to reunite.

Sure enough, Barbara is soon trapped in the weirdly angled corridors of the city, which suggest a kind of high tech version of *The Cabinet of Dr Caligari*. She is then sealed behind an assortment of closing doors. We later learn that she's actually been carried down under the city in an elevator, hence all those closing doors, but this is far from clear in these sequences and, without the subsequent dialogue, we might never have guessed it. Throughout this sequence, Raymond Cusick's design remains exemplary.

The episode ends on the requisite cliff-hanger when *something* closes in on Barbara. We can't see what it is because the scene is shot from the menacing intruder's point of view, but we know it's got to be pretty horrible because Barbara screams lustily, in a manner that would come to be expected of *Doctor Who* companions. When I joined the show as a script editor in 1986, I inherited a companion called Mel, played by Bonnie Langford, who was known for her ability to scream and precious little else.

While Barbara is screaming at the first appearance of this first (unseen) Dalek, the Doctor and the others are blundering through some moodily lit rooms where they discover a Geiger counter, complete with a "Danger" label in English. This isn't a clever sign of a connection between Skaro and Earth, it's just a prop foul-up in what is otherwise a story full of well thought-out designs. Most of the other Dalek equipment features suitably abstract or alien symbols. In any case, the Geiger counter tells them the same story that the bright flashing light in the Tardis would have conveyed if they'd paid any attention to it. They've all been exposed to high levels of radiation and will soon begin to succumb.

Ian wonders how their environment can be so drenched with radiation yet show no signs of a bomb blast and, in a startlingly modern response, the Doctor says it was a neutron bomb, which destroys living things without damaging machinery or buildings. Then he admits that there was nothing wrong with the fluid link after all, and that his passion for investigation has led them all to their deaths. Ian calls him an old fool.

Oddly it's only now, almost halfway through the second episode, that we get to see the Daleks. They're presented to us as they cluster around Barbara, whom they've taken captive. Initially it's a rather undramatic entrance. Then they begin to talk, in their distinctive sinister, synthesised voices, and suddenly the Daleks are *here*. Ian tries to flee from them and they fire at him with the guns that are one of their three limbs (if you count the eyestalk as a limb). The flash of the Dalek guns throw the image momentarily into negative, a spooky effect, and Ian collapses, temporarily paralysed. He's gotten off lightly, by Dalek standards.

The four travellers are now united again, but as prisoners in a cell where Barbara asks some very perceptive questions. She wonders if they're machines through and through or whether they contain an organic occupant.

The Daleks learn that their captives are suffering from radiation poisoning and decide to send one of the four out to get the drugs that will save their lives. This isn't a piece of Dalek altruism. Instead they hope to copy and synthesise the drug and use it themselves. The source of the drug is the other species that inhabits the planet Skaro, the Thals. Susan is sent out to fetch the antiradiation drug.

This drug, along with that pesky fluid link, is one of the McGuffins that clutter up Terry Nation's story and lead to some rather mechanical to-ing and fro-ing. Like being cut off from the Tardis, or routine separation of characters, unashamed use of McGuffins would tend to be the bane of Doctor Who stories.

Susan finally encounters the Thals, who have been built up as some kind of loathsome mutations, and discovers instead that they're humanoids of an Aryan standard of blonde physical flawlessness. She exclaims that they're perfect. It's a gratifying plot twist, but the Thals are wearing rather strange costumes. The males have leather trousers with holes up the side of the leg that might, to more modern viewers, suggest membership in the Village People, while the females wear a kind of modified Playboy bunny outfit and nutty headpieces.

More damaging than the costumes is the dialogue that the Thals are given. It's typical of a certain kind of clichéd science fiction writing in which inhabitants of an alien planet, or denizens of the future, all talk like Roman senators in a second-rate play. The Thals even have mock classical names that echo Greek and Latin (Antodus, Elyon, Dyoni, Alydon, Temmosus).

Back in the clutches of the Daleks, Susan makes the mistake of laughing and is told to stop making that noise. She is once again incarcerated with the Doctor and the others and, between these captivity scenes and some very dull interludes with the Thals, the story is in danger of grinding to a halt altogether. One almost longs for a bit of standardized companion-separation to get things moving again. But a classic, iconic set piece is only moments away.

The Doctor and the others lure a Dalek into their cell and overpower it (rather too easily) and then unscrew its lid (even more easily). What Ian sees inside this metal shell causes him to hastily send the womenfolk out into the corridor, ostensibly to keep watch. With the Doctor's help Ian scoops out the hideous living occupant of the metal machine, keeping it discretely covered with a cape, and dumps it on the floor of the cell.

Then, in a ludicrous sequence, Ian *climbs inside the empty Dalek*, has the lid sealed on him, and begins to operate it like an old hand. Never mind the unlikelihood of him being able to work such a machine, how could he possibly fit into a vehicle designed for a blob not much larger than a squashed cat? It doesn't really matter.

What matters is that in this guise he can help the Doctor and the girls escape and, more importantly, as they leave the cell, we get a shot of the cloth shrouding the displaced Dalek, and a pseudopod comes squirming out, giving a hint of its horrid form.

It's an unforgettable moment and one that agreeably scarred the minds of a generation.

The rest of the story is largely anticlimactic. The fluid link is summoned up yet again as a McGuffin after their successful escape, to send the Doctor and his team back to the Dalek city. It's been confiscated by the Daleks and the Doctor can't operate the Tardis without it (this time we assume he's telling the truth). With the help of the Thals they set off to retrieve the damned thing.

Without this device (in both senses of the word) "The Daleks" could have been a tight four-part story. With it, the narrative sprawls to seven episodes, involving a lot of talk, some swamp monsters and some fairly heavy-handed clichés. The Thals are a peace-loving people who have forsaken all warlike ways. So Ian teaches them how to punch people. (At the end of the story, perhaps as a compensating gesture, the Doctor will teach them how to shake hands.) Meanwhile, back at the city, we learn that the only thing more boring than two Daleks talking to each other is *more than* two Daleks talking to each other.

However, there are some amusing and cherishable sequences when the Daleks discover unforeseen side effects of the antiradiation drug they stole from the Thals. Specifically, it causes the Daleks to freak out. They spin around shrieking and begging for help in their robot way, lamenting that they are going out of control. We also get some

subjective shots of their hallucinatory point of view that suggest the
Dalek equivalent of a bad acid trip.

The Daleks conclude that the drug doesn't work on them because
they have become dependent on radiation. They need it to survive. In
fact, they like radiation so much they decide to use another neutron
bomb to completely wipe out the Thals. Fortunately the Thals and the
Doctor's crew are busy infiltrating the city. The penultimate episode
features a literal cliff-hanger in which Ian is clinging to a ledge above
a vertiginous drop in a network of caves (nicely designed and realised
by Cusick and his team).

Meanwhile the Doctor spends too long gloating about having a superior intellect and gets himself and Susan recaptured by the Daleks.
When he learns of their plan to ethnically cleanse the Thals, the Doctor suddenly becomes quite impressive. William Hartnell rises to the
occasion as he delivers a speech condemning them for their blood-
thirsty ways. Luckily, Ian and the Thals cavalry arrive in time to stop
the genocide and cut the Daleks power, effectively eliminating them
once and for all.

*   *   *

No one expected "The Daleks" to be a hit. Terry Nation lamented
that he had wiped the Dalek race out at the end of this first adventure,
thus theoretically shutting the door on any notion of a sequel. He is
quoted by Howe and Walker as saying, "Nobody has ever killed off
their brainchild as thoroughly as I annihilated mine—with the possible exception of Sir Arthur Conan Doyle trying to rid himself of Sherlock Holmes." The allusion to the Reichenbach Falls isn't entirely apt
since Conan Doyle had grown tired of his great and enormously popular character only after some seven years. Terry Nation was still looking forward to a long and fruitful partnership with his creations.

In any case, the annihilation he describes isn't actually so thorough
at all. If some of the Daleks had survived in a dormant state after their
power was cut, then bringing them back to life would have been as
simple as throwing a switch and restoring a trickle of electricity.

But the problem was solved simply enough by invoking some plausible sounding business about time travel—the first adventure on
Skaro had taken place millions of years in the future. So that meant
there might still be Daleks active *now*. "Now" being some time after
the year 2164, which is when the second Dalek adventure is set.

"The Dalek Invasion of Earth" by Terry Nation

"The Dalek Invasion of Earth," first broadcast on 21 November 1964, is in many ways the ultimate Dalek story. Admittedly, it's not the first one—yet in a way it is. You could argue that it is the first *true* Dalek story, in the sense that no one suspected what they had on their hands the first time. In the debut story the Daleks were expected to be just some prop. Now people knew what they had. They understood the potential of the Daleks.

"The Dalek Invasion of Earth" is also the first time that substantial location shooting was permitted on *Doctor Who*. The story benefits tremendously from this, most notably in the sequences where the resistance fighters flee through the deserted streets of London, dodging the deadly spectres of the Daleks. Among the atmospheric London locations used are Hammersmith Bridge, which also features heavily in the television writing of Dennis Potter, notably *The Singing Detective* and St. Katharine's Dock, the grim site of the derelict warehouse at the beginning of "Dalek Invasion," which is now, amusingly, a luxury marina in twenty-first century London. So much for prophecy.

But in the London of 1964, which was passing for the London of 200 years in the future, the riverside warehouse is a striking, atmospheric slum. The black and white photography adds powerfully to the mood in the opening shots as a man wearing a strange metal helmet stumbles down to the water, pulls off the helmet and proceeds to drown himself in the dirty grey water of the Thames. He is in direct contravention of a huge poster on the wall behind him, which grimly advises IT IS FORBIDDEN TO DUMP BODIES INTO THE RIVER. This poster with its suggestion of government propaganda in a bleak future dystopia, along with the suicide in the desolate location and the science fiction trapping of the head garb, all suggest Orwell, perhaps in the admirable film version of *1984* directed by Mike Radford or the BBC television adaptation of the same scripted by Nigel Kneale.

After the suicide—a dark but brilliant opening—the Tardis appears and the Doctor comes out, with Barbara and Ian and Susan. Because the Doctor is still not in full control of his ship, it remains a game of Russian roulette trying to return Barbara and Ian to their native time and place. No sooner have they emerged to see if this just might be 1960s London than a girder from the derelict bridge above comes crashing down to instantly bury the Tardis and prevent them from getting back in.

This is an unashamed example of a trope already evolved by the show, making the Tardis inaccessible and closing off the escape route. It's also a knowing gesture by the writer. Ian sets off to search the abandoned warehouse nearby, looking for a cutting torch or something similar. He says to the Doctor that they must make sure they can get back in the ship before they start looking around, just in case they encounter danger. It's the voice of experience.

The Hartnell Doctor is busy being a crotchety old man. When Susan sprains her ankle trying to climb a wall, he rather alarmingly advises the young woman that she needs a spanking.

Aside from the striking riverside locations, the first panorama we see of future London is Ian's glimpse of Battersea power station. Sadly, this is an unconvincing still photograph. In a nice bit of dialogue, Ian suggests that London has converted to nuclear power because the power station is missing two of its familiar chimneys. He also discovers a calendar in the abandoned warehouse that suggests the local date is at least 2164.

The opening scenes of the story are distinguished by good location photography (Peter Hamilton was the film cameraman) and some interesting, martial music by Francis Chagrin. Director Richard Martin establishes a mood of grim tension. However, much of this mood is squandered by an immensely inept shot of a flying saucer soaring over London, heading for Sloane Square. The saucer is a risible piece of work on a par with one of the cheesier 1950s flying saucer movies.

In this story William Hartnell is, as ever, occasionally fluffing his lines. One is willing to forgive him this for some satisfyingly Doctorish behaviour. For instance, he is coolly interested in what is going on in this grim urban wasteland, while Ian just wants to escape back into the Tardis.

In an effective piece of writing, the corpse of the suicide comes bobbing up in the dirty river water to be spotted by our heroes. The Doctor finds another helmet like the one worn by the drowned man and identifies it as a device to pick up radio waves.

It isn't long, however, before the companions are splitting up, and the subplots are proliferating around them. Barbara and Susan are taken under the wing of some mysterious strangers. Meanwhile the Doctor and Ian are hived off into a different narrative stream where they are confronting a group of menacing men wearing those strange headsets. We discover that these are the Robomen, mental slaves to the Daleks. This is a clever idea by Terry Nation and virtually foolproof.

I say virtually. It's clever because it allows the production team to use normal-looking human beings in contemporary costume; the denizens of London in 2164, under the Dalek tyranny, are a shabby lot who look just like shabby Londoners of two centuries earlier. In other words, the forces of the Daleks can be supplemented by these threatening, alien minions who nevertheless look virtually human apart from those headsets, a successful enough piece of design. It seemed a cheap yet dramatically effective way of adding variety to the opposition. And a new *Doctor Who* monster.

Unfortunately, the Robomen aren't very successful, and they fall down for an unexpected reason. The way they talk.

The essential problem with the Daleks, their Achilles heel you might say, is that they talk in these flat, sinister metallic voices. It isn't long before these metallic voices become boring instead of sinister. They are deadly dull to listen to, and it is difficult to use them to do much more than utter a terse phrase or two. After that, the audience stops listening, and who can blame them?

So to supplement the ranks of the boring-talking Daleks with some equally boring Robomen proved to be a tactical mistake. Instead of an asset, the Robomen swiftly became a liability in dramatic terms.

As Ian and the Doctor turn to flee from the Robomen at the end of the first episode, they are confronted by the muddy waters of the Thames when suddenly, arising from the river, is the uncanny shape of a Dalek, aiming its gun at them.

This is a terrific, eerie scene, a *tour de force,* and a great cliff-hanger. It's like some kind of corrupt version of the Excalibur legend. It's also a case of out of the frying pan and into the fire for Ian and the Doctor.

But the climactic arrival of the Dalek, like some messenger of Death from the River Thames, is seriously undermined when it croaks a threat, and Ian responds as if he's only just registered that a Dalek is present, despite the fact that he and the Doctor have just watched one emerging, dripping from the water, pointing its gun at them.

It's possible that this is simply a case of the script and the action on the screen being at variance. Maybe Terry Nation intended for the Dalek to arise from the depths unseen, behind the backs of the Doctor and Ian, as they were preoccupied with the Robomen approaching them. Another more intriguing possibility is that Nation envisaged these Daleks as looking quite different from the ones in the previous story. This notion is supported later, when the Doctor and Ian are taken under guard to the landing zone for the Daleks' flying saucer at the "Heliport Chelsea" (one of the few gestures the script makes towards imagining a London of the future). In this scene Ian's dialogue actually suggests that these Daleks appear considerably different from the ones he's seen before. The designer for this story, Spencer Chapman, knew better than to tamper with a winning formula. Other than the unobtrusive disc on the back, these Daleks are virtually Cusick's original design.

The new metal disc on the Daleks was necessary because this allowed the Daleks to move freely. They are "energy collection discs." In the previous adventure the Daleks were only capable of moving backwards or forwards along smooth metal floors, from which they took their power in the form of static electricity. Now here they were emerging from rivers and scooting all over London. There had to be some innovation to explain this new mobility.

Some would argue that this is why Terry Nation's time travel argument begins to crumble. The Daleks in this story seem more advanced than the ones in the previous adventure. Yet that story, in which they were wiped out, took place in the future. So these more technologically advanced Daleks are in fact, *earlier* than the other ones. Of course, one could argue that the future Daleks are a degenerate race. Or maybe the Daleks have mastered time travel . . .

In a separate strand of story, we discover that the people who have taken Susan and Barbara are members of an underground resistance force fighting the Daleks. We gradually learn that the Daleks have taken over London, and indeed the world. Barbara and Susan are led into the secret underground lair of the resistance fighters who are trying to throw off the Dalek yoke. There are torn posters on the wall with the single word "Veto" or "Vetoed" emblazoned on them. These read like some kind of political message boiled down to an essential distillate. They also once again suggest Orwell.

Meanwhile the Daleks are croaking threats in a characteristic fashion. On a radio broadcast to the oppressed humans, the Daleks demand obedience. This is when Dortmun, the wheelchair-bound resistance leader (Alan Judd), makes a crack about them resembling dustbins and gets a good laugh from the resistance fighters.

When Barbara is introduced to these hard-bitten characters, their first question, presumably because she is a woman, is whether she can cook. This is an attitude that seems dated well before 2164. However, Dortmun is an interesting character, pluckily arranging mayhem for the invaders from the confines of his wheelchair.

Dortmun also oddly prefigures Davros, the leader of the Daleks, who turns up later in the Dalek mythology that unfolds through *Doctor Who* over the years. Davros is a kind of half-man, half-Dalek. A sort of centaur. He rolls along in his half-Dalek shell, strangely like a man in a wheelchair. (Another plausible source of inspiration for Davros is suggested by still photographs of actors inside the Daleks, resting between takes, with the top half of the Dalek armour removed. Put some alien makeup on the actor, and you pretty much have Davros.)

We hear how the Earth was initially softened up by a meteorite storm spreading a plague before the Daleks landed and invaded in person. This is a clever idea that bears comparison with the meteor shower in the *Day of the Triffids* that blinds most of humankind, making them easy prey for the carnivorous plants. As we gradually learn the Daleks' behaviour on Earth, we begin to wonder about their motives. They are busy converting Bedfordshire into a kind of giant mine. But why? What are they digging for? The Doctor, for one, doesn't seem to care. He tells the others to ignore all this nonsense about Bedfordshire.

This goes beyond tetchy. It suggests a fundamental lack of interest in crucial questions that seems downright odd coming from the same character who not long ago was so coolly attentive of the situation.

On the other hand, if this was the sort of trickster Doctor, of the kind later exemplified by Sylvester McCoy, it might all just be a stratagem, concealing a razor sharp mind deeply preoccupied with vanquishing a deadly foe.

Back among the resistance fighters we meet Jenny, who doesn't believe in sentiment. She's a modern woman, unlike Barbara. Yet Jenny and Barbara will be paired off together in one of the subplots that is about to ensue as the companions are separated from the Doctor—and separated from each other—at regular intervals. Inside one of the Dalek's flying saucers, the Doctor is busy admiring the technology in a Doctor-ish way. At the same time, the viewer can admire Spencer Chapman's designs. On the outside it might look like a flying pie plate, but inside this Dalek saucer is a convincingly futuristic, sparse, and technological environment.

As soon as the Doctor has finished admiring it, he is suddenly in jeopardy, dragged away from Ian and taken to the part of the saucer where people are turned into Robomen. The Doctor is thrown down in an undignified manner and is about to be robotised, providing a cliff-hanger ending.

The Doctor isn't robotised. Not quite. Nobody could pull that on him. But he does subsequently disappear from the story for long stretches, and remains unconscious for much of the time while the three companions are being paired off with a proliferation of subsidiary characters. Perhaps this is meant to give the story scope, an epic feel, but it has the effect of diluting the essence of the show. Who cares about these minor characters? Where's the Doctor? Perhaps, in the shape of William Hartnell, having a well earned rest.

One of Terry Nation's masterstrokes was making the Daleks sort of futuristic metal fascists. He never denied that he had the Nazis in mind when he created them and, in "The Dalek Invasion of Earth," this is made amusingly explicit by the Daleks' Nazi salute in front of the Albert Memorial.

The London location photography is one of the strongest assets of "The Dalek Invasion of Earth," evoking a real time and place. It's never really in any doubt that it's not London in 2164, but London in 1964, that we're looking at. There are a few attempts in the story towards creating a sense of the future. One such is the old woman who offers shelter to Barbara and Jenny when they are on the run from the Daleks in the countryside. She reminisces about having visited London and seeing things like the moving sidewalk. In any case it turns out that the woman's actually a treacherous old crone. She has betrayed Barbara and Jenny to the Daleks, who take them away. The old woman gloats, examining the reward with her accomplice. Not thirty pieces of silver but some fruit and sugar.

This well realized scene stands out in Dalek "Invasion." It is also pleasingly reminiscent of stories set in occupied France during World War II, where there were also resistance fighters at war against an alien invader in constant danger of betrayal, reinforcing parallels between the Daleks and the Nazis.

Barbara and Jenny's flight to the countryside, and their capture by the Daleks, follows one of the most exciting and wholly successful sequences in "Dalek Invasion." The unaccustomed location shooting gives spectacular results in a sequence that dramatises fear and flight in a barren and threatening London. We see the deserted Embankment, eerily empty London streets, Daleks crossing Westminster Bridge, prowling and gathering in Trafalgar Square accompanied by Francis Chagrin's martial music. Here are some of the most astonishing scenes in the story as Barbara and Jenny and the disabled Dortmun flee through the streets. The women whisk Dortmun along at high speed in his wheelchair. They race down the eerily deserted streets dodging sinister clusters of Daleks set against familiar London landmarks. The gritty documentary look of the photography here makes for some extraordinary scenes that haven't dated at all.

It is always unsettling to see a great metropolis with its streets empty. Films like *Seven Days to Noon*, *The Day the Earth Caught Fire* and *28 Days Later* have managed this feat with London while American films like *The Omega Man* (Los Angeles) and *The Devil's Advocate* (New York) also achieved striking effects.

Adventure stories that are told in serial form often involve a group of characters being routinely separated then reunited. That's certainly the case in "The Dalek Invasion," somewhat to its detriment. Apart from the above-mentioned tendency to dilute the narrative with a flood of minor characters, there is also the matter of excluding the Doctor from the story. Indeed, the Doctor is notably absent for large sections of the plot, and when he does appear he is distinctly feeble, even fainting when he learns that a firebomb has been planted nearby. The justification for this is that he has recently been almost—but not quite—robotised while on board the Dalek saucer. Nevertheless, he's unforgivably ineffectual. Instead of passing out at the mention of a bomb, the Doctor should be the one to defuse it. Or, failing that, the companion (in this case Susan) should do the honours. But it is left largely to a nonentity called David to defuse the bomb.

Later on David and Susan actually end up kissing, and later still she elects to stay on Earth with him instead of pursuing her adventures with the Doctor in the Tardis. (Carole Ann Ford's contract ended with the final episode of this Dalek story.)

Throughout much of the London sequence, however, the Doctor is abandoned, quite literally. He is left lying, unconscious, like so much baggage. While he is on his back, comatose, Susan is sneaking through the sewers, and Barbara commandeers a fire truck (its Borough of Ealing insignia perfunctorily disguised) and literally smashes her way out of London through a line of Daleks in a highly cathartic moment. The Daleks, however, get their revenge when a pie plate flying saucer blows up the fire truck, or at least a model of it.

Finally, the scattered band of heroes reunite at the Dalek mine in Bedfordshire. Here Ian, who seems to have spent most of the story eavesdropping on the Daleks from concealment (albeit in some damn fine sets), is finally taking direct action and is formulating an attack on the Daleks.

The mine is introduced in a striking scene in which the Daleks stand guard and their Robomen straw bosses follow, wielding whips as a tattered group of human slaves laboriously pull a railroad car along with ropes. The notion of human labourers working for alien masters here is agreeably reminiscent of Nigel Kneale's *Quatermass II*.

The question of what exactly the Daleks are digging for in the mine is the story's big mystery. Eventually we learn that they are digging down to the Earth's core, which they intend to replace with a propulsion unit. The Daleks will then fly the Earth around the galaxy like a giant spaceship.

The less said about the science of this, the better. But it certainly is a grand scheme, fitting for such grand villains. And it does evoke the golden age of space opera, the science fiction pulp magazines of the 1930s and 1940s that featured the writing of such genre stalwarts as Edmond Hamilton and E. E. Doc Smith.

In due course, the Doctor and his companions seize control of the mine and foment insurrection. Having taken possession of the control unit for the Robomen, Barbara amusingly thinks she has to speak into it in a Dalek voice and tries hard to do so. The Doctor impatiently takes control (about time) and enunciates clearly into the device, exhorting the hordes to overthrow and destroy their masters. There then ensue some rousing sequences in which the Robomen and the slave workers do indeed turn against their masters and kill them. It's not quite *Battleship Potemkin* with the Daleks, but it must have been exhilarating stuff to viewers at the time, after six episodes of alien tyranny.

The mine blows up, the Tardis is cleared of debris, and Big Ben once again tolls above the London skyline, symbolically ending the silence of the Dalek repression. The Doctor and his companions prepare to leave, but with one change to the line up. Susan is destined to stay with David, the bomb-defuser. The Doctor gives her his blessing and goes.

The Tardis disappears, leaving Susan with David. She stares down at her Tardis key, lying abandoned on the ground, and the shot mixes through to a vista of distant galaxies against the blackness of space. It's a moving image and would be even more powerful if it was clear to the viewer *what* that damned thing lying on the ground actually *was*, and they didn't have to consult a reference book to find out.

*   *   *

When I learned that the elegiac, unusually lyrical leave-taking scene in "The Dalek Invasion of Earth" was actually written by David Whitaker, then script editor of the show, and added to Terry Nation's script as a kind of coda, I felt an enormous sense of relief. Scenes of companions saying farewell to the Doctor would become something of a staple of the show over the decades and, as script editor, I was responsible for writing one myself when Bonnie Langford said good-bye to Sylvester McCoy in 1987. I had written it as an audition piece and never actually intended it to end up in a script. But Sylvester became very attached to it and, at his insistence, it was eventually tacked on to "Dragonfire," an extremely good script by Ian Briggs.

It assuaged my feelings of guilt to learn that this sort of thing had been going on since *Doctor Who* began, with the script editors dramatising the coming and goings of the companions and adding them to scripts written by other hands.

In a move reflecting their popularity, the second season of *Doctor Who* featured two Dalek stories, the second one being "The Chase." Perhaps more interesting than "The Chase" are the Dalek stories that followed in the third season, "Mission to the Unknown" and "The Daleks' Master Plan," both transmitted in 1965. The former is a one episode oddity, a curtain raiser to the epic twelve episode "Master Plan."

It would be instructive to consider these third season Dalek stories in some detail, unfortunately it is impossible to do so. As mentioned in chapter one, there are certain lacunae in the history of *Doctor Who*, gaps left by episodes that are lost forever, and it is here that they begin to be felt most keenly. We'll look at this situation is some detail in the next chapter, but for now suffice to say that "Mission to the Unknown" is gone in its (brief) entirety and all that survives of the dozen "Master Plan" episodes are parts 2, 5, and 10. At least we can consider these.

"The Daleks' Master Plan" by Terry Nation and Dennis Spooner

Episode 2 of "The Daleks' Master Plan" is entitled "Day of Armageddon." It opens on the planet Kembel (a damned strange name for a planet and not as punchy as Terry Nation's original suggestion, Varga) in an evocative alien jungle setting where the Doctor is crouched, watching the Daleks snooping at the door of the Tardis. One is immediately struck by the superior sets and costumes in this story (making the loss of three quarters of its length all the more keenly felt), but the clarity of the videotape image, as restored on DVD, reveals some embarrassing flaws, such as the battered carapace of some of the Dalek props. These death-dealing machines are starting to look positively tatty.

We are soon introduced (in a very impressive set) to an alien entity called Zephon, Master of the Fifth Galaxy. Unfortunately this sort of ineffectual exotica proliferates throughout the story. It's the sort of unconvincing half-baked cliché that gives science fiction a bad name. One has the strong sense that Terry Nation has no idea what the Fifth Galaxy is, let alone the other four. In any event, Zephon is a menacing hooded figure, rather resembling a monk, whose sinister aspect is undercut by the ridiculous seaweed style fronds that he has instead of hands. Matters aren't helped by the undistinguished would-be science fiction dialogue that ensues about the intergalactic congress in Andromeda and so on. Whereas "The Dalek Invasion of Earth" was founded in a certain gritty reality, with its recognizable London setting, here we are adrift in an unconvincing futuristic milieu of inadequately imagined other worlds. The whole thing is a hair's breadth away from *The Hitchhiker's Guide to the Galaxy* style parody. Or perhaps not even that far away. One might charitably assume that Terry Nation, a talented writer and one with a sense of humour, had his tongue in his cheek here.

Any notion of comedy is undercut, though, by the intermittent ruthlessness and violence of the story. "Master Plan" featured the startling innovation of having the Doctor's companion, Katarina (Adrienne Hill), dying in the course of the adventure. What's more, her replacement Sara (Jean Marsh, whom I'd later work with on the story "Battlefield") is also killed off, though not before shooting and killing her own brother.

Nonetheless, despite the downbeat nature and cold-bloodedness implied by this high body count, "The Daleks' Master Plan" also features large dollops of broad humour, and not necessarily to its advantage.

On the plus side of the equation, the story has some very good music by Tristram Cary, and there are some nice small touches that do genuinely convey a sense of the alien, as when we see the Guardian of the Solar System holding a pen and writing in a very strange fashion. The Guardian is called Mavic Chen, an intriguingly bizarre name that conveys a certain sense of otherworldly reality in a fashion that looks back to the works of Edgar Rice Burroughs and forward to the creations of George Lucas. There is also some laudable design in evidence (courtesy of the ever-reliable and often inspired Raymond Cusick). The composite noise of unseen creatures crying out in the jungle also gives us a real sense of an otherworldly environment. It is in this jungle that we see the Daleks use their guns as flamethrowers. These flames flicker eerily on the face of Bret Vyon, a Space Security Service agent who will later, in a piece of manipulation by the sinister Mavic Chen, be killed by his own sister Sara. The ill-fated Bret is played by Nicholas Courtney, a talented actor who will later earn a major place in *Doctor Who* history as the Brigadier, one of the Doctor's longest running allies.

The Daleks proceed to burn down some alien looking trees in an impressive display of pyrotechnics that probably had the floor managers in the studio in a cold sweat. They are setting a wall of fire to flush the Doctor and his friends out of the jungle. These sequences are also marked by some notably fluid camera work.

As the story develops and various alien delegates gather on Kembel we're treated to some imaginative and interesting costume design (seaweed hands not withstanding), and one of the delegates from the Outer Galaxies has some amazing pointed teeth which must have inspired a few nightmares in younger viewers. There are also some intriguing, if not entirely convincing spaceships, seen sitting on a landing pad. William Hartnell, however, has found a new way to mess up his lines, saying "revelant" instead of relevant.

Despite this clear mismatch between the time-travelling alien genius and the very down-to-earth actor who plays him, the character of the Doctor has by now acquired considerable authority. Sadly, the story he's involved in features such sub-pulp science fiction concepts as the most valuable mineral in the universe and one senses the hoariest kind of McGuffin taking shape.

But "The Dalek Master Plan" is beautifully photographed (the film cameraman is again Peter Hamilton) and strikingly well directed by Douglas Camfield. The noteworthy design of this mammoth epic was shared between Raymond Cusick and Barry Newbery ("The Aztecs"), making a fortuitous pairing of two of the BBC's outstanding designers.

By the time we reach the next surviving fragment of "Master Plan," episode five, entitled "Counter Plot," Katarina has met her death on a spaceship while Bret has fallen by the wayside, shot by his sister. The Doctor and his surviving companion Steven (Peter Purves) stumble into an experimental chamber where an exercise in teleportation is being carried out, and we are once again reminded of the ingenuity and originality of Terry Nation. Teleportation was by no means unknown in science fiction literature at this time, but it wasn't exactly a television staple, and it would be a year yet before *Star Trek* gave us Captain Kirk being beamed up by Scotty, in September 1966. Sara, the female Space Security agent, who at this point in the story is still a villain (albeit an innocent one, being used by Mavic Chen as his cat's-paw), arrives in the chamber on their heels, just in time to be accidentally teleported with them. The chamber is one of many excellent sets in the story and the beginning of the teleportation sequence is a memorable solarization effect—a kind of psychedelic negative image.

Teleportation carries the Doctor, Steven, and Sara, along with the proper subjects of the experiment (some non-speaking laboratory mice), to the planet Mira. Here they encounter a race of invisible monsters, the Visians. This unseen menace is evoked by moving vegetation and through the reasonably effective technique of footprints appearing on the ground (an old ruse used, for instance, in *Forbidden Planet*). Effective or not, the Visians point up one of the basic flaws of "Master Plan." A Dalek story should be about the Daleks. Obviously there's a need for an interesting cast of supporting characters. Yet Terry Nation had also, from the beginning, shown a tendency to include some secondary exotic menaces in his Dalek stories: the swamp monsters in "The Daleks," the Robomen in "Invasion," something called the Mire Beast in "The Chase." In some cases, as with the Robomen, these were potentially interesting additions to the mix. In the case of the Visians in "Master Plan," these secondary menaces merely distract from and dilute what should be a story about the Daleks. It's hardly surprising, though, that such examples of plot padding turn up in a story that spans twelve episodes.

But if "Master Plan" is padded, it's not necessarily Terry Nation's fault. The workload involved in scripting such a massive story led to Nation dividing the writing chores between himself and former *Doctor Who* script editor Dennis Spooner. Nation wrote episodes one through five and seven. Spooner wrote episodes six and eight to twelve, with a credit line that reads "from an idea by Terry Nation."

By the time we reach the last surviving remnant of "Master Plan" (episode ten, "Escape Switch," the only surviving example of Dennis Spooner's contribution) things have begun to go seriously awry. For a start, we are now in ancient Egypt, messing around amongst tombs and pyramids. While this does provide an opportunity for some typically high quality design work by Barry Newbery, it also suggests a certain desperation in the ideas department. Further evidence of last ditch measures is the reappearance of a comedy relief villain called the Monk, who had turned up previously in a non-Dalek story called "The Time Meddler," also written by Spooner, at the end of Season 2, in July 1965.

The Monk is, in theory at least, an interesting character and, in some senses, a pivotal one. Like the Doctor he is a traveller through space and time. In fact, he is described as coming from the same planet as the Doctor—although that planet is not yet named. The Monk has his own Tardis, one with a working chameleon circuit, which means it can assume any shape, unlike the Doctor's, which is stuck in its police box form.

In other words, the Monk is a Time Lord in all but name, and he comes from Gallifrey, just like the Doctor. These other words are anachronistic, because the concepts of Time Lords, and the naming of Gallifrey have not yet been formulated. They are ideas that await us further down the line in the history of the show. Nevertheless, the Monk is tantalising character, especially for hard core fans, pointing as he does to certain central tenets of the mythos that are yet to emerge. He is also significant in that he is the first character, other than the Doctor and companions, to return and appear in more than one *Doctor Who* story.

It's rather disappointing to report, then, that at least in the one episode of "Master Plan" that survives, the Monk is rather a tedious fellow, an obvious charlatan and double-crosser with a regrettable habit of talking to himself. He makes his debut in this episode swathed in mummy bandages and emerging from a sarcophagus in a tomb while the companions—at this stage Steven and Sara (who is now among the good guys)—look on in trepidation. This is the payoff of what is decidedly one of the weaker cliff-hangers in the show.

"Escape Switch" is not without its compensations. The Doctor strolls among the sunlit pyramids (all studio creations courtesy of Barry Newbery) wearing a Panama hat which makes him look like a suavely patrician Edwardian tourist. He is confronted by the Daleks who have captured Sara, Steven, and the Monk and are seeking to exchange them for the taranium core. Taranium is the rarest mineral in the universe, and the Daleks need it to create the time destructor just as Terry Nation needed it to create another plot McGuffin. "Master Plan" was the lengthiest *Doctor Who* story to date and is certainly some kind of epic. It is also much lauded by the fans. But the entire "epic" expanse of "Master Plan" is really just a massively padded chase, predicated on these routine McGuffins.

In "Escape Switch," the Doctor is powerful and commanding in his confrontation with the Daleks, laying down the terms of the exchange of the taranium core for the hostages. (William Hartnell does have a bit of trouble saying "Mavic Chen," but who can blame him?) Jean Marsh is excellent as the short-lived companion Sara. The Egyptian setting is less than entirely convincing. Despite Barry Newbery's adept design work, the intense studio lighting needed to suggest Egyptian sunlight also tends to point up the theatricality, and artificiality, of the environment. The earlier existing episodes set on alien planets, benefited from the story being largely set at night and in darkness, which provided an atmosphere conducive to suspense and menace while also concealing any of the shortcomings inevitable on such a modestly budgeted show. In the full glare of the studio lights, ancient Egypt is simply less convincing than the planets Mira or Kembel. Nonetheless, there is an interesting and vivid sequence where ancient Egyptian warriors attack the Daleks with spears and rocks.

This episode ends with the Doctor double-crossing the Daleks and escaping in possession of both the taranium core and his companions. The Daleks are apoplectic, swearing revenge and unending pursuit. Their strident, synthesised voices are perfect for such pronouncements, and we are reminded again how much the success of these strange villains is due to their grating vocals.

The Doctor has also managed to dispense with the annoying Monk by stealing the directional unit from his Tardis (yet another McGuffin) thereby sending him into exile on a freezing, desolate ice planet.

The threat of the Time Lords, as well as the threat of the Daleks, has been dealt with for the time being . . .

chapter 3

Regeneration

On 21 April 1987 I was embroiled in the final day of shooting on my first *Doctor Who* story, the sorely troubled and deeply compromised "Time and the Rani." It had been a long, fraught day in the studio culminating in us blowing up a giant brain (don't ask). As I wrote in my diary at the time:

"We get the shot. We blow up the brain. We finish the show. In the taxi back home, the driver reminisces about Doctor Who as we drive through the empty night streets. He went to the cinema to see the first movie with Peter Cushing in it (*Dr Who and the Daleks*), and all over the cinema, parents were having to explain to their kids who were saying, 'That's not him. That's not the Doctor.'"

Well, the tots were just going to have to get used to it . . .

Because the fourth season of *Doctor Who*, which began transmission on 10 September 1966, saw William Hartnell bowing out of the role of the Doctor (albeit reluctantly) to be replaced by Patrick Troughton. Although it's never easy to arrive at the precise truth about such situations, it's possible that Hartnell departed for reasons of ill health. It's also possible that the production team had had enough of a rather cantankerous leading man. In any case, it was decided that the show could, and would, continue without him. The ruse that made this possible was the invention of a concept called *regeneration*.

The notion was that the Doctor, being an alien, could periodically undergo a kind of metamorphosis in which his body was renewed and assumed a new shape . . . the shape, that is, of a different actor. It's a brilliant yet simple idea, though it might not have been so simple to arrive at. In *Doctor Who: The Sixties*, Howe, Stammers, and Walker cite script editor Gerry Davis as giving credit for the concept to the triumvirate of producer Innes Lloyd, writer Dennis Spooner, and writer and series science advisor Kit Pedler. These are the men who came up with regeneration, although it wasn't called that yet.

It's deeply ironic that at the precise juncture when this device appears in the show's lengthy narrative—a device that allows for the show to be endlessly renewed and go on forever—that the real world intervenes. Because it is in the fourth season where the gaps in the *Doctor Who* archives really begin to make themselves felt. It's almost as if the fates are saying, "The character may be able to go on forever but no one will be able to see the shows featuring him . . . because they're going to be *gone* forever."

It's a classic example of the curse of *Doctor Who*, and it takes some explaining. In fact, it takes considerable explaining to anyone who comes from a television culture like that of America, where the notion of deliberately and systematically destroying great swathes of television classics like (say) *The Twilight Zone*, *The Outer Limits*, and *Star Trek* is pretty much unthinkable.

But that is what happened to *Doctor Who*. For several years during the late 1960s, the tapes of the original *Doctor Who* stories were systematically wiped. Apparently this was standard practise. After broadcast the tapes were returned to the BBC Engineering Department where they were cheerfully erased. The justification for this extraordinary procedure was that videotape was expensive and that re-using it made good economic sense. Just how it's good sense to obliterate a commodity that could be sold again and again, all over the world, for decades and quite possibly even centuries to come, in return for a tiny short-term saving of money, is difficult to say. It might be argued that at the time the Engineering Department was diligently erasing *Doctor Who* with an electromagnet, no one actually knew that *Doctor Who* was such a commodity.

Yet even then the series was being sold, and shown, all over the world. Indeed, this is why the devastation of the show isn't even worse than it is. Because before the tapes were wiped, they were transferred onto film stock for sale to TV markets all over the world. Don't heave a sigh of relief yet, though. Because once foreign broadcasters had finished with the films, they were instructed to destroy them (and provide a "Certificate of Destruction"—a *Doctor Who* title if ever there was one) or return them to the BBC. Once they were returned to the BBC, the BBC would then destroy them. The thinking apparently being that once a show had proved itself popular enough to be shown all over the world, then it must be so worthless that it wasn't even worth storing. Such Alice in Wonderland logic suggests a rather sinister and surreal *Doctor Who* plot.

In any event, the results of these policies were that any *Doctor Who* episodes that had managed to survive on film after being erased on videotape in the late 1960s were diligently and carefully *burned* during the 1970s. (I swear I'm not making this up.)

The results of this *auto-da-fé* mean that there are missing *Doctor Who* stories and episodes that date back to the first Hartnell series, disfiguring it like gap teeth in the smile of a beautiful woman. Say goodbye to "Marco Polo," for example, in its entirety. And the French Revolution story "The Reign of Terror" is missing two episodes. The second Hartnell series has only one mutilated story, "The Crusade," for which only two episodes exist. With series three the fun really begins. Out of ten stories, only three survive intact.

And the situation for the Patrick Troughton Doctor is much, much worse. A list of episodes from the Troughton era reads like a roll call of the lost; the first story, the one that introduced him and pitted him against his nemesis, "Power of the Daleks" is completely destroyed. The second story, "The Highlanders," which introduced Frazer Hines as the companion Jamie, is also completely destroyed. Of the next story, "The Underwater Menace," only one episode survives. Next is "The Moonbase." Two (nonconsecutive) episodes of that survive. Next is "The Macra Terror." None survive. Next, "The Faceless Ones." Two nonconsecutive episodes survive. The next Dalek saga, "The Evil of the Daleks," has fared little better than the first Troughton Dalek story: only one episode survives. Then we have "The Tomb of the Cybermen" that, astonishingly, is completely intact. For "The Abominable Snowmen," however, the film-burners are back on form with only one episode escaping their attention. By the time we reach the next story, "The Ice Warriors," it almost seems cause for celebration that only two of the six episodes have been destroyed.

The film-burners are in full swing for the next story, though. "The Enemy of the World" has only one episode surviving. The same for "Web of Fear." Then for "Fury from the Deep" there are none. For "The Wheel in Space," two survive. "The Dominators," again, astonishingly, is complete. So is "The Mind Robber." For "The Invasion" (eight episodes), only episodes one and four were destroyed. Then "The Krotons" and "The Seeds of Death" are intact. For "The Space Pirates," though, all but one episode has been destroyed. Then "The War Games" (which introduces the concept of the Time Lords) is miraculously intact.

Then we're out of the woods and the purge is at an end. Like a nerve transmission finally working its way into the pea-sized brain of some great armoured creature of the Cretaceous, the notion that this might not be a good thing to do dawned at last, and policy was changed. All subsequent stories are complete (although some only exist in black and white copies).

The damage has been done, and reviewing the Troughton era is necessarily like visiting an art gallery where vandals have been beavering away with razor, blowtorch, and spray can. It's a heartbreaking business. There is virtually nothing left. Out of a total of twenty-three stories in the three Troughton seasons only six survive intact. Or, to put it differently, there is not a single complete story from Season 4 (Troughton's debut). There is only one complete story surviving from Season 5. So, in Season 6, one is pathetically grateful that five out of seven survive.

If this seems like something of a diatribe, I can only say that I was hard-pressed not to preface the word "destroyed" with the word "deliberately" every time I used it. The mentality behind such behaviour certainly takes some understanding. It would be wrong to think that *Doctor Who* was the only victim of such organised and officially sanctioned vandalism. Nigel Kneale's first *Quatermass* story was subjected to similar mutilation and his classic science fiction plays *The Creature* and *The Road* are both gone forever. (Though the former at least survives as the film *The Abominable Snowman*.)

In utter contrast to the thoughtless devastation that was wrought at the time, the BBC has recently compiled a painstaking DVD collection (appropriately entitled *Lost in Time*) which lovingly collects and restores all the surviving fragments of the incomplete episodes. It's a splendid piece of work and the thoughtful and well written notes that accompany the set do their best to explain and justify what happened, stating that the individuals responsible for this pillage were "just ordinary people doing their jobs in terms of the need and assumptions of the day."

While obviously it would be insane, not to mention inappropriate, ridiculous, and tasteless, to invoke the shadow of the Third Reich here, one can't help observing that virtually any human activity could be excused under such a rubric.

This is an even greater shame than it seems on first consideration. Because the Troughton era was in many ways a unique high-water mark in *Doctor Who*. There would be better scripts, equally appealing actors to play the Doctor, more fascinating concepts, but in series four to six certain high points were reached in the *Doctor Who* saga that can never be repeated.

If we regard the Hartnell years as a kind of shakedown cruise, then the Troughton era was a case of a show that had settled in and found itself—the format had been established and now, with a new actor in the lead role, old boundaries had been obliterated and experimentation could begin. Perhaps, more importantly, the Troughton *Doctor Who* seasons would be the last ones in black and white. There is something unique about monochrome photography, especially for a science fiction series with a less than mammoth budget. Black and white disguises and forgives a multitude of sins. It also adds a mystique, a mood, or atmosphere which lends immeasurably to even barely competent stories, making them seem vast and mysterious and unknowable. With the advent of colour photography, all this would be lost.

On a more technical level, the shift from black and white photography to colour resembles the change from silent to talking pictures. The constraints of a new technology, primitive and in its infancy, would put paid to sophisticated photography and visual techniques that had come to their full-flower under black and white. (Though it's hard to argue this point too forcefully when one considers the diabolically bad design work in "The Krotons," for instance.)

*   *   *

From a *Doctor Who* point of view, the years 1966 to 1969 are the Troughton years. A broader point of view might also embrace some of these other events. May 1967 saw the release of the Beatles' *Sgt. Pepper's Lonely Hearts Club Band*, a seminal rock LP and one of the first concept albums. The following month the Six Days' War erupted between Israel and her Arab neighbours. Later, in June 1967, Mick Jagger and Keith Richards of the Rolling Stones began a three-month sentence at Brixton prison on drugs charges; a week later, as the result of an overwhelming public outcry, they were released.

The beginning of 1968 marked the start of the Tet Offensive in Vietnam, with intensive fighting as the North Vietnamese struck back against the American-supported South. February 1968 witnessed the supersonic jet Concorde's maiden flight. April 1968 offered the grim spectacle of riots in Washington following the assassination of Martin Luther King. In May 1968, there was rioting in the streets of Paris, initially led by students but soon spreading to other sectors of society.

August 1968 saw the Soviet invasion of Czechoslovakia in response to a liberalization of the regime in that country.

In October 1968, black American athletes John Carlos and Tommy Smith were suspended for giving the black power salute at the Olympics in Mexico City. Throughout 1968 there were deepening doubts among the American public about the US involvement in Vietnam. In 1969, Samuel Beckett won the Nobel Prize for Literature. In March of that year, John Lennon and his wife Yoko Ono took to their bed for a week in protest against violence.

In July 1969 Rolling Stone Brian Jones was found dead in his swimming pool. On 16 July 1969, Apollo 11 was launched into space, and on 21 July Neil Armstrong walked on the moon, an event that began to put many of the science fictional doings on *Doctor Who* in a new perspective.

*   *   *

"The Tomb of the Cybermen" by Kit Pedler and Gerry Davis

The earliest Patrick Troughton story to survive in its entirety is "The Tomb of the Cybermen." The eponymous Cybermen were a foe that the Doctor, and the viewers, had first encountered in "The Tenth Planet" (1966), William Hartnell's final story. They were created by Gerry Davis, a *Doctor Who* script editor and writer, and Kit Pedler, a medical doctor and writer who was the show's informal scientific adviser. Unlike the mutated Daleks, the Cybermen were once men (there is precious little mention of Cyberwomen in the canon) and have voluntarily forsaken their humanity, turning themselves into men-machine hybrids with coldly logical minds. Kit Pedler had done research on computer simulations of the nervous system, and this may well have informed his thinking about the man-machine interface. Pedler and Davis would go on to create the classic eco-thriller series *Doomwatch* in 1969.

The Cybermen are widely held to be a *Doctor Who* monster on par with the Daleks. Frankly this is a huge overstatement of the case. The Cybermen are a run of the mill alien adversary, lacking the brilliant design that characterised Raymond Cusick's pioneering work on the Daleks. The costume supervisor Sandra Reid was responsible for the original design of the Cybermen, a look that hasn't varied hugely in the subsequent decades. The Cybermen costumes aren't bad. They have the virtue of simplicity and they look fairly eerie in black and white. Later, in colour, the silver outfits just look cheap and kitsch-futuristic.

Altogether the Cybermen lack the qualities that made the Daleks a timeless classic. Indeed, the public at large seem to subscribe to this perception. There have never been any Cybermen spin-off films, and only a trickle of tie-in merchandise to compare with the flood that accompanied the Daleks.

Under other circumstances, the Cybermen could very easily have put in one appearance and then vanished from the series forever. However, they proved sufficiently popular to reappear in a Patrick Troughton story called "The Moonbase," a 1967 story of which only two episodes survive, and since then have been a regular villain of the show.

"The Tomb of the Cybermen" is not only the first Troughton story to come down to us intact, it is also the first complete Cyberman story ("Tenth Planet" is missing one episode). It begins with the Doctor introducing a new companion to the Tardis, Victoria Waterfield (played by Deborah Watling). Victoria is from 1867, a native of Victorian London whose father was killed in the previous story, "The Evil of the Daleks." The Doctor explains about his ship to her, that it's his home and has been for a long time. Troughton is charming as he tries to remember his exact age, eventually confessing to being about 450 years old. Victoria declares that she is impressed by all the knobs on the Tardis's elaborate control panel (dialogue that must have occasioned considerable ribald laughter during the studio shoot).

Already on board the Tardis is a male companion, Jamie McCrimmon (Frazer Hines), a young man from eighteenth century Scotland who joined up six adventures ago in a story (now lost, of course) called "The Highlanders" and who is, frankly, a breath of fresh air. Jamie observes with a certain wry amusement the Doctor's attempts to put Victoria at her ease. He suggests that the Doctor endeavour to achieve a smooth takeoff so as not to alarm their new passenger. The Doctor bridles at the suggestion that he's a bad driver.

He sets the Tardis in motion and we cut straight to a quarry (in Gerrard's Cross). Disused or temporarily empty quarries were always a cheap, though deeply unimaginative, option to stand-in for a barren alien landscape on *Doctor Who*, and they would become a standing joke. ("It wouldn't be Doctor Who without a quarry," said Malcom

Kohll when I told him we'd be filming his script "Delta and the Bannermen" in a slate quarry near Rickmansworth.)

This quarry at least features some effective dramatic music (from stock) which suggests an alien location, and some nice effects design (by Michaeljohn Harris). We get a convincing shot of a spaceship which has evidently landed some time earlier. We will discover that we are on the planet Telos, which luckily has an Earth-like atmosphere and we're straight in at the deep end with a rather interesting group of characters. They are all human, all from Earth, and are apparently here on some kind of expedition. The first few lines of dialogue establish a diversity of agendas and a variety of conflicts within the group. Best of all, nobody states baldly what they are doing here, and we have to pick up information as we go along. This is smart, realistic writing and we learn soon enough that the group is on an archaeological expedition.

They are looking for the entrance to the city of Telos, we're told. Then an explosive charge is detonated high on a rock face. The explosion is huge, and to the casual observer it seems likely that any number of priceless artefacts have been destroyed. In another neat piece of writing, the explosion seems at first to have accomplished nothing at all. Only after a dramatic pause does a rock-slide reveal the entrance to a tomb. The party—which surprisingly, and refreshingly for Doctor Who, contains a black member (and there's even a woman, too)—scramble up the rock face, excitedly hurrying to the find. The photography in this sequence (once again by Peter Hamilton) is tremendous, and along with the on-the-fly introduction of the characters and the sudden discovery of the tomb, we begin to feel that we might be in for a really exciting adventure.

What has been exposed on the cliff face is the entrance to an Egyptian-style tomb, flanked by impressive images of Cybermen. As with all good Egyptian tombs, breaching it proves to be a dangerous business. The first man to touch the doors is electrocuted and drops down dead. As this moment of peak tension the Tardis's arrival is signalled by that familiar hoarse noise. The expedition members react by pulling guns and when the Doctor, Jamie, and Victoria wander into view they are stopped by a barked command, "Hold it right there, friend." The Doctor looks around at all these guns pointing at him and says, "If you put it like that, I certainly will."

But he has hardly said these words when he notices the dead man and flings himself forward, into the thick of the narrative. Hurrying to the body he says, "He appears to have been electrocuted. Trying to open these doors, perhaps." This is all good Doctor-ish behaviour and bodes well for the story.

And as soon as the Doctor hears that the expedition is here to study the tomb of the Cybermen, wild Daleks couldn't drag him away. "I can open these doors for you," he says. It seems that it is now safe to touch the entrance. "The poor fellow who died drained all the electricity out of his body," explains the Doctor, getting subject and object, not to mention basic physics, a bit muddled up. The doors may be safe to touch, but they need someone physically stronger than the Doctor to open them, even stronger than Jamie, who puts the best face on his failure ("I haven't been getting much exercise lately").

So to open the tomb's doors they turn to Toberman (Roy Stuart), the black member of the party. Depressingly Toberman, whom one hoped might be an astrophysicist, an archaeological expert, or possibly the leader of the expedition, turns out to be a servant. And not just a servant, but a bodyguard-cum-muscleman. One can almost hear the jungle drums beating. Toberman strains his mighty thews and opens the huge tomb doors.

Even at the time "Tomb" was made, this sort of stereotyping was bordering on toe-curling. It makes one queasy to realise that Martin Luther King had been leading civil rights marches for years before this story was made and, a few months after it was transmitted, would be assassinated. It could be argued that this is too great a weight to put on a science fiction story that was largely aimed at children. On the other hand, children were the last people who should have been exposed to a character as clichéd and generally negative as Toberman.

Basically, Toberman is a black brute, all muscle with a bit of basic cunning thrown in. In fairness to the writers of "The Tomb of the Cybermen," in *The Television Companion* Howe and Walker describe Pedler and Davis's original script as featuring Toberman with a hearing aid, and presenting him as a kind of deaf mute. It's hard to know whether this interpretation would have improved the character hugely (it was dropped at the request of the director Morris Barry), but it at least would have got Toberman out of the rut of stereotype.

If hints of racism in the script are only arguably present, there's no question about the sexism. As the group enters the tomb and further exploration begins, Victoria and Kaftan (Shirley Cooklin), the female member of the party, are greeted with the injunction, "I think the women had better remain here." Happily, Victoria dismisses this ridiculous suggestion (she comes from at least a couple of centuries earlier, and even *she* thinks this attitude is terribly out of date). Eventually the women are allowed to come along, provided they're under the protection of a man. "The Tomb of the Cybermen" is also a tomb of 1960s attitudes.

The Patrick Troughton Doctor is sardonic and sarcastic. With his black cloak and his unruly dark hair he looks a trifle like Barnabas Collins (the vampire hero of the horror soap opera *Dark Shadows*, which first aired in June 1966). When the Doctor proves startlingly au fait with the control panels that open the inner doors of the tomb, he explains snappishly, "I used my own special technique . . . Keeping my eyes open and my mouth shut."

The tomb itself, designed by Martin Johnson, is a highly impressive set. Occasionally a door wobbles, indicating flimsiness under the well wrought exterior, but that can't be helped. Among the clever and nicely executed details are decorative images of Cybermen's heads on the walls (these being more Mayan than Egyptian in style). The studio lighting by Graham Sothcott is also suitably creepy, and that stock music is surprisingly effective, adding to the tension. Of course, by now the explorers have split up into subparties (and subplots). Jamie asks why there is constant interior light in the corridors and the rather interesting reply goes, "Alpha meson phosphor . . . works by letting cosmic rays bombard a layer of . . ." We don't hear any more because Jamie hastily cuts off the explanation with a casual "Oh aye, that," as if he's heard it all before. Of course, he plainly doesn't have a clue but also doesn't have any desire to hear the rest of a lengthy technical explanation. It's occasional subtle little performance gems like this that make Jamie such good value as a companion and indicate Frazer Hines's adroitness as an actor. It's a great character moment.

Meanwhile Patrick Troughton is fairly convincing in a mathematical conversation, talking about power series. Unfortunately, this provides the vital clue for the others to activate the tomb. "You fools," says the Doctor. "Why couldn't you leave it alone? . . . Perhaps the Cybermen aren't as dormant as you imagine." After all that mathematical chat, the viewer is beginning to hope that this is exactly the case.

Soon the tomb is pulsing to life in its various chambers, and we gradually discover that it's a kind of trap for human beings, so that the resident Cybermen can use them as raw material for creating new members of the Cyber race. This imaginative story twist anticipates

Robert Holmes "The Krotons" and also bears a certain generic resemblance to Paul Anderson's film script for *Alien versus Predator* nearly forty years later. Jamie is exposed to hypnotic flashing lights in one room, while in another Victoria is trapped in a kind of upright cyber sarcophagus. She's soon freed, though.

Although "The Tomb of the Cybermen" is a highly regarded story, deemed a classic, it's in fact pretty poor stuff. The script, after its strong beginning, turns out to be rudimentary and dull. The characters are a particular weakness. Besides the thankless Toberman we have Captain Hopper (George Roubicek), the commander of the rocket that brought them to this planet. Hopper is a faux-American of the worst kind, speaking in a way that suggests the English writers have never travelled across the Atlantic and have paid precious little attention to films or books that have flowed the other way. He keeps saying "guy" and using odd fake American idiom like "It's not exactly peaches."

There is also a great deal of exposition in the script, dull and lacking in suspense, a fault which the completely offstage sabotage of the rocket ship does little to rectify. Nor do the discussions of Boolean logic do much to inspire excitement. Then, God help us, we get the ancient science fiction cliché of a futuristic meal. Victoria is offered dinner ("Veal or chicken?"), and it turns out to be a tiny tablet, which she declines.

Soon, fortunately, the Cybermen's frozen tombs are thawing out (one of the working titles of the story was the evocative "The Ice Tombs of Telos") and the Cybermen are stirring. "This is unique in archaeology," says the expedition's Professor Parry (Aubrey Richards), who is rather missing the point as he watches the monsters come to life. Sadly, it takes the Cybermen what feels like forever to thaw out and burst through the membranes that hold them. Only some deft use of that high quality stock music prevents the scene from being hilarious as they fumble their way to freedom.

While they take forever doing this, our heroes all stand around and watch, oddly disinclined to flee or do anything useful. The climactic entrance of the Cyber Controller, the Cybermen's leader who is distinguished by an odd, veined helmet, is mildly interesting. The standard design of the Cybermen is nothing very impressive, and their faces are just joke shop masks. However, many accounts of terrified children watching Cybermen adventures suggest that there is something about the dead, hollow eye sockets and the motionless, ever-open mouths of these aliens that is actually quite effective.

Undeniably pathetic, though, is the Cybermat, a sort of Cyberman's pet which is about the size of a rat (indeed, its name sounds like Cyberrat for the first few repetitions) and looks like a mechanical trilobite. When it jumps on Kaftan's shoulder and she screams in terror, we are unfortunately deep in comedy territory.

Back at the ice tombs the Cybermen stand around talking in their synthetic voices (distinct from the earlier Daleks and the later Krotons, but still a chore to listen to, at least as dreary as they are eerie) before getting down to cases and starting to beat people up and electrocute them in earnest. In the fight scene that ensues, one Cyberman lifts Toberman over his head, presumably to demonstrate the Cyberman's awesome strength. All that is really demonstrated is the wire that lifts Toberman towards the studio ceiling. This wire is so obviously and explicitly visible that for a moment we assume it must be a plot point, a Cyberhoist perhaps, but instead it's just a botched effect.

All the earlier promising characterisation is by now similarly botched. Hopper, the tedious American rocket captain is back. He peers down an open hatch towards the realm of the ice tombs, with Victoria at his side. "It's very quiet down there," says Victoria. And, to the script's eternal discredit, Hopper replies, "Yeah, too quiet." He then sets off to investigate. When Victoria tries to follow him, she's prevented from doing so, because she's a woman.

Soon the tiresome rocket jockey is creeping around the ice tombs, getting ready to throw smoke bombs and get the drop on the Cybermen, enabling the others to escape. Suddenly this nonentity is a hero while the Doctor has been left standing around doing absolutely nothing. This is simply poor plot mechanics. Or perhaps all that endless chat about power series and Boolean logic has left the Doctor tuckered out.

The high quality of the set design continues to pay dividends, however, and there's a good suspenseful scene where the Doctor is the last one out of the hatch, fleeing the ice tombs, and a Cyberman grabs him and starts dragging him back down. The battle to free the Doctor and close the hatch on his pursuer is moderately exciting. Then everybody is safe, except Toberman, the black member of the party, who has been captured by the Cybermen. No one seems too concerned about this, perhaps accepting it as his lot.

Next, the Doctor and the others proceed to sit around, doing nothing except talking. There is an unusual, intimate scene where the Doctor has a heart-to-heart with Victoria, and he describes what it's like wandering through time and space in the Tardis. Meanwhile, locked beneath the hatch, in a building of their own devising, the Cybermen are surprisingly ineffectual. They decide to send their Cybermats to do their bidding. The little creatures scurry through apertures up to the higher level, like rats in a drainpipe. The tiny Cybermats then proceed to attack the sleeping humans.

With their ludicrous appearance, fake motion (like mobile shoe brushes), and comedy fangs, all the scary music in the world can't make the Cybermats seem dangerous—though Troughton's excellent acting almost does the trick. The Cybermat's attack is utterly ineffective in dramatic terms. What is worse is that it bears an intriguing similarity to a sequence in *The Outer Limits* story "The Zanti Misfits," directed by Leonard Horn and written by Joseph Stefano (creator of *The Outer Limits* and screenwriter of *Psycho*). First transmitted on 30 December 1963, almost four years before "The Tomb of the Cybermen," this *Outer Limits* episode is a true television classic. It was original, striking, and terrifying, making an impression on the author in his childhood that easily surpassed that first glimpse of the squishy thing inside a Dalek. It also bears a distinct resemblance to the Cybermat attack in "Tomb," with tiny insectoid creatures attacking humans and being beaten off and shot at. Possibly this is a case of parallel evolution, but it is remarkably similar, right down to the nasty little teeth that the Zantis and the Cybermats share. Whereas the Zanti attack was frightening and unforgettable, the Cybermat scene is just majestically inept.

The Doctor saves the day with a power cable that "generated an electrical field and confused their tiny metal minds."

Down in the ice tombs, poor Toberman has been "prepared" by the Cybermen. He has gone from being a manservant to a zombie. The Cybermen exert mind control over him, a process illustrated by animated sine waves that weave luminously through the ether. Even this doesn't do much to flog the story to life. After a renewed assault on the humans the Cyber Controller stands confronting the treacherous Kaftan, who thought she could play him off against her friends. "You have broken your promise," she says. "The Cybermen do not promise," responds the Controller. "Such ideas have no value." The Controller and Kaftan then proceed to have a shootout with drawn pistols, old west style, while the Doctor and friends and the semi-Cyber Toberman look on. The Controller shoots Kaftan down like a dog. Having done nothing to stop this, the Doctor then immediately scuttles over to talk persuasively to Toberman. He tries to shock him out of his Cyber state, indicating Kaftan's smoking corpse and saying, "Look what they've done. You're not like them. You're a man like us."

It works and Toberman reverts to his loyal strong man role. In a scene that provides a kind of symmetrical incompetence to the one where he was hoisted on highly visible wires, Toberman now picks up the Cyber Controller and throws him across the room. No need for wires here, because the Cyber suit he throws is obviously empty.

The Doctor, who so recently stood by and saw Kaftan shot dead without lifting a finger, now pluckily volunteers to go down into the ice tombs and make sure that the threat of the Cybermen is at an end. He elects to take Toberman (who, as the only black member of the party, is obvious cannon fodder) with him. He talks Toberman into it thus: "They tried to make you their slave. They just want to use you." One wonders how this makes the Cybermen any different from the white people in the story.

As the Doctor and the trusty black strongman descend into the perilous ice tombs, the insufferable rocket captain turns up again, the repairs on his (unseen) ship complete. "We can blast off any time . . . Hey, what gives?"

What gives is a final battle between Toberman and Cyberman, a brutal fight in which he disembowels the Cyberman and causes white foam to spew out of his solar plexus. The black beast has slain the silver monster. The Doctor contemplates the results with satisfaction, tempered by concern about the continuing danger presented by the Cybermen. "Last time they were frozen for five centuries. This time it must be forever."

Astonishingly Toberman, who seemed so transparently groomed for sacrifice, has survived. He returns to the upper levels with the Doctor and they seal the hatch behind them. Then, in a surprise late twist, the Cyber Controller lurches back to life. This sort of false ending, with a final jolt of menace just when everything seems wrapped up, is now a Hollywood cliché (descending largely from the bravura shock ending of De Palma's Carrie). At the time of "Tomb of the Cybermen," it was still a clever piece of plotting.

The Doctor and the others are forced to stop the Cyber Controller by shutting him in the huge tomb doors, which are now electrified again. Or, rather, Toberman is forced to do this. He sacrifices himself, cannon fodder after all.

The last shot is of Toberman's body, lying outside the tomb.

"The Mind Robber" by Peter Ling

"The Tomb of the Cybermen" was the only intact story from Season 5. In Season 6 (starting transmission on 14 September 1968), one of the few other surviving complete Troughton adventures is "The Mind Robber," written by Peter Ling (with an uncredited contribution of one episode by script editor Derrick Sherwin).

It begins with the Doctor and Jamie doing a kind of Laurel and Hardy double act as they fling themselves into the Tardis to escape a mammoth flood of lava on the planet Dulkis. Zoe is already waiting inside for them, and they attempt to make good their escape before the lava hits the ship. But those unreliable fluid links just won't take the load. The controls start to smoke.

Since the fluid links are ostensibly filled with mercury (the search to refill them motivated the first Dalek story), Zoe correctly points out that this smoke is mercury vapour. Of course, if it was, the Doctor and his companions would be breathing in some very toxic stuff (though this might go a long way towards explaining the ensuing adventure they experience). As they struggle to depart from the violently volcanic Dulkis, the Doctor glances at the scanner and can't help admiring the spectacle. "What a wonderful sight," he says, as they are about to be buried in lava.

The Tardis won't work, but an alternative does exist. It involves moving the Tardis out of reality. With one eye on that encroaching ocean of lava, Jamie hastily agrees. He doesn't much like his current reality. When the Doctor persists in his reluctance, Jamie begins to lose his rag. He disrespectfully forces the Doctor to push the button. And out of reality they go . . .

(Or maybe it's just those mercury fumes.)

As the emergency unit cuts in, strange things begin to happen. Jamie is appalled and hugs the Doctor in fear, again in Laurel and Hardy fashion. We get a remarkably effective exterior shot of the Tardis succumbing to the lava, the light on its roof just sinking under a flood of foam.

Then they're gone. The Tardis scanner just shows a blank screen. The Doctor issues an assortment of dire warnings about the strange situation they are in. Yet Zoe, plucky girl of the future, wants to go outside and investigate. While they're thrashing this through, Jamie is staring at the scanner, on which he believes he can see the rolling (presumably green) hills of Scotland. Of course, when Zoe joins him, the screen is blank again. Jamie rationalises that the mist must have covered it over. "Aye, you get a lot of mist in the highlands."

Now Zoe sees a futuristic city that is *her* home, and naturally Jamie can't see a damned thing. This doesn't stop Zoe stepping outside of the Tardis and into luminous white blankness. You might say, in fact, that she's been lured outside. Indeed, when he finds out what has happened, the Doctor says as much. Jamie too is lured, dashing out the door to rescue Zoe. The Doctor is left behind, wrestling with some kind of psychic onslaught.

This goes on for the rest of the episode. Outside Jamie finds Zoe in the luminous, featureless void (or, as Derrick Sherwin puts it in *Doctor Who: The Sixties*, "a white cyclorama cloth [and] lots of smoke"). Jamie doesn't cheer things up by saying that he's got a funny feeling he's being watched.

They are indeed being watched by some angular, vaguely Cybermen style robots, later to be known as the White Robots, which are actually recycled costumes from another BBC SF series, *Out of the Unknown*. They are accompanied by a rather groovy electronic noise as they watch the companions, then disappear again, unseen. Jamie and Zoe are tempted by mirages of home again, Jamie's vision accompanied by the sound of bagpipes. It vanishes when Zoe, possibly annoyed that her vision was silent, slaps him in the face. Then the White Robots loom again . . .

Back in the Tardis, the Doctor is hearing voices tempting him to go out and "save" his companions. He succumbs, heading out into the white mist where he has strangely little trouble finding Jamie and Zoe, considering they have wandered out into a nebulous gleaming void. They seem to be in a trance—as well as white costumes. The Doctor tries to hustle them back into the Tardis, but then the robots intervene, accompanied by assorted low budget psychedelic effects.

The Doctor finally manages to usher his companions back into the safety of the Tardis.

By now it's all getting a bit tedious and the novelty of a story set nowhere is starting to wear off. While the Doctor struggles with his still malfunctioning vehicle, Jamie is busy dreaming of being attacked by a white unicorn. We only know this because he wakes up and tells us, thereby concluding one of the cheapest action sequences in *Doctor Who*.

But things pick up, and we finally get an effective sequence. We see the Tardis floating in a black void, and suddenly it's *ripped apart*. The walls, ceiling, and floor go flying off like playing cards discarded from the hands of a cosmic dealer.

The control console goes hurtling off into the blackness, the companions clinging to it. Zoe looks particularly alluring crouched on the spinning console in her skintight, spangly catsuit. She sees the Doctor floating off in the void in the other direction and gives an exemplary girl companion's cliff-hanger scream . . .

It's worth pausing and considering this first episode. According to *The Television Companion*, production exigencies meant that "The Mind Robber" was forced to expand from four parts to five. That extra episode had to come from somewhere, and, as so often happens, it came from the imagination of the script editor.

Howe and Walker describe how Sherwin wrote the first episode of "The Mind Robber," but being still in office as script editor, he couldn't be credited as a writer. Thus "The Mind Robber," part one was transmitted with no writer credit on it.

Knowing this, one is a lot more forgiving of the longueurs and absurdities of this story fragment. We begin to realise that the reason that the Tardis goes "nowhere" is because there was really nowhere for it to go. There was no extra money in the budget for this episode, falling as it did between two stories.

This makes Sherwin's use of limited resources even more admirable. It's a story that goes nowhere and is about nothing for very good reasons. The sequence where Jamie goes to sleep and dreams of a white unicorn turns out to be cheap for an equally good reason. More importantly, this will prove to be a reference to a scene in the next episode, in fact a kind of premonition. This is a clever touch by Derrick Sherwin, a resourceful script editor in a corner.

Episode two opens with Jamie and Zoe lost in a forest and separated. They only know of each other's presence by calling to each other. They can't seem to meet. This forest is a very strange place. The "trees" seem to be kind of rough-hewn oblongs, like crudely carved blocks of wood.

Our heroes climb up one, only to find that the trees actually form the sides of huge raised alphabetic letters that point up at the sky, like type in a printers' tray. Standing on top of one of the trees, we're high enough to look down at the other letters and realise they form a pattern of words. Words like *slow,* in the phrase *slow but sure.* The Doctor seems to be lost in a forest of platitudes.

In another part of the forest, Zoe comes on a door in what looks like the wall of a castle. She opens it, steps through, and immediately drops out of sight. The story begins to feel like one of those tediously surreal episodes of *The Avengers,* where some sinister mastermind is tampering with the sanity of Steed and Mrs Peel.

And, indeed, this is where the plot seems to be headed, when it eventually kicks in. We see our baffled heroes watched on a monitor screen by an ominous half-seen figure who muses, "Good. Good. Excellent."

The Doctor is looking for Jamie and Zoe. He and his companions have undergone the traditional separation. He can hear their voices but cannot see them. When he complains, exploring in the dark, the lights suddenly come on (or at least they would if the cue wasn't laggard). The Doctor blinks in the new illumination and offers his thanks to whoever is responsible.

Whoever they are send out a squad of marching robots in pursuit of the Doctor with orders to find him. The Doctor meanwhile meets an Englishman in a three-corner hat, brandishing a pistol and hailing from 1699. Then the Englishman disappears. "An hallucination?" says the Doctor, perhaps edging towards the mercury vapour hypothesis.

What ensues is more riddles, puzzles, and wordplay. The Doctor and Jamie hear Zoe crying out from behind the door in the castle wall. They hurry to it and find that they can't open it because it's a *trompe l'oeil* door, a brick wall with a door merely painted on it. "When is a door not a door?" muses the door, and he comes up with the old punch line to an old punning riddle. "When it's ajar." A jar. Zoe duly appears in a giant jam jar. This sort of Alice in Wonderland logic definitely has its charm, but it wears thin with surprising speed.

The Doctor and Jamie hoist Zoe from the jar. (At least no one makes a gag about getting her out of a jam. In *The Avengers* they wouldn't have missed the chance.) And the Doctor says, "I think we may be in a place where nothing is impossible." As if to emphasise this point, Jamie scales one of the "trees" and glimpses the landscape of words they are manoeuvring through.

The seventeenth century Englishman in the three-corner hat turns up again, uttering cryptic and somewhat menacing pronouncements. More life-size toy soldiers turn up, but these ones are not remotely as humanoid as the one Jamie encountered earlier. They are also a nice piece of design. The designer for "The Mind Robber" is Evan Hercules and the costumes are by Martin Baugh (episodes one to four) and Susan Wheal (episode five).

The toy soldiers escort the Doctor and his friends into a black void. Here at last Jamie's unicorn turns up. It's a splendid beast, pretty damned convincing and dynamically photographed (film cameraman for the story is Jimmy Court). Here's an original cliff-hanger. The Doctor and the companions are being charged by a white unicorn.

They don't need to worry about being impaled, though. The cliff-hanger is resolved by the simple expedient of the Doctor insisting, while Jamie and Zoe are yelling in terror, that unicorns don't exist. His firm conviction on the matter causes the unicorn to freeze and turn into a photograph. It seems the Doctor is beginning to get the measure of this bizarre game. The unseen villain with the observation screens briefly stops gloating to praise the Doctor's intelligence. Then he starts gloating again that he's set a trap for the Doctor.

The Doctor and his companions enter an old cobwebbed house. They are in an agreeably gothic labyrinth of candle-lit tunnels, where Zoe suddenly gets spooked. We move in for a striking close up of her terrified face as she hears a sound that reminds her of a mythical creature said to stalk human prey in a labyrinth. The Minotaur. Sure enough we see a pretty good Minotaur shadow lurking on the wall nearby. Unfortunately, the creature doesn't live up to its shadow. It's just another bad *Doctor Who* monster, though mercifully briefly glimpsed.

The Doctor and Zoe get rid of it by denying that it exists. The same stratagem as used on the unicorn, rather boringly repeated. They then meet the three-cornered hat man again, and this time they finally learn who he is. Lemuel Gulliver. From *Gulliver's Travels*. As he leaves them, Zoe asks why he talks so strangely. The Doctor says it's because he can only use the dialogue from the novel he appeared in. He explains to Zoe that Gulliver is a fictional character, come to life. They've entered the world of fiction.

Zoe then asks why she's here. It's a question that doesn't bear too close examination considering that Zoe, too, is a fictional character, played by an actress called Wendy Padbury. Even without getting into these metafictional (and metaphysical) questions, "The Mind Robber" is an intriguing story.

It also cleverly dodges the endemic *Doctor Who* problems of bad sets, costumes and props by making them minimal, symbolic, or surreal. Disappointingly, a world of the imagination ceases to appeal when imagination goes into short supply. Jamie is soon busy climbing up Rapunzel's hair and into a castle tower. The sinking feeling one gets on seeing these old fairy tales dragged out is somewhat tempered by some nice dialogue. Rapunzel takes one look at Jamie and says it's a pity he's not a prince.

Jamie climbs through the window to find not a princess's castle but a futuristic control room where a ticker tape device is chattering out a narrative. Jamie reads it and discovers that it is an account of the subplot involving Zoe and the Doctor in the labyrinth, which is taking place even now. It's like something out of a John Barth novel.

These are terrific ideas, self-referential and postmodern in a way one doesn't expect from *Doctor Who*, especially in 1968. Jamie reads the ticker tape haltingly, "The Doctor and Zoe, unable to find their companion in the labyrinth, decided to return to the cave in search of him where a new terror awaited them . . ."

In the control room, Jamie is contending with Lemuel Gulliver and an assortment of robots. The Doctor and Zoe have hardly gotten clear of the Medusa before they are doing battle with plastic rocks, cheap explosions, and a silly pop-art effect that heralds the appearance of "the Karkus," a kind of costumed superhero. Zoe exclaims that the Karkus is superhumanly strong. He's a comic strip character of the year 2000. Then she goes all Emma Peel and uses martial arts to throw him around the place.

The Karkus is actually a clever ploy, because his silly looking futuristic costume is *intended* to look silly (it features fake musculature that looks like a low budget precursor of Tim Burton's *Batman*). After defeating him, the Doctor and Zoe reunite with Jamie and seek to confront the Master, who is behind all this. The Doctor studies the ticker tape trailing from the machine and sees how he departed from the plot laid down for his encounter with the Medusa. He concludes that if they'd fallen into the Master's trap they would have become fiction.

Finally, they meet the Master face-to-face. "This is a great pleasure," he says in a classic suave villain greeting, before filling us in on his background. He looks like an amiable schoolmaster from a second rate boarding school. He explains that he left England in the summer of 1926. He was a writer of adventure stories for a boys' weekly magazine (the pulp fiction of English middle class adolescence).

He waxes nostalgic about how prolific he was. "For twenty-five years I delivered five thousand words every week." Zoe does the arithmetic and says, "That's well over half a million words."

"Yes, yes," says the Master smugly. "It was probably some kind of record."

Without wishing to bring things to a screeching halt, it's worth pointing out that Zoe, mathematical genius though she is, has got her sums wrong here. In fact, she's off by a factor of ten. The total is six and a half million words. The Master is also wrong about it being a record. To cite just one example, the English popular novelist John Creasey wrote over six hundred novels in his lifetime, weighing in at something over thirty million words.

Nevertheless, it was the Master's prolific pulp output that qualified him for his job here. Now, lest things are in danger of getting too cosy, we notice that there is a cable attached to the Master's head that runs back up into the huge spherical device hanging above him that looks like some kind of mechanical brain (it is, in fact, the Master Brain).

The Master Brain suddenly compels the Master to get writing, and he responds promptly, like a rat with an electrode in its grey matter. He gives Zoe the creeps, and us too.

Now we learn what is really going on. The Master wants the Doctor to take his place.

"As you refused to take over my post at the controls, we have been forced to absorb you into the computer itself." This is an extraordinarily modern notion, anticipating such virtual reality epics as *The Matrix* and even *Tron* by decades. There are some slight issues of consistency and set design, though. The computer—or Master Brain—is behind the Master and up in the air, encased in Perspex. The Doctor is in front of the Master and on the floor, also encased in Perspex. Are they both in one giant computer?

The White Robots now menace Jamie and Zoe, who have fled to the library. As the Doctor watches on a screen, the robots prepare to shut his companions between the pages of a giant book. It's like something out of *Batman* (the TV show, or the vintage Bob Kane DC comics). It's another way out cliff-hanger.

From his vantage point in the computer the Doctor finds he can fight back, encouraging Zoe and Jamie to free themselves from the realm of fiction, as symbolized by that giant book. They do so, only to find themselves menaced by the toy soldiers. The Doctor strikes back, narrating in perfunctory pulp fashion, "Suddenly the Karkus came to their rescue."

The Master ripostes with Cyrano de Bergerac, huge nose and all. The Doctor responds with Dartagnan and a swordfight begins, complete with ripely dramatic swashbuckler music (the music, surprisingly, is stock).

This duel of fictional improvisation between the Doctor and the Master is surely one of the strangest story climaxes in *Doctor Who*. Soon Blackbeard the Pirate supplants Cyrano and, in a positively Pythonesque flourish, the Doctor replaces Dartagnan with Lancelot, in full armour on horseback.

Now is when we discover that the Master is really no master at all but merely a flunky of the Master Brain, which must be protected from overloading at all costs. He abandons the fictional duel and sends in the robots after the Doctor. Zoe overhears the remarks about overloading the computer, and she and Jamie set about making sure it overloads, racing to a control panel and hitting the keys on it like a bebop piano duo.

Now in a Hitler-in-the bunker mode, the Master Brain launches its robots on a scorched earth mission. They begin to sprout (pathetic) chest guns and rake the control room with (pathetic) gunfire. In the ensuing havoc, the Doctor rescues the Master, unplugging him from the computer. He decides to destroy the computer and see if that will take them back to reality.

We see the Tardis appear, in fragments, and reassemble itself. And the story ends.

Peter Ling, the writer responsible for this extraordinary postmodern pop culture collage (or at least four fifths of it, with the help of script editor Sherwin) was the co-creator of the long running English soap opera *Crossroads*. In *Doctor Who: The Sixties*, Howe, Stammers, and Walker write, "Part of the inspiration for the story was Ling's observation that many fans of soap operas . . . come to believe that the characters are in fact real people."

As a postscript, I should add that every mention of the Master in this story really ought to be replaced with "the Master of the Land of Fiction," to distinguish him from *the* Master, an evil reengaged Time Lord who will crop up later on in the canon. He will recur as a running character, turning up most recently in 1996, contending against the Paul McGann Doctor.

*   *   *

While Terry Nation was certainly the most influential writer in the history of *Doctor Who*, he wasn't necessarily the most characteristic. Among other writers who more closely caught the spirit of the show, understanding its possibilities, the best may be Robert Holmes, a reporter and journalist who moved into television script writing, for which he showed an extraordinary flare.

Holmes would later write episodes for *Doomwatch* and scripted his own 1981 BBC science fiction serial *The Nightmare Man*, adapted from the novel by David Wiltshire.

Besides regularly writing for *Doctor Who*, Holmes worked as a script editor on the show from 1974 to 1977. He died in harness, still writing *Doctor Who* on 24 May 1986. In December of that year, I went for my first interview for the post of script editing the show and a month later I started work, arriving just too late to meet the man I would come to regard as one of the great *Doctor Who* writers.

If Terry Nation was the ultimate ideas man, Holmes was the ultimate character writer. Holmes had his share of fascinating ideas, but his great strengths were dialogue, characterisation, and a feel for science fiction. He had a unique influence on the development of the show and wrote a classic adventure of the Tom Baker Doctor, "The Talons of Weng-Chiang."

After a buildup like that, it's ironic, but perhaps inevitable, to say that his first *Doctor Who* story is a fairly undistinguished one, the work of a tyro writer just beginning to find his voice. Robert Holmes had originally submitted it to *Doctor Who* three years earlier, under the more evocative title "Space Trap," and it had been rejected by then script editor Donald Tosh. Holmes tenaciously (and serendipitously) resubmitted it and Terrance Dicks, a new script editor on the show, liked it and encouraged him. Together Holmes and Dicks set about working on the story.

"The Krotons" ended up as the fourth story to be transmitted in Season 6, and, as chance would have it, it's one of the Troughton stories to survive in its entirety (four episodes). It begins, like so many *Doctor Who* adventures, with the Tardis materialising in an English quarry (in Malvern, Worcestershire). Yes, another quarry.

But even before we get to the quarry in "The Krotons," the story is in deep trouble. The episode opens in a kind of underground chamber or cave with rough-hewn walls among a group of humanoid (i.e., totally human-looking) aliens we will learn are called the Gonds. They are arguing about the fact that two of their brightest young people are about to be sent on a strange rite of passage (the young couple pass through a silly looking doorway). In a way, it doesn't matter what they're arguing about. Because their costumes are so laughable that the whole enterprise is already in jeopardy at this early stage.

When the Doctor appears from the Tardis, his first words are "Lovely, lovely, lovely," as he sets about exploring. He is accompanied by Jamie, who is refreshingly disrespectful. "Where are we?" says Zoe, and Jamie replies, "You don't expect him to know, do you?"

The Doctor accepts this insult affably and opens an umbrella against the beating glare of the planet's twin suns (a competent special effects shot). Troughton looks splendid picking his way across this bleak, rocky landscape with his umbrella, humming happily in a way that Hartnell would never have done. They spot some buildings, a set of uninspired miniatures. "Fascinating architecture," says the Doctor, gamely.

The trio find a ramp and door complete with would-be exotic angles and glittery decorations to signify their futuristic, or alien, nature. The Doctor says this is not part of a building, but of a machine. Either way, he could have added, it's terrible design.

Then a man emerges and what appear to be guns suddenly poke out of the wall on either side of him. They fire what looks like smoke and this smoke causes the man to disappear. The Doctor, Zoe, and Jamie show good sense by fleeing.

The next thing you know, jarringly and without proper explanation or transition, we are in that set of the underground chambers, or cave, with its rough-hewn walls. We never see how the Doctor and his companions got here from the quarry outside. This ellipsis may well be explained by the fact the production simply couldn't afford the necessary set. "We were underbudgeted," said Terrance Dicks, the script editor, in what was probably an understatement and would be a perennial complaint on *Doctor Who*.

After single combat, the ice is broken between the Doctor's crew and the locals and the Gonds explain a little about their culture. "The Krotons live in the machine—so we're told." The machine is where the young couple went. Unlike the Gonds, the Doctor and his friends know the fate of the young man who appeared in the quarry: he was disintegrated by the smoke guns.

But this still leaves the young woman, who was also fed to the machine, unaccounted for. "Vana is joining the Krotons," the Gonds assure us. "It's a great honour." The Doctor suspects otherwise.

The Gonds are deeply skeptical of any suggestion that the Krotons are up to no good. "Why should they kill the best of our students?" It seems that only the top students have the honour of being sent into the machine. They are trained for the honour by the teaching machines that the Krotons thoughtfully provide. There are some great shots of Zoe's delighted face as she uses one of the learning machines.

The Doctor discovers what she's doing and is outraged, fearing that the Krotons use these machines not just for education but also for mind control.

But the dial unquestionably registers a record score. "Zoe is something of a genius, of course," sighs the Doctor. "It can be very irritating at times."

In a neat piece of plotting from Robert Holmes, the machines turn out to be organic. "Some crystals do resemble virus forms," muses the Doctor, straying dangerously close to intelligent science fiction.

Unfortunately, the design team seem to have taken the crystal notion and used it as an occasion to put sharp angles on everything. But because the props and sets are metallic and not transparent, any notion of crystalline form is lost.

An alarm gong sounds. "Great jumping gob stoppers!" says the startled Doctor, invoking the name of a popular children's sweet (though they don't actually jump). Troughton is loveable and engaging in a way that Hartnell never was, yet he doesn't sacrifice the mystery of the Doctor or, oddly, his stature.

Of course, the gong comes from the machine (which we will learn is called the Dynatrope) and it signifies that the Krotons want Zoe. The Doctor can't possibly let her enter the machine on her own, so he sets about using the learning machine, trying to get chosen, too. But he is so brilliant that he trips himself up, overcomplicating his interpretation of the questions and getting the answers wrong. Troughton's flustered demeanour is a delight in this scene. And, without wishing to berate William Hartnell for not being something he was not, it's a scene the first Doctor couldn't have played with much success. Troughton has charm.

Despite his foul-ups, the Doctor scores as a top student, too, and he enters the machine with Zoe. More fascinating Robert Holmes concepts are revealed. The machine is a spaceship—with no crew. The

Doctor and Zoe are suddenly subjected to a strange force. We get some agreeably distorted close-ups of their faces in what is an otherwise uninspired montage. The montage is meant to signify that the Doctor and Zoe's mental energy has been drained and used to operate a "thermal switch." "Zoe, I think we've gone and done it," says the Doctor.

What they've gone and done is awaken the Krotons. More specifically, they've caused them to emerge from a state of dormancy in liquid crystal forms, coming out as solid crystalline entities. It is well beyond the competence of the special effects to express this clearly. What we get instead is a bunch of clumsy metal robots stumbling around in some of the worst costumes we are ever likely to see. Howe, Stammers, and Walker quote Terrance Dicks as saying "[The] Visual Effects [department] could not make the Krotons live up to our expectation."

In fact, the Krotons have heads that look like those angular wasp-waisted Italian coffee pots. The coffee pot heads are set on shoulders and torsos that look like inert lumps of furniture with Robbie the Robot-style arms. It's hard to look at them without thinking how wonderful the Daleks were by utter contrast, and perhaps also somewhat cruelly thinking, "There but for the grace of God, or the scheduling of BBC design staff . . ."

The Krotons' voices, highly admired in some quarters, are not much better. They are so undifferentiated that it's impossible to tell whether two of them are conversing or whether one is babbling in a schizoid soliloquy. At least the Daleks had flashing lights on their helmets to indicate which one was talking. What's more, the Krotons sound oddly South African, which at least adds to their sinister aspect.

With Jamie and Zoe's help, the Doctor triumphs over the Krotons. The Gonds are whipping themselves into rebellion. They are willing to attack the apparently invulnerable machine that houses the Krotons. "We have slings and fireball," says one hothead. "Weapons that will destroy the strongest building to rubble." This bizarre piece of phraseology almost succeeds in making the Gonds sound genuinely alien for a moment.

The Gond subplot finally perks up when the Doctor joins them to help lead their rebellion. These scenes in the underground chambers are well lit and moodily shot, lending some suspense and atmosphere to the silly sets and props. The Gonds succeed in damaging the machine. In perhaps the only nod to its organic nature, the Dynatrope starts to bleed.

The Doctor and Zoe reenter the machine, where the Krotons coffee pot heads are spinning around in an amusing fashion.

We learn why the Krotons need the brainy Gonds they've been training up. "You've discovered a way of using mental power," says the Doctor. Another intriguing and original science fiction idea from Robert Holmes. The Krotons need mental energy to power the Dynatrope, and mental energy of a sufficiently high standard. There are two Krotons surviving on the ship, which was once part of a battle fleet. "Two of our crew were exhausted by enemy fire . . . ceased to function." They need a total of four high brains to power their spaceship and fly it home. That is why they've been educating the Gonds, in the hope of creating a suitably high standard of intelligence among these primitive indigenous people. The Gonds whole civilization has been built to service the Krotons' attempt to get their ship home.

It's a great concept, and one can only regret it wasn't better executed.

In any case, the Doctor and Zoe use sulphuric acid to sabotage the ship—and its inhabitants. The Doctor intends them to melt, which they do passably well. The Krotons and their ship simply melt away. Tellurium dissolves in sulphuric acid, the Doctor tells us smugly. The Gonds realise they are free at last. They turn around to ask the Doctor a question. But, like the Lone Ranger, he is gone. "We have to find our own answers now," says a Gond.

One of the weaknesses of "The Krotons" is its lack of a music score. This may well have been an economy measure, but if so it was an error of judgement. If ever a visually weak story needed musical support, this was it. The special effects for "The Krotons" is credited to Bill King and Trading Post. The costumes were by Bobi Bartlett. The designer was Raymond London.

The moody and commendable lighting was by Howard T. King.

"The Tomb of the Cybermen" was pulp science fiction; "The Mind Robber" was an Alice in Wonderland romp, and "The Krotons" was failed pulp science fiction—but presented some fascinating ideas.

But among the few surviving intact stories of the Troughton era, one towers above all others. It comes dangerously close to being the greatest *Doctor Who* story of all time—"The War Games."

chapter 4

War Games and Time Lords

"The War Games" by Terrance Dicks
and Malcolm Hulke

"The War Games" starts brilliantly with the writers' credits
(Terrance Dicks and Malcolm Hulke, more power to them) flashing on
the screen intercut with grainy war newsreels of bombardment footage. Then the Tardis appears in the sordid mud of no-man's-land. It's
already clear that we're at the height of the monochrome heyday of
Doctor Who. There is an atmosphere and an expressionist force to the
black and white stories that is unrecapturable in colour. "War Games"
is the last black and white story, and up to episode four, at least, it's a
masterpiece. There's noteworthy photography (the film cameraman is
Alan Jonas) with the Tardis first appearing reflected in a muddy pud-
dle in this war torn wasteland. Director David Maloney (who directed
both "The Krotons" and "The Mind Robber") also excels himself in
this story.

The Doctor and his innocent young companions make their way
through no-man's-land, heartrendingly unaware of what it is. Jamie
cuts his finger on a barbed wire fence. "Barbed wire," says the Doctor.
"Filthy stuff." Then an artillery barrage begins. Zoe's terrified face is
pressed to the ground. There is a beautiful authenticity to these scenes
and, because of the World War I setting, a sense that the story is actually *about* something.

It might be the best *Doctor Who* opening episode ever. A perky English ambulance woman called Lady Jennifer comes up and finds our
heroes cowering in the mud. "That was just a softening up barrage,"
she says, looking at the curious trio. "This is no place for civilians,
between the lines."

Lady Jennifer is a note-perfect decent sort, an upper class girl
caught up voluntarily in the horrors of the Great War. She is played

by Jane Sherwin, wife of Derrick Sherwin, script editor and, by the time of "The War Games," producer of the show.

Then gas-masked Germans turn up looking like goggle-eyed *Doctor Who* monsters, taking all of them captive. At which point an entire subplot is apparently excised, presumably for reasons of length, and the Doctor and the others are miraculously free again, being driven along in a fantastic vintage vehicle, Lady Jennifer's ambulance, through a credibly war torn landscape.

After this, the move into the studio for the trench sequences is a little jarring. We've become accustomed to the savage muddy realism of no-man's-land. The Doctor explains that they've landed in the midst of one of the most horrendous wars in human history. Then he gives a quick account of the trench warfare system.

Inevitably, our heroes are suspected of being spies. The notion of the Doctor and his companions caught in the machinery of military justice is quite scary. They are sent to the officers' chateau where we sense that there's something wrong at the top of the chain of command when General Smythe moves a painting on the wall to reveal a futuristic communications device.

Elsewhere in the chateau, Lady Jennifer and Lieutenant Carstairs begin to compare notes. They both seem to have lost their long-term memories. This is all great stuff, and only improved by the fact that General Smythe is a very sinister figure, especially when he puts on a pair of hypnotic eyeglasses to impose his power over his junior officers, reinforcing their false memory and obedience conditioning. "You were at school together," hisses Smythe. This suggests an echo of a brilliant scene in *The Manchurian Candidate*, which will only be reinforced later.

Soon the Doctor and company are taken under martial law and summarily sentenced at a court–martial, and things begin to seem more reminiscent of Kubrick's *Paths of Glory*. This is engrossing stuff and evokes a strong sense of injustice with these time-travelling innocents caught up in the brutal machinery of military justice. We share their sense of outrage when they're sentenced to death. (Zoe is let off leniently with a mere ten years of hard time because she's a girl.)

The Doctor goes down fighting. Troughton rises to the occasion with impressive strength and power. "This is all just a mockery," he thunders. "I demand the right to appeal to a higher authority."

"There is no right to appeal," spits Smythe. Which is a relief because we thought he was going to say there was no higher authority.

The Doctor and the others are hustled off to their shocking fates. Even Smythe's junior officers are outraged by the injustice of this summary sentence, and the General is forced to whip out the old hypno-specs again.

Zoe being a woman not only means she was spared the death sentence, she also doesn't have to spend the night in a dank cell in the chateau's dungeon. Instead, she bunks in with Jennifer, and when the Lady is asleep she sneaks out. She steals into Smythe's private quarters, where too damned quickly and without proper motivation she finds the communications device. Maybe she always looks behind paintings.

This is a wonderfully dark story, strengthened immeasurably by the evocative black and white photography. Zoe frees the Doctor, and they turn to escape—and run straight into the arms of the execution detail. He's escorted out to the firing squad in the courtyard. In an incredible cliff-hanger, which evokes the Hollywood serials of the 1930s, we actually hear a gunshot and think we've seen the Doctor killed.

The way the cliff-hanger is resolved at the beginning of episode two is quite amazing, and amazingly frustrating. The gunshot turns out to have come from a high window of the chateau. Apparently a mutinous British soldier is firing on the others. We never see the sniper but the power of this scene, with its suggestion of insurrection, a shocking willingness to shoot at one's own and overthrow the establishment, is reminiscent of Lindsay Anderson's *If*.

Frustratingly, we never do learn who the deus ex machina sniper was. Maybe the uncertainty is a Lee Harvey Oswald homage. I suspect instead that the Doctor was saved by a member of the Resistance, although the concept of the Resistance hasn't even arisen in this story yet.

Soon the General is using the hypno-specs again. One of his officers has just walked in and seen the General disappearing in a Tardis-style space-time travel device. The officer soon recovers his conditioning. "General Smythe? . . . Of course. He's gone to that meeting."

In a subplot, Jamie has been thrown in with another perceived deserter. It turns out to be a Redcoat, his sworn enemy from 1745. This is an inventive idea but the proliferation of subplots seems to slow the main story down. Much more interesting is the Doctor and Zoe story, in which the Doctor barges in on a complacent, tea-drinking commanding officer. The Doctor takes the high ground. "How dare you

treat me like this?" he demands of the astonished man. "I am the ex-
aminer from the War Office. I am here to inspect the military prisons." Troughton brilliantly puts a little tremor in his voice to suggest
he's improvising as he goes along. "This young lady is my secretary,"
he adds. And then, my favourite, "You were expecting us, surely?"

When the man timidly demands to see his papers, the Doctor erupts
again. "How dare you? You send no car to meet us on our arrival!"
And now the man has insulted him by questioning his credentials.

The commander crumbles. "It's probably my adjutant's fault." The
wonderful thing about this scene is that it shows the Doctor's re-
sourcefulness and intelligence. Having chosen to present himself as an
inspector of prisons, he can set about finding Jamie (who is in a
prison). It also evokes the otherworldly power of the Doctor without
recourse to dodgy special effects. It's all done through character.

The trouble with the Jamie subplot is that it begins to feel that we're
in a different movie, or TV show, whenever it crops up. This is because it isn't properly integrated. We're more interested in the competing subplot of Carstairs and Lady Jennifer. They're only minor
characters, but they're at the heart of the mystery, groping towards a
realisation of their plight. If Jamie could somehow have been worked
into this subplot it would have kept him at the heart of the story.

But Jamie soon links up with the Doctor and Zoe. The Doctor has
used his (purely self-appointed) clout as Inspector of Military Prisons
to get Jamie freed. There's a brilliant comic moment between Troughton and Hines, when the Doctor has to stop Jamie revealing that they
know each other. By now even the thick-witted commander has
begun to suspect something, and Zoe gets the pleasure of breaking a
flowerpot on his head.

Then, clumsily, we get a reprise of the previous thwarted escape.
They walk straight into the arms of a party of officers. And back into
captivity. Apart from some new dialogue, it's a reprise of the earlier
scene.

With a sinking feeling we begin to suspect that the writers have hit
reset and that we're about to go in a protracted story loop, milking
every situation, as tends to happen in long running serials. In fact, the
plot leaps ahead when the Doctor and Zoe begin to convince Lady
Jennifer and the Lieutenant about the strangeness of their situation. In
a cleverly staged scene they show them the communications device in
the General's quarters. Jennifer and Carstairs have to overcome their
conditioning. Initially they can't see it. Then, in a wonderful touch,

Jennifer begins to get it first. The image of the communications device begins to appear on the blank wall. Lady Jennifer wonders who or what is on the other end. A scary concept. She and Carstairs join forces with the Doctor and his friends. They all head out the door . . .

Only, for the third time, to walk into the arms of an adversary. In a neat twist, Carstairs bluffs their way out of it, and soon they are fleeing in the Lady's ambulance. Smythe finds out and furiously orders a barrage laid down on the road where it is speeding. His junior office is appalled by this, so out come the hypno-specs, and soon it's, "A very good idea sir. Creeping barrage. Stop them dead." The dialogue in this World War I story is consistently of a high standard, showing a very good ear for the period.

Fleeing the barrage, the ambulance vanishes into a mist that the Doctor identifies as a kind of a force field. Suddenly they find themselves in Roman Europe, facing a charge by Roman soldiers who have taken an instinctive dislike to these strangers. They stare in wonder as the ambulance reverses back through the force field and disappears. It appears again in 1917, back into the barrage. This is wonderful science fiction adventure, and the writing shows real flair. It elevates "The War Games" to the status of a classic.

It has its imperfections, though. No sooner have the Doctor and his entourage escaped the chateau than they decide to head back. They've concluded General Smythe has a map of the different time zones that they need. On the one hand, this is audacious and amusing plotting; on the other, it's a wearisome McGuffin, blunting any sense of forward impetus in the story.

But what ensues is an incredible sequence. The vital map is in a safe and the Doctor becomes a safecracker to get at it. He takes a grenade and in a nail-biting sequence removes the explosive core to put into the lock of the safe. Once they've got the maps, it's back to the ambulance and an attempt to get through the German lines which results in yet again being arrested as spies . . .

Exasperated by the persistence of the German interrogator who insists on being given a name, the Doctor says he's called John Smith, his *nom de guerre*. While he is being questioned, the shells keep falling and Zoe is sexy and vulnerable, clinging to Jamie in a German trench that is rocked by explosions.

To convince his German captor that he's from the future the Doctor demonstrates the sonic screwdriver. This device would eventually develop into a kind of cosmic get-out clause, a handy invention that could do almost anything. Finally, it had to be disallowed from *Doctor Who* stories for the same reason that Kryptonite had to be introduced into Superman. An all-powerful hero is a dull hero.

It's gradually creeping back in, though. The Russell T. Davies version of the Doctor is known to use it on occasion. At this early stage the sonic screwdriver is just a screwdriver, every handyman's dream. Demonstrated to the German, it convinces the man that the Doctor is from the future. He goes to his superior to report and promptly gets his memory wiped for his trouble—rather than hypno-specs the German general has a suitably sinister hypno-*monocle*—which comes and goes from his face rather weirdly in the editing.

Since the man has had his memory wiped, the writers cheekily get the Doctor to demonstrate the sonic screwdriver to him *again.* As the German general reports back we begin to see more of the futuristic base that controls the war games—a base inhabited by humanoids who are only ever known as the Aliens. This generic designation is carried over to their individual designations. Rather than being given names, the characters have titles like the Security Chief, the War Chief, and (top dog in this particular kennel) the War Lord. The war games they are conducting are taking on an Earth-type planet which is also never identified by name. It's not the Aliens' home planet, which is referred to as precisely that and which is elsewhere.

As the show moves into this more explicitly science fictional territory the design and lighting seem initially less convincing. They will become more sure-footed later on, with some magnificent 1960s futurist sets worthy of Roger Vadim's *Barbarella* or Mario Bava's *Diabolik* (the designer was Roger Cheveley and studio lighting was by Howard King), and there are interesting new plot developments. "Time travellers? I want them brought here immediately."

But the Doctor and friends have escaped in the ambulance, and driven straight into the American Civil War. Sadly, it's "You are spies and you are going to be shot." Here we go again. After the World War I scenes, the Union soldier's dialogue falls heavily on the ear.

It's a relief to go back to the Aliens' base and hear about the five percent failure rate they have on the conditioning of the soldiers in the various eras. This low-sounding figure still gives "pockets of resistance." It's a potential revolutionary movement. The political satire apparent in the writing here is biting. There is a revolutionary nucleus among the troops who can throw off their conditioning and stop fighting their masters' wars. Indeed, they can turn on their masters.

Lady Jennifer and Jamie are being held prisoner in a barn, under the guard of Confederate soldiers who suspect them of espionage. Suddenly, out of the shadows a black man appears. He seizes Lady Jennifer's lily-white flesh, folds a hand over her mouth, and points a gun at Jamie. "Not one sound," he says.

It's the Freudian white race nightmare come true!

But it turns out that the black man, who wears a Union soldier's uniform, is their saviour. He's come to rescue them from the Confederates. The warm aura of utopian racial harmony inspired by this excellent scene is bolstered by the revelation that the black soldier, Harper (played by Rudolph Walker), isn't really from the Union, either. He's from the Resistance. After he helps Lady Jennifer and Jamie to escape, he is captured by the Confederates. Their commander, a captain this time for variety's sake, has his own set of hypno-specs. The black soldier, Harper, says dismissively, "That stuff doesn't work on me." He's one of those pesky members of the proletariat who are resistant to brainwashing.

We learn more about what is really going on through the mischievous use of a lecture in the Aliens' control zone that Zoe and the Doctor gate-crash. Here we get the exposition about difficult specimens who insist on thinking for themselves. A particularly virulent example is wheeled out. It turns out to be Lieutenant Carstairs, who was missing, presumed dead. He actually has been busy (offscreen) fighting for the Resistance. The lecturer tells us that in Carstair's case, "The process has completely lapsed and he is fully conscious of his surroundings."

This is where we really get into *The Manchurian Candidate*. This scene is an interesting echo of a bravura sequence in that classic movie. Directed by John Frankenheimer, and scripted by George Axelrod from Richard Condon's extraordinary novel, *The Manchurian Candidate* is a blackly funny political satire about the McCarthy era that is also a compelling thriller with an assassination plot. Its use of brainwashing, to create obedient and unquestioning assassins, almost puts it across the genre line into science fiction.

There is an extraordinary scene in *The Manchurian Candidate* where we see captive American soldiers in an auditorium full of Russian and Chinese communist brass. The communists have brainwashed the Americans (this was written at the height of Cold War paranoia) and they have been conditioned to believe that instead of an auditorium in Manchuria, they are waiting out a rainy afternoon in a hotel in America where some nice ladies are having a meeting of their garden club. From their point of view, the Commie nabobs and scientists are a bunch of nice, fat, boring old ladies talking about the growing conditions for hydrangeas, and when the Reds are presented from the soldier's point of view, that is exactly what we see.

"The War Games" doesn't essay anything this elaborate. But the same ideas are alive in this scene where Carstairs is made to describe his surroundings, an Alien lecture theatre, and then is subjected to a machine that reconditions his mind. He emerges from it with the controlling delusion once again intact. He identifies the Alien audience in their bizarre costumes and eyepieces (which again call to mind Bava's *Diabolik*) as "My brother officers."

But the writers have the imagination to add a new spin to this brainwashing idea. Carstairs spots the Doctor and Zoe in the audience and correctly identifies them, in the terms of his conditioning, as German spies.

Carstairs is still screaming about spies when he is dragged away, in a kind of straitjacket. The Doctor has brazened his way through this dangerous moment, rather in the way he presented himself as the Prison Inspector earlier. Both Troughton as an actor, and the Doctor as a character, are at their glorious best in scenes like this. He goes on the offensive against the lecturer. "The man was obviously unhinged as a result of your experiment." He starts examining the conditioning machine. "Will you leave the apparatus alone," say the lecturers. The Doctor, far from leaving it alone, begins to dismantle it. "This circuits overload the neural paths," he says with confidence.

And, as in the Prisoner Inspector scene, he is paving the way to take action on behalf of his friends. In a masterly stroke, he gets the lecturer to show him how to use the machine to reverse the conditioning process, preparing to rescue Carstairs.

When we cut away from this story, it would normally be a matter for annoyance, but the subplot we go to now is about the black Resistance fighter in the Civil War, Harper. He is now being held prisoner with Lady Jennifer and Jamie. Harper shows how profoundly he has left his own brainwashing behind. He indicates the Confederate soldiers guarding them. "You see those guys over there? They think they're fighting the war between the states," he says with disgust. "This isn't even America."

With his sardonic intelligence and his rebellious refusal to be deceived, Harper's a great character and a necessary corrective to

Toberman, the fetishistic near-brute of a manservant in "The Tomb of the Cybermen."

While it's always dangerous to assign responsibility to a particular member of a two-man writing team, it seems likely that Malcolm Hulke, a gifted left-wing polemicist, was responsible for elements in the script such as Harper (still the most right-on black character ever to appear in *Doctor Who*) and the speech about the five percent of the cannon fodder who won't be deceived. Meanwhile Terrance Dicks, who was known for his scrupulous historical research, may well be the man behind the evocative World War I terminology and detail, and scenes, such as the dismantling of the hand grenade.

In any case, the Resistance bursts in and rescues Harper and Lady Jennifer and Jamie. They're soldiers from all different periods in different uniforms and the only thing that links them is the desire to overthrow their oppressors. Throughout this scene the cheesy accompanying music posits the unity of man. When the dust settles Harper turns out to be the one in charge, at least temporarily. However, Jamie and Lady Jennifer soon realise the limits of the understanding that the Resistance members have of their situation. They are looking for a "tunnel" in the barn, to account for the hordes of troops who have been seen emerging from it. The poor souls don't realise that the troops are pouring out of space-time machines that vanish afterwards, leaving no trace. Jamie tries to explain to them, and his veracity isn't abetted by talking about green machines in a black and white show.

There is soon dissension amongst the ranks of the Resistance (no revolutionary movement is perfect) and while they're fighting among themselves, Lady Jane and Jamie start to sneak off. It's got to be easier than explaining about the space-time machines. Then they walk smack into another one of their captors arriving and are recaptured.

This is the fourth time this particular gag has been used, with only one feeble variation (Carstair's bluff) being worked upon it. It's possible, though, to be a little more forgiving of such infelicities when one hears that Malcolm Hulke and Terrance Dicks wrote all ten scripts for "The War Games" in approximately twenty days . . .

Meanwhile, back among the Aliens, the Doctor is cunningly suckering the lecturer into telling him everything he knows while the sets are becoming Op Art masterpieces (and period pieces) reminiscent of *The Avengers*. The costumes, by Nick Bullen, are also first rate.

Amongst the Aliens, Zoe and the Doctor have at last become separated by the writers (after a surprisingly good run together as a double act), and she has been, yet again, taken prisoner. This time, however, the Security Chief of the Aliens is interrogating her by using a rather nicely designed mind-reading helmet that enables him to probe Zoe's thoughts—and he learns more than he bargained for. She isn't just a member of the Resistance.

The Doctor can't help Zoe because he's busy trying to free the re-brainwashed Carstairs. Troughton is terrific in these scenes, fast and physical, darting mischievously around the Alien's base. He comes on like a trickster, or a clown, whose demeanour conceals deadly serious motives. He manages to get the lecturer to decondition Carstairs and then, with Carstair's help, traps the lecturer in his own machine. "Better leave him on simmer," muses the Doctor as he leaves the Alien egghead twitching in the grip of the mind control unit.

Now the story strands begin to intertwine as the Resistance troops commandeer a Tardis (which, we will learn, is exactly what the Aliens' space-time machines are) and are carrying the fight to the enemy. They arrive at Central Control, with its stylish moiré pattern sets (like wall murals by Bridget Riley) and launch an ambitious and somewhat foolhardy attack. Lady Jennifer and Jamie have been roped in, and they are taken prisoner along with the Resistance fighters when the attack fails. Meanwhile, the Doctor and Zoe are free and close at hand.

The final major subplot of "The Wargames," and the one that makes it such a significant part of the *Doctor Who* canon, now comes into play. We learn some crucial facts about the War Chief (Edward Brayshaw), up to now not much more than a highly effective bad guy with a nice line in facial hair. It seems that "his people have the secret of time travel." In fact, he is something called a Time Lord (just so you can keep track, the War Chief is a Time Lord, but the War Lord isn't. He's just an Alien). What is more important, we will learn that the Doctor is also a Time Lord.

This is a crucial fact, and one that carries the *Doctor Who* mythos into whole new realms. For the first time in six years, we will be given some concrete facts about the Doctor's background. It's been a good run, but it seems his personal mystery couldn't last forever. The Doctor is a Time Lord, according to "The War Games," and he comes from a planet of other Time Lords.

This was the beginning of the end for the Doctor as a cosmic enigma; he was given a backstory. This provided access to new story material but also eventually led to a loss of moody, majestic uniqueness.

What if the Doctor had remained unexplained, enigmatic, and slightly menacing?

The only television drama I know to successfully attempt this was P. J. Hammond's 1979 cult science fiction series *Sapphire and Steel*, which featured David McCallum and Joanna Lumley as sort of interdimensional time detectives, troubleshooters called in by an unseen higher authority to investigate cosmic anomalies. The show uncompromisingly refused to offer anything but the most shadowy hints of its characters' mysterious origins and was all the more powerful for that.

But *Sapphire and Steel* only ran for three seasons. I imagine if they approached *Doctor Who*'s twenty-eight years of transmission, they might have begun to explain a thing or two about their protagonists.

(Incidentally, Don Houghton, whom we'll encounter as the writer of the Pertwee story "Inferno," also co-wrote a *Sapphire and Steel* adventure. Anyone interested in that series would be better advised to first view some of Hammond's work, though.)

In any case, the notion of the Doctor as a Time Lord would give rise to endless elaborations and an accretion of detail on what was once the smooth and singular enigma of the Doctor, like seaweed, barnacles, and marine parasites encrusting the hull of a ship. Like such an encrustation, as it grew over the next two decades, the concept of the Time Lords would become such a hindrance and irritation that, by the time I joined the show as a script editor in 1986, it was time for some serious hull-scraping.

By 1989, twenty years after the Time Lords were first introduced on *Doctor Who*, we had achieved this, restoring some of the Doctor's original singularity and authority. (In the current series, Russell T. Davies has gone a step further, wiping out the Time Lords and their planet completely in an offstage Ragnarok and thereby providing a clean slate.)

It's intriguing to speculate that the Time Lords might never have come into being if writers Malcolm Hulke and Terrance Dicks hadn't found themselves in the position of trying to script a ten-part *Doctor Who* adventure in a matter of days, and were desperate for ideas to pad out their plot . . .

By now the story has slowed down and is losing energy in endless complications of fighting, escaping, and being taken prisoner. There is little feeling of forward movement, and it will gradually become clear that "The War Games" has peaked around episode five. For the re-

maining half of its running time we get, largely, more of the same—
with the notable exception of the Time Lord subplot.

This is a pity, not just because the Time Lords would arguably
prove more of a liability than an asset to the epic narrative of *Doctor
Who*, but also because up to the halfway mark "The War Games" was
pretty much an unqualified masterpiece and possibly the best *Doctor
Who* story ever. Even compromised as it is by an extended and weak
denouement (if you can call five episodes a denouement), it is still
probably the greatest of the black and white stories.

And one can't be too unsparingly critical of a script that was written under such pressure. "The War Games," like so many *Doctor Who*
adventures, was composed with the writers' backs to the wall as a last-
minute replacement for another story that had fallen through. In this
case, several planned scripts apparently fell through. The knock-on effect of this sudden gap in the schedule was that a story proposed by
Malcolm Hulke had to be expanded. Accounts vary; Hulke's original
story may have been intended to be a four-parter, or even a six-parter.
But in any case, the sudden expansion to ten episodes led to Hulke
collaborating with assistant script editor Terrance Dicks on a whirl-
wind writing session to create a new story.

Given all these exigencies, one should perhaps be generous about
"The War Games." Yet it's still difficult to forgive it for coming so
close to being a work of unalloyed genius for its first half and then
settling for mediocrity touched with flashes of inspiration for its second half.

At four, five, or perhaps even six episodes, "The War Games" could
have been the ultimate *Doctor Who* adventure. At ten episodes, we
have to settle for it merely being one of the most memorable.

The War Chief confronts the Doctor, and tries to initiate a candid
discussion man-to-man, or Time Lord-to-Time Lord. "You may have
changed your appearance," says the War Chief, alluding to the recast-
ing of Troughton for William Hartnell and the regeneration gimmick,
"but I know who you are."

This seemingly innocent comment sends a shiver down the spine.
After all, this is enigma incarnate that he's talking to, the Doctor
whose very name (or title) is a question. "I had every right to leave,"
says the Doctor, jumping to the defensive. "Stealing a Tardis?" says
the Warlord. "I had reasons of my own," replies the Doctor. Obviously, the enigma is not to be eroded too quickly.

The tide is now turning and it looks as though the Aliens are going to be defeated by the Resistance, which leaves the Doctor with a thorny problem. When the war games are stopped, there are thousands of kidnapped, brainwashed humans who need to be relocated to Earth and their proper times. Since the War Chief's Tardis fleet is swiftly running out of power (a McGuffin looms into view), there is only one solution, and it's not for the Doctor to use his own vessel to take everybody home one at a time.

The War Chief guesses the solution the Doctor is suggesting and it frightens him. "Doctor, you mustn't call them in or it will be the end of us. They'll show no mercy."

Again the mention of the Time Lords sends shivers emanating down susceptible spines. Even the Doctor isn't too cheery about his decision, but "I'm afraid there's no alternative . . ." Only the Time Lords have the resources to repatriate the hijacked humans, so the Doctor must summon them.

He proceeds to do so in one of the most extraordinary scenes in the long history of the show. The Doctor takes out six squares of white paper and sets them on the floor. Then he sits facing them, crosslegged and apparently meditating. Without touching the paper, through use of his mental powers (powers that we have never seen before), he proceeds to assemble the six squares into the six sides of a cube. It's a box. A box that now contains all the information about the situation plus an appeal for help.

We're still reeling from this psychic box assembly when the War Chief makes an attempt to get the hell out of there before the Time Lords arrive. However, in at least the fifth occurrence of this trope, he runs straight into the people he least wants to see, the War Lord and his Guards, who summarily execute him. "Remove the traitor's carcass," says the War Lord dispassionately. It's an historic moment. The first dead Time Lord in the series (assuming that the Monk didn't freeze to death on the ice planet where the Doctor stranded him in "The Dalek Master Plan").

Back in the Doctor's Tardis, he and Jamie and Zoe hear the disembodied voice of a Time Lord telling them there is no escape and advising the Doctor to return his stolen Tardis immediately. He has broken the Time Lord laws and now must face trial.

This last injunction is particularly hair-raising to any modern viewer who happens to be familiar with the truly diabolical tedium of the story "Trial of a Time Lord," which will appear a couple of decades later. Fortunately, this trial is not remotely in that league. It displays merciful brevity.

The Tardis materialises on the Doctor's home planet (still nameless), and we glimpse the Time Lords for the first time. They wear strange robes (well realized costumes if a trifle ecclesiastical). The sets are also very alien and effective, exotic but minimal (by now the budget must have been running on empty). It transpires that the Warlord is on trial too, for his mass slaughter of humans in the war games. The Time Lords' dialogue tends towards declarations like "Brutal methods of mental processing were used which contravened all the galactic laws" as charges are read out against the War Lord. At this point we begin to feel that the title of the story could as easily have been "The War Crimes."

The Doctor is summoned as a witness, and the War Lord, vindictive to the end, does his best to implicate him as a collaborator. The Time Lords see through him. They proceed to sentence the Warlord and his flunkies in a rather harsh, no-nonsense manner. "You will be dematerialised. . . . It will be as though you never existed." Except for the more civilized inflections of the Time Lord's voice, this brutal prescription could have been uttered by a Dalek, Cyberman, or Kroton.

And so the War Lord and his men are perfunctorily disintegrated. Now it's the Doctor's turn, and he is cheeringly defiant. He not only admits his transgressions, he is proud of them. While the Time Lords have been content to observe the evil in the galaxy, he has been fighting it.

There then ensues a kind of magic lantern show of the Doctor's greatest monsters and foes, a cavalcade of inadequate and laughable costumes, including a Yeti, a Cyberman, and of course the Daleks (the only impressive ones in the batch). At this point, we're reminded irresistibly of those clip-show compilations that *The Simpsons* shamelessly include in a season when the budget or schedule comes up short.

Now it's time for the Doctor to say farewell to Zoe and Jamie and even a cynical viewer might feel a little saddened. The Doctor is taking his leave of two of the finest companions ever to share the Tardis. He gives them advice that is a kind of summary of their character notes. He tells Jamie, the hot-headed man of action, "Don't go blundering into too much trouble, will you?"

"You're a fine one to talk," says Jamie. And he has a point.

To Zoe, the scientific intellectual, he says goodbye, and when she asks if they will meet again he replies, "Again? You and I know time is relative." Then we see Zoe back in the space station she came from, experiencing a strange sense of déjà vu as she tries to recall the adventures she shared with the Doctor before she seamlessly rejoins the flow of her life. Jamie is back in his clan tartan, swinging a Claymore and dodging Redcoat shot.

The Doctor watches them go on a screen, shaking his head fondly. Then it's time to be sentenced by a jury of his peers. Since the War Lord and his Guards have been disintegrated, the worst that the Doctor's likely to face is some long, boring speeches lecturing him about his errant behaviour.

He gets some of that now, as the Time Lords say they've taken on board some of his arguments about fighting evil. They will let the Doctor continue to do so, but on their own terms. He will be returned to one of his favourite places and times (the Earth circa 1970), where he will be exiled and deprived of his Tardis.

These last injunctions sting a little, but perhaps not as much as the command that his appearance will once again change, a neat way of writing Patrick Troughton out of the series and the next Doctor in . . .

The last we see of the Troughton Doctor is a fun house mirror effect as his face distorts. He cries "No!" as he disappears from view.

chapter 5

Exile and Freedom

In 1970 a tall, solid, rather powerful looking man came lurching out of a police box and without ceremony fell facedown in some shrubbery. The wig he was wearing suggested a passing resemblance to the Patrick Troughton Doctor, but this man's posture, his movement, his physical presence indicated someone entirely different . . .

From a *Doctor Who* point of view, the years 1970 to 1974 are the Pertwee Years. From a less narrow perspective, these years also include the following events: In April 1970, President Richard Nixon invades Cambodia. On 4 May 1970, the National Guard shoots dead four students and wounds nine others during a peaceful protest against the invasion at Kent State University in Ohio. August 1970 the Isle of Wight Pop Festival was a blazing success. March 1971 saw Joe Frazier beat Muhammad Ali at Madison Square Garden for the world heavyweight boxing championship. On 30 January 1972, Bloody Sunday, British troops killed thirteen civilians in Londonderry. In August 1972, American swimmer Mark Spitz won seven gold medals at the Munich Olympics. A few weeks later Black September terrorists murdered eleven Israeli athletes at the Olympic Village in Munich. In 1973, US troops finally left Vietnam. On 11 September 1973 President Salvador Allende of Chile was killed and his government overthrown, with a little help by the CIA. In February 1974 Alexander Solzhenitsyn was exiled from the USSR as a result of the publication of *The Gulag Archipelago*. In October 1974 Muhammad Ali defeated George Foreman in the Rumble in the Jungle in Zaire. Also in 1974, Nixon found that a little matter called Watergate was making his second term as president problematical.

"Spearhead from Space" by Robert Holmes

Back in 1970, on 3 January, as the new decade began, a new series of *Doctor Who* appeared on TV screens. The colour title sequence came as a shock, after seven years in black and white, and, though it was stylish and well executed, it makes one nostalgic for the great, iconic, original logo.

Some viewers even compared this series unfavourably with the new American import *Star Trek*.

In the first story featuring the new Doctor, Jon Pertwee stepped into Patrick Troughton's shoes. Still reeling from his sentence of exile by the Time Lords, he falls out of the Tardis and into a story about aliens invading the Earth. The deft script for "Spearhead from Space" is by Robert Holmes, in many ways the ultimate *Doctor Who* writer. Somewhat cheekily, it bears some points of resemblance to the effective black and white British science fiction film *Invasion* (1965, directed by Alan Bridges) that was scripted by Roger Marshal, but for which Robert Holmes wrote the original story.

Holmes's "Spearhead" resembles *Invasion* not only in frightening the audience with the prospect of an invasion from space, but also by having an injured "person" taken into hospital, where it becomes dramatically apparent that the patient is actually an alien. Perhaps more acutely, "Spearhead from Space" resembles *Quatermass II*, with fifty meteorites landing in Essex. They become affectionately known to the locals, and to the authorities dealing with the matter, as thunderbolts. In *Quatermass II*, the strange projectiles (for they turn out to be anything but meteorites) are called overshots; they are odd hollow objects from outer space that contain a parasite that can exert control over human beings. This subtle sort of alien invasion moves rapidly up the local hierarchy and begins to infiltrate the government.

Holmes's story also posits an infiltration, but one that owes more to earlier *Doctor Who* stories than to Nigel Kneale. David J. Howe and Stephen James Walker point out how the story resembles "The Abominable Snowman" with a disembodied cosmic intelligence (in this case called the Nestene consciousness) manipulating some synthetic local heavies to achieve their ends.

In "Spearhead from Space" the "meteorites" that land are made of a substance resembling plastic, and the Nestene has an affinity for plastic. It creates humanoid beings out of plastic, using a mannequin factory. These creatures are called Autons. They are made so lifelike that when animated they can pass as humans. They also come in cruder versions, which aren't much more sophisticated than shambling display mannequins come to life. This latter form is useful for scaring the bejesus out of people when the special effects hold up, as they do in the early part of the story. When they burst out en masse later on, erupting from department store show windows, they are rather obviously fake. The Autons, particularly in their cruder form, are also reminiscent of the Cybernauts who were a popular adversary in *The Avengers*, created by writer Philip Levene.

Holmes's frequently witty and effective writing is one of the distinctions of "Spearhead from Space." Another is the realistic Earth setting, which helps immensely in giving the story authenticity and impact. This return to earthbound locations was a deliberate move. Derrick Sherwin was still influential in the show's development. He had served at various times as a writer, script editor and producer. According to *Doctor Who: The Seventies*, Sherwin had studied Nigel Kneale's *Quatermass* stories, and he and producer Peter Bryant had determined that *Doctor Who* would benefit from a return to Earth for a while.

One of the great strengths of Kneale's writing in general, and his *Quatermass* stories in particular, had been their sense of realism, which was achieved by grounding the extraordinary and alien in the familiar and everyday. Sherwin and Bryant determined they should bring their stories down to Earth, quite literally.

So the Doctor was exiled to the Earth, and his Tardis effectively wheelclamped. The creative minds behind *Doctor Who*, like Sherwin, were astute enough to know that the Doctor now needed more than just a companion or two. Once he was confined to Earth, he could benefit from an entire organisation built around him.

This was the era of international organisations, preferably accompanied by a snappy acronym. NATO, UNICEF, the World Health Organisation (WHO), and the UN in all its myriad forms, loomed large in the post-war mind. Organisations designed to make the world a safer place.

Of course, there was a sinister counter world of nefarious organisations such as SMERSH, and everybody's favourite, SPECTRE. These latter were mostly the work of the fertile mind of Ian Fleming, the same mind responsible for James Bond. Fleming also had a hand in creating *The Man from UNCLE*, a television series with the most groovy of 1960s acronyms. Honorary mention should also be made of the Tower comic, THUNDER Agents, if only for its great artwork. THUNDER, straining at every letter, was The Higher United Nations Defence Enforcement Reserve.

UNIT stood for United Nations Intelligence Taskforce.

The third great asset of "Spearhead from Space" is that it is shot entirely on film. It was the only *Doctor Who* story since its inception to have this honour. Traditionally on *Doctor Who*, as on most BBC dramas, location sequences were shot on film while scenes shot in the studio were recorded on videotape. In the days of black and white, this distinction was apparent, though not as shockingly apparent as it would become now, under the unmerciful eye of the colour camera. Later episodes would feature the Doctor running outdoors on film, straight into an interior shot on video and the transition was so jarring that the viewer almost felt thrown out of one story and into another.

But "Spearhead from Space" was the unintended beneficiary of a strike that made studio space unavailable for *Doctor Who* for the duration of this first adventure. Being shot entirely on 16mm film gives this story a unity and a verisimilitude (give or take a dodgy Auton) that make it stand out among the adventures of the Third Doctor. Use of adventurous techniques, like a handheld camera during a press conference, give the story some engrossing authenticity.

The man at the centre of the press conference, very much against his will, is Brigadier Lethbridge-Stewart. *Doctor Who* viewers have met him twice before. In "Web of Fear" where he was still a mere Colonel and in "The Invasion" (written by Derrick Sherwin, from a story by Kit Pedler, which introduced UNIT). Both these stories featured the Patrick Troughton Doctor, and both were decimated in the great purge.

As the Brigadier explains to Elizabeth Shaw, an attractive lady scientist, "We're not exactly spies here at UNIT . . . We deal with the odd, the unexplained." He refers to the earlier stories where he encountered the Doctor and explains, not quite accurately, that since UNIT has been formed there have been two "attempts to invade this planet" and that a mysterious someone called "The Doctor" helped on both occasions. In short, UNIT is a military organisation designed to deal with the threat of alien attack, and the Brigadier is up to speed on the fifty odd meteorites in Essex. He has summoned Miss Shaw because of her expertise in such matters.

Nicholas Courtney as the Brigadier looks young and dashing in his UNIT uniform (despite its phoney-looking cap badge) as he uncharacteristically finds himself caught in the limelight later at a country hospital. The press are badgering him with questions, because they've got wind that an alien has been admitted to the hospital. This is true. The Doctor has been brought in, after emerging from the Tardis and collapsing, still in post-traumatic coma after the Time Lord's sentence. An X-ray has revealed that he has two hearts. What's more, his blood sample isn't human. "I don't know if that makes me a doctor or a vet," quips the attending physician.

Robert Holmes's writing here is vivid, concise, and witty. He seems much more at ease with the mechanics of a mystery and suspense story in a realistic Earth setting than he was among the exotic science fiction impedimenta of "The Krotons." He does a good job of evoking the intramural bickering of the medical fraternity. There is a sense of real medic people working together at a real hospital here, a social and medical hierarchy. Especially in the later scene where the Doctor makes his escape through a door mischievously labelled Doctors Only.

The attending physician is bemused by the Doctor. "His whole cardiovascular system is quite unlike anything I've ever seen."

"Splendid," says the Brigadier. "That sounds like the Doctor." The contrast of the Doctor's utter alienness and the hidebound military normality of UNIT is an inspired stroke. As further medical examinations of the bedridden Doctor ensues, the Autons infiltrate the hospital. They knock the physician unconscious and kidnap the Doctor, who wakes up sufficiently to escape from them in a wheelchair in a great scene. The villains are forced to pursue him in an ambulance (in what now appears to be a lost scene) as Pertwee wheels the chair athletically away down the hill.

This vigorous and athletic, though silver haired, new Doctor manages to escape both the Autons and UNIT, who have had him under a kind of house arrest. He doesn't look like the old Doctor and the mechanics of regeneration (let alone its name) are not familiar yet.

Who can blame the Doctor for wanting to escape and flee back to the Tardis. He abandons the wheelchair in the woodlands and does just that. Unfortunately, he gets shot for his trouble, by the guards the Brigadier posted. The Doctor of "The War Games" might have made an acerbic comment here about the military mentality. But this new Doctor is lying in the bracken, his head bleeding, fortunately just from a graze. Then it's back to the hospital in a rather unexciting plot loop.

Meanwhile the Autons have taken over a mannequin and plastic doll factory. There are shots of eerie doll heads without bodies and then some deeply sinister footage of the naked doll bodies on the assembly line conveyor belt, clever visual equivalents for the mass produced Autons who will soon be pouring out into the world to infiltrate and then to seize by force. These moments reflect well on director Derek Martinus.

The invading aliens are emanating from the hollow (but not empty) plastic spheres that crashed into the Essex woods. They look like glowing crystals and make a strange noise that now sounds oddly like a cell phone ring tone. This odd object tempts a rather tiresome poacher to dig it up and cart it home with him before attempting to sell it to UNIT. The meteor houses the Nestene Swarm Leader and the Autons are busy trying to recover it. The Swarm Leader's presence is required at the mannequin factory so that the serious business of taking over the world can proceed.

While the avaricious stereotype of a poacher is preoccupied trying to make the military mind take on the concept of payment for services rendered, his wife is being violently attacked by one of the monstrously mannequin-like Autons. The Doctor, the Brig, and some UNIT troops arrive in time to encounter the malign dummy. The UNIT troops fire the first in what will seem like an endless series of futile volleys of small arms fire to be directed against an assortment of alien invaders in the next two seasons of the show.

As the Auton invasion progresses, the Doctor has asserted his independence by escaping from the hospital again, stealing his new costume and a cool vintage car along the way. Pertwee is very much the action hero Doctor, not hampered by the shy protestations, dithering, or clowning that sometimes disguised Troughton's steel-trap mind and powerful will. Pertwee has a great face, craggy and full of character. His background was in comedy and light entertainment, and this comes through in the exuberance and comic energy of his performance. He makes for a dashing, heroic Doctor and is a far cry from crotchety William Hartnell, but he doesn't display the depth or range of performance of Patrick Troughton.

The new companion for this new Doctor is Liz Shaw (Caroline John). The Brigadier is too much plugged in to the establishment, too much a company man to qualify as a full-blown companion. To be one of the Doctor's companions you have to renounce your ordinary life and make him, and his erratic odyssey, your first loyalty. Both Nicholas Courtney as the Brig and Caroline John as Liz Shaw make valuable foils for Pertwee. Liz is witty and shares the Doctor's jaundiced ambivalence about the military. She has an acerbic relationship with Lethbridge-Stewart. "Am I interrupting?" he asks her as he visits her lab. "Yes," says Liz. She hits it off with the Doctor immediately, despite his first order of business being to try and escape in the Tardis (which has been brought to the lab for study). The Time Lords weren't kidding about immobilising it. His efforts merely result in some straining, grunting noise from a constipated-sounding Tardis and a laboratory full of smoke.

The aliens' plan is to replace key figures in the power structure with facsimiles ("Facsimiles" was Holmes's original title for the story), and there is an adroit and spooky scene where the pompous General Scobie, the army's liaison to UNIT, answers the door to find his double standing there.

We learn that the plastic meteorites that fell on Essex contain organisms that are part of one big gestalt entity, a collective intelligence. This critter begins to grow inside a transparent plastic box in the mannequin factory while it is extending its influence through a whole wax museum (Madame Tussaud's was used as a location) full of government muckamucks and senior civil servants (as if anyone ever bothered to make a life-size model of a civil servant). The Doctor and Liz investigate the wax museum and Robert Holmes demonstrates a good instinct for the creepy potential in the situation. "Funny how their eyes seem to be following you," says the Doctor. "Hilarious," says Liz.

Back at the factory there are some surprisingly good effects as the Squad Leader is added to the plastic box with the rest of the Nestene cluster. The pulsating thing we see inside is actually quite impressive.

To stop the invaders, the Doctor solicits Liz's help in the laboratory. She's an intelligent collaborator and a refreshing change from some of the more helpless female companions. (Zoe may have been a genius but she chiefly seemed to spend her time pouting.) With Liz's assistance, the Doctor constructs a machine that drives the Nestene off the planet. He takes it to the factory for the big showdown, activating his device while the UNIT troops continue their tradition of pouring futile gunfire at the alien bad guys.

When the Nestene consciousness confronts the Doctor, it thrusts tentacles out of the tank and tries to strangle him. All the earlier sterling special effects work goes out the window here, and Pertwee has to gamely hold the green tentacle to his own throat in an attempt to convince us it is really throttling him. (Sylvester McCoy would later be called upon to do exactly the same thing with a squirmy Dalek organism attacking him from inside its opened armour in "Remembrance of the Daleks.")

It is left to Liz to save the day by repairing the device the Doctor built and reactivating it. After the invaders have been routed, there is a technical explanation of just what the device is, and does. But the Brigadier isn't interested and neither are we. "It worked," he says succinctly.

"Spearhead from Space" ends as the Doctor has proved himself to Lethbridge-Stewart and feels in a position to haggle with the Brigadier about the terms of his future employment by UNIT. Chiefly he wants a vintage car like the one he requisitioned at the hospital, to roar through his subsequent adventures in.

When the Brigadier cautiously agrees to this condition, the Doctor immediately asks, "When can we go and choose it?"

"Inferno" by Don Houghton

Jon Pertwee's first season as the Doctor concluded with one of the great *Doctor Who* stories, "Inferno," a masterpiece that almost matches the best episodes of "The War Games," and is more consistent as an overall piece of work. "Inferno" begins its seven episode run (first transmitted 9 May 1970) very promisingly, and is rather reminiscent of "The War Games," with the writer's credit over lurid footage of red-hot flowing lava. "Inferno" was written by Don Houghton, a writer who did a considerable amount of movie work for Hammer Films, including *Dracula AD 1972*, *The Satanic Rites of Dracula* and *The Legend of the Seven Golden Vampires* (a vampire-kung fu hybrid). His television credits include, notably, the previously mentioned *Sapphire & Steel* story.

"Inferno" begins with the Doctor singing as he careens along in his yellow vintage automobile (yes, the Brigadier made good his promise) affectionately nicknamed Bessie. He sweeps past a sign that reads Keep Out into a rather grim and threatening industrial landscape.

We soon learn that the Doctor, and UNIT, are peripherally involved in an ambitious project to drill deep into the Earth's crust to tap sources of natural gas to provide unlimited and inexpensive energy. As sinister events begin to cluster around this high tech venture, it will begin to seem a bit like *Quatermass and the Drill*, which is no bad thing. Again the story benefits from the sense of a real organisation with real people caught up in plausible and convincing conflicts.

Rather less convincing is the green slime that comes bubbling up the drill shaft and stains the hand of an engineer doing maintenance work. Before you know it, the engineer is transformed into a violent zombie and begins to metamorphose physically into a creature called a Primord.

"Inferno" is well edited and well directed (by Douglas Camfield, with uncredited contributions by Barry Letts). In one memorably neat sequence we cut from the Primord smashing a technician with a wrench to a shot of a hammer bashing a nail into the wall. The nail is for hanging up a group photo featuring the Brigadier among other troops in his younger days. The Doctor tries to identify him in the picture and is told that the Brigadier didn't have a moustache in those days, a joke that will pay off later.

Pertwee is engaging in these scenes, and there is a nice interaction between him and Nicholas Courtney as the Brigadier. The Doctor is now characteristically attired in frilly shirt, black velvet jacket and trousers, and a black cape with red lining that makes him look like a superhero.

"Who's the gentleman in the fancy dress?" is a valid question asked by the drilling team as the Doctor comes to witness the initial penetration of the Earth's crust.

In the scenes near the drill machinery, the actors have to shout to be heard, which seems an unnecessary bit of self-flagellation by the production team, since there really is no drill and the noise of it had to be specially dubbed in for the sake of verisimilitude. Greg Sutton, a drilling consultant (played by Derek Newark), is impressed when he learns how deep the drill is going. "Twenty miles? You're liable to wake up Old Nick going that deep," he says, foreshadowing the diabolical nature of what will ensue. The Doctor is agreeably insolent with Professor Stahlman (Olaf Pooley), the arrogant originator and director of the project, who comes equipped with a beautiful and loyal assistant in the shape of Petra (Sheila Dunn).

After watching "Spearhead from Space," which had the luxury of being shot entirely on film, "Inferno" is occasionally dismayingly uneven in its visuals. When the Doctor drives Bessie into the hut where he works, there is a jarring transition from film to video tape. In the hut, Liz Shaw is waiting and so is the Tardis console, the crucial control cluster for his ship. The Doctor has not abandoned his attempts to get the Tardis working again, and he has detached the console for some further experiments. It rapidly becomes clear that he is primarily interested in using the power supplied by the drilling plant's nuclear generator for his own experiments.

By now the Primord engineer has mutated further, acquiring some genuinely unsettling face makeup but also some hilariously hairy Lon Chaney Jr style hands that we are forced to inspect in some misjudged lingering close-ups.

There is a power surge, which serves to briefly carry the Doctor and the Tardis console away into the realm of some efficient special effects (the visual effects for this story are by Len Hutton) and also serve to prepare us for a major plot development later on. Liz manages to cut the power and he reappears again, telling her that he seemed to be in some kind of limbo while he was gone. It seems the power surge was caused by problems in the generator control room, where the Primord has broken in.

Accompanied by UNIT troops, the Doctor confronts the Primord. "There's nothing to be frightened of, old chap," he says, a wonderfully Doctor-ish line when you consider that he's confronting a dangerous, subhuman monster. The military presence again helps to ground the story in reality and also heighten the drama. Naturally, it is a soldier who panics and shoots the creature. The thing turns out to be searingly hot, its body scorching the wall where it lies.

Throughout the ensuing technical dialogue, Pertwee comes across as efficient and meticulous, but there is no sense of any profound understanding. As the Doctor, he is forceful and likeable but lacks Troughton's depth.

The Doctor is called in to examine the green goo that keeps oozing up from the drill. It's unfortunate that whenever some weird substance is required in a science fiction story that the design team think it ought to be a bright luminous green. As an enervating cliché, this ranks with silver zip suits and characters called Zarb. On the other hand, "Inferno" scores some points for having a black face among the extras who make up the team of drilling technologists.

The story as a whole is engrossing, realistic, and suspenseful, though the Doctor's use of Venusian Karate (basically a rip-off of Mr. Spock's Vulcan nerve pinch in *Star Trek*) is dismayingly childish—why Venusian? When he's not using his knowledge of interplanetary martial arts to subdue miscreants, the Doctor is pursuing his research on the Tardis console, which now disappears again, along with the Doctor and his car Bessie.

This time the Doctor really has vanished, to another dimension. Unfortunately the special effects for this transition sequence are abject, some cheap shots of what appears to be an out-of-focus disco ball spinning and reflecting light. These ropy effects presage an exemplary and gripping sequence. The Doctor wakes up on the floor of what appears to be the same hut he left, but there are some subtle differences. On the wall, for instance, hangs an Orwellian poster with the image of a grimfaced leader and the slogan Unity is Strength. (The face on the poster is an in-joke. It belongs to Jack Kine, a visual effects designer who had worked on "The Mind Robber" and became head of the visual effects department—their leader.)

The Doctor ventures outside the hut and finds a fascist insignia emblazoned on the door; there are also uniformed guards who are eager to shoot him as a saboteur. It looks like the same drilling plant he left, but there are some unsettling (and potentially lethal) differences.

We now have two stories running in parallel in "Inferno." First, there was the plot about the drilling project with its hints of technological doom and the strange substance welling up to change people into Primords. That in itself was gripping and (give or take a close-up of a hairy hand) quite effective. Now we have a whole other storyline concerning a parallel universe, and it's utterly enthralling.

The Doctor leaps into his car and tries to escape the fascist soldiers. There's some terrific chase music (amazingly, from stock) which audaciously plays against the frenetic physical action, being dreamy and eerie and slow, a subtle way of telling us that something is terribly wrong here. One of the pursuing troops leaps onto the car and Pertwee fights him off in a way that Troughton would never have attempted. The Doctor is now a dashing, physical hero—and also an accomplished comedian. When the soldiers give up the hunt, the Pertwee Doctor emerges from hiding in the waste bins, wearing a garbage can lid on his head, like a Chinese coolie's hat.

As he tries to escape across a high metal walkway, we discover that there are savage green-faced Primords on the loose in this dimension too, and the Doctor fights one off using a fire extinguisher (reasoning that these superheated creatures are like flames that need quenching). The Primords, at this stage, are extremely well realised (the makeup design is by Marion Richards). In fact, they are genuinely scary, something that you can't often say about a *Doctor Who* monster.

A woman walks past the Doctor, and he emerges from hiding to greet her. It's Liz Shaw—yet it isn't. She's a kind of uniformed, militaristic doppelganger of Liz. The Doctor wonders aloud what is going on, asking her why she is wearing such odd clothes. For a fellow who travels through time and space in a trans-dimensional vehicle, he is surprisingly slow to catch on. The Liz Shaw in this world is no friend of the Doctor's, and he promptly finds himself taken prisoner (it's that time again) and confronting the Brigadier.

In this dimension the Brigadier (or, more correctly, the Brigade Leader) is clean-shaven, with a sinister eye patch and an impressive scar. Nicholas Courtney looks great in this fascist getup, and the uniforms are excellent (the costume design is by Christine Rawlins). Now the Doctor finally begins to catch on. "I come from a parallel space-time continuum," he tells them. Not surprisingly, this alibi doesn't convince them.

We are now in episode three of "Inferno" and, again unusually for a *Doctor Who* adventure, the story hasn't put a foot wrong. The Doctor is dragged into the drilling control room, and he dryly registers the advantages of a regimented society, ruled by fear: this team is a lot more advanced with the drilling. He meets the counterparts of the technical team. This is a wonderful concept, the same cast but in different costumes, and with subtle differences in characterisation. Sutton, the roughneck drilling consultant who wore casual clothes back on our Earth, is here neatly dressed in a suit and tie.

It becomes clear, even at this early stage, that "Inferno" is a classic *Doctor Who* adventure and, in a series where there was often a shortage of story material, it appears to be blessed with an abundance of it. Interestingly, according to Howe and Walker, Don Houghton's original storyline concerned the drilling project and an alternate universe, but all the material about the green goo and the Primord creates was added at the behest of the production team (possibly being the contribution of script editor Terrance Dicks).

Dyed-in-the-wool *Doctor Who* fans have complained about the alternate dimensions story getting in the way of the monster subplot, but I'd make the counter argument. This story of a parallel world, with its England under fascist rule, is far stronger and more sophisticated and more frightening than the intermittently scary Primords. (We learn that Britain is a republic and, chillingly, that the royals have all been executed. "Pity," says the Doctor. "A charming family.")

But given that "Inferno" is a seven-part adventure, it clearly needs both alternate world and Primord plot strands to provide sufficient plot material. The basic drilling and monster story was gripping enough, but this new idea adds another dimension, quite literally. "Inferno" ends up as a hybrid of subtle, cerebral science fiction and conventional monster scare-fest, but perhaps that's not a bad combination.

It transpires that the infallible central records of this police state don't have a file on the Doctor. He tells them that he doesn't exist in their world. "Then you won't feel the bullets when we shoot you," says the Brigadier, a very nasty piece of work in this incarnation.

Any occasional infelicities of the low budget video shooting are easily forgiven and forgotten in this gripping narrative. Like the title sequence, this story is the best since "The War Games." It's great to see Liz and the familiar, friendly UNIT personnel transformed into these cold and threatening counterparts. "A parallel space-time continuum," reiterates the Doctor. "A twin world," he adds, for the benefit of dullards. It's a grim and frightening place, though Petra has a better hairdo here.

The Doctor is brutally interrogated by the Brigadier and Liz (who is a security officer in this world), but holds up manfully under the abuse. He courageously tells them that they're wasting their time and calls their behaviour childish. They keep demanding to know where he came from and how he got here. The Doctor's reply that he slipped sideways in time doesn't please them, and Liz suggests proceeding to a more intensive interrogation. The Brigadier demurs, saying he might die before he talks.

The Doctor is dragged off to the cells by this world's equivalent of UNIT Sergeant Benson, here a brutal flunky, whereas his counterpart in our world is a nice guy, as the Doctor tells him. He's locked up and we go back to the other Earth, via that execrable glitterball effect. However, it's a marvellously curious sensation to return to the original group of these characters and requires a mental somersault to distinguish them from their fascist counterparts. It must have been an equally interesting challenge for the actors.

Both worlds are now moving towards the moment when they will break through the Earth's crust and harvest the fiery chaos within. The Doctor warns his captors about releasing undreamed of, deadly forces. But the drilling continues inexorably in both dimensions and, because the Fascists are so darned efficient, they break through first, unleashing hell on Earth.

There is a wave of earth tremors and full-blown earthquakes. The Doctor tells them that the forces they have released would make an atomic bomb's explosion seem "like a summer breeze."

The most chilling thing about "Inferno" is that once the crust has been penetrated and this cataclysm begun, there is no turning back, no cosy solution. For once, the Doctor has no answers. Doomsday really is here. This world is at an end. It must be written off. There is, how-ever, one grim way to balance the equation. Everyone here must die, but the Doctor tells them at least they can save their other selves. If he can get back to our Earth, with its woolly, inefficient democratic social system, the drilling will still be lagging behind and he might have time to save *that* world.

While the Doctor is struggling to do this, which entails re-routing power from the nuclear reactor to the Tardis console, Director Stahl-man and a group of his underlings have metamorphosed into full-blown Primords. This involves not just green skin and hairy hands but also massive amounts of facial hair and huge fangs. Sad to report, this Mr Hyde style of makeup is a step too far, and considerably less frightening than the earlier stage.

Fire extinguishers aren't up to the task of fending off these hot monsters, but there is a pipe full of coolant to be deployed, a kind of giant fire extinguisher. A little too convenient, perhaps, but this appa-ratus is satisfyingly difficult to set up and provides some good sus-pense, though nothing compared to the nail-biting complications as the Doctor and his new allies try to send power to the Tardis console in the last few moments of this dying world. When a series of red lights finally flash on to indicate success, it's a rousing moment and even the most cynical viewer might be tempted to cheer.

The Tardis console, and the Doctor and his beloved car Bessie, all disappear at the last possible moment, as documentary footage of lava flows menacingly towards the doors of the hut. In fact, we never actu-ally see the Doctor leave. It seems that some shots from the story are missing, or proved unusable. The Doctor simply begins the final epi-sode waking up on the floor of his hut in our world (a resolution again reminiscent of the cheats used in the cliff-hanger Hollywood serials of the 1930s). He greets his old friend by saying, "Brigadier, you really do look better with that moustache."

Even when he is safely back here, with the drilling not yet at critical point, the Doctor faces an uphill battle. The intractable and pigheaded Professor Stahlman must rank as one of the great *Doctor Who* villains, all the more loathsome for being so plausible and recognisable in his selfish fanaticism. When the Doctor, in an excess of frustration, takes a monkey wrench and smashes the control panel, it's a great cathartic moment. And when the Brigadier is forced to constrain him for this apparently unaccountable behaviour, the suspense ramps up agreeably.

Finally, Stahlman is up to his elbows in green goo and he transforms. The makeup is better in this scene, and more dramatically lit than the earlier hairy-face prosthetics. When the Brigadier and the others are presented with this apparition, all doubts about the Doctor's bizarre story evaporate, and they set about stopping the drills.

In the end, this is achieved with thirty-five seconds to spare. A quaint, old-fashioned and very English safety margin. In any self-respecting modern Hollywood film, we'd go down to the wire and wait until the very last second before the world was saved. And quite right, too. But this was 1970, after all.

"Carnival of Monsters" by Robert Holmes

Jon Pertwee was a major success as the Doctor and would play the part for five seasons. By his fourth year, the show began to manifest some major changes. Liz Shaw was now gone and had been replaced by Jo Grant (Katy Manning) introduced during Season 8 in "Terror of the Autons." Jo was a return to the rather more fluffy companions of yesteryear after the acerbic, intelligent, and relatively hard-edged Liz Shaw. But, as Ben Aaronovitch has pointed out, as soon as they try to dumb the companion down, she starts getting intelligent and independent again, and Jo Grant could be enjoyably feisty.

With the first story of 1973, the Doctor's exile on Earth came to an end, and his close association with UNIT also began to wind down. The second story of that season, "Carnival of Monsters," written by Robert Holmes, saw the Doctor and Jo Grant exploring his new freedom by taking the Tardis on a test flight and, of course, promptly getting into trouble.

The story begins with some hilariously terrible special effects of a spaceship landing on the planet Inter Minor. The denizens of this world, the Minorians, are grey-skinned and wear grey uniforms, an outward manifestation of their rather grey, bureaucratic nature, which is neatly sketched in Holmes's script. His witty writing presents them

as boring, flattened-out personalities obsessed with protocol and reg-
ulations and obsessively fond of using the pronoun "one." These self-
effacing nonentities are well drawn, but the downside of their characterisation (and appearance) is that it's hard to tell them apart. The
scheming Kalik and Orum, and their superior Pletrac, may be differentiated in the writing, but the fact that they are all grey-skinned, wear
grey clothes and speak in the same colourless idiom makes them hard
for the viewer to identify and separate.

The Minorians also wear baldhead prosthetics, and as the show goes
on some shots of these would prove so unconvincing that the producer
insisted on making cuts from the print of the show for all future
screenings. (If only similar care had been lavished in an earlier era to
remove the wires attached to Toberman in "Tomb of the Cybermen.")

Generally speaking, the makeup of the Minorians isn't bad, although that hardly matters when the set representing their world is so
brightly lit and cheesy it looks like something from a downmarket
game show. The music (by Dudley Simpson) does its best to achieve
what the lamentable visuals fail to do. Meanwhile Minorian lower
classes (known as Functionaries) are busy unloading a machine from
the ship that's just landed (the "miniscope," which will prove to be
absolutely central to the unfolding story). It's clear from the way the
costumed extras carry it that this prop weighs nothing. Any sense of
reality has long since headed south, and Robert Holmes's good dialogue and characterisation has to do a lot of hard work to recapture a
sense of atmosphere and audience involvement.

It's immediately clear why the earlier production team (Derrick
Sherwin and Peter Bryant have now moved on, and the show is produced by Barry Letts and script edited by Terrance Dicks) chose to
specialise in Earth-based settings. It was an intelligent decision given
the limitations of design and photography at the time, and "Carnival
of Monsters" suggests that setting the Doctor roaming in a larger universe again is perhaps a disastrously bad idea.

The costumes for the Minorians (by James Acheson) are effective,
but the same can't be said for the two humanoids who arrive on their
planet, the male and female entertainers Vorg and Shirna. Vorg wears
a transparent plastic bowler hat and has a cluster of multi-coloured
grommets stuck to his lapels. Shirna is in some kind of crazed futuristic nightmare of a showgirl outfit with small coloured foam balls
attached to her head. There is a certain justification for these terrible
travesties they're wearing, since they're itinerant entertainers and are

supposed to have a colourful showbiz air. A time would come, all too soon, with Colin Baker as the sixth Doctor, when the Doctor's own costume would be a similarly camp travesty: the addition of a transparent bowler hat to Colin Baker's ensemble would have done it no appreciable harm.

Having established the Minorians' world, and Vorg and Shirna as fish out of water in it, we move on to another strand of story, featuring the Doctor and Jo Grant. They step out of the Tardis (on its shakedown cruise) and, to no one's surprise except possibly the Doctor's, incorrigible optimist that he is, discover that they have not reached their proper destination. Instead they are in the hold of what looks like an ordinary human ocean-going ship. The Doctor tries to maintain his high hopes, greeting a crate full of chickens on the possibility that they're a gaggle of intelligent extraterrestrials. Sadly it transpires that they are on board the *SS Bernice* in the Indian Ocean (actually the Robert Dundas filmed in the Naval Dockyards at Chatham) in what seems to be the year 1926. The Doctor reluctantly concedes that they haven't managed to get off the Earth, though they have at least travelled in time.

The connection between the two story strands, set on the planet Inter Minor and aboard the ship in the tropical seas of Earth, is not immediately apparent. When it is finally revealed, it will prove to be a gratifying shock and one of the major strengths of the story.

The Doctor and Jo continue to poke around on board the ship, and we learn that the *SS Bernice* was a famous maritime mystery on the order of the *Marie Celeste*. It just disappeared without a trace. This sequence is rather slow in developing and talky, and matters are not helped by the appearance of an outrageously and wretchedly fake sea serpent. The Doctor identifies it as a Plesiosaurus, but he might more accurately have labelled it a mess of papier-mâché that looks like it was made as a school project by a child, and not a very gifted child at that.

Soon, the Doctor and Jo are (naturally) taken prisoner by the ship's suspicious crew. Escape proves relatively easy because the passengers and crew of the *Bernice* are caught in a time loop. They are doomed to re-enact the same behaviour patterns over and over again and have the sort of long-term memory problems that might interest Oliver Sacks. Or, as Jo puts it, their behaviour resembles a record stuck in a groove. This ruse also enables the writer to recycle a lot of dialogue, but one doesn't begrudge Holmes because it's a clever and intriguing idea and, enacted by the engaging and colourful characters he's created, comes across as rather audacious and surreal. Not as audacious and surreal, though, as the *giant hand* that suddenly reaches down from above and plucks the Tardis from the hold of the ship.

The working title for "Carnival of Monsters" was "Peepshow," and that's exactly what the story is about. The miniscope, operated for profit by the showman Vorg and his beautiful assistant Shirna, is described as being wholesome old-fashioned entertainment, showing the drama of real life events. The device is malfunctioning, however, and Vorg has to open a panel and rummage around inside to see what's wrong. He says he thinks he's found the trouble, a bit of junk in one of the circuits. He takes out the Tardis. Or, rather, a miniature model of the Tardis.

There is a slight problem of scale here—the toy Tardis removed by Vorg is, proportionately, so large that there's no way the miniscope could accommodate the ship carrying the Doctor and Jo and the others, let alone all the assortment of other living creatures who exist in the mechanism. Apart from that, it's an ingenious plot. The miniscope is full of creatures that have been miniaturised and placed in realistic looking environments, where they live and re-live their miniature adventures for the entertainment of paying customers. The miniscope is billed as a "carnival of monsters" in Vorg's spiel, and it contains not only the humans on the SS *Bernice*, but an assortment of other life forms, including Cybermen and some vicious giant worms we'll get to in a minute.

The immorality of this mercantile voyeurism is hammered home when Vorg offers to spice up the live show for a Minorian audience. By adjusting the controls on the machine he can make the tiny humans inside behave more aggressively. The Doctor is not immune to this manipulation and indulges in fisticuffs with a ship's officer. Things rapidly escalate, and the Doctor and Jo are on the point of summary execution when Vorg fortuitously dials down the aggression again. He can't leave it on too long or the specimens inside start damaging each other—and his income.

The Doctor and Jo manage to escape into the inner workings of the miniscope by exiting the *Bernice* through a metal plate in the deck (in another imaginative piece of plotting, the ship's crew and passengers are mentally conditioned so that they can't see the plate, rather like the denizens of "The War Games" and their communications device). They wander around the giant-sized circuitry (some nice sets by designer Roger Liminton) and the Doctor is fascinated, comparing it to roaming around inside a giant wristwatch. Well, yes, if it's an electronic wristwatch with a minimum of moving parts.

The Tardis, a toy-sized artefact when removed from the miniscope by Vorg, starts to swell back up to its normal size. We learn that anything taken out of the device and its "compression field" for long enough will similarly return to normal—and we begin to discern how the plot might go.

But the Doctor and Jo don't manage to escape from the scope just yet. Instead they merely make it into one of the other inner chambers. This one consists of apparently deserted marshland, but soon enough we discover it's home to the Drashigs, screaming needle-toothed giant worms. These monsters are somewhat like perverted and vicious Muppets but are far better executed than the earlier sea serpent and in several sequences aren't bad at all. (Incidentally, Robert Holmes was fond of anagrams and Drashigs is a rearrangement of "dishrags." Another set of Holmes's alien villains were the cannibalistic Androgums—gourmands.)

But by the time they've pursued Jo and the Doctor back into the innards of the miniscope and then onto the *Bernice*, in another neat plot development by Holmes, the Drashigs begin to look increasingly fake and cumbersome. However, there is an agreeable moment when the passenger, Major Daley, stops drinking Scotch long enough to blast a Drashig with a tommy-gun before reverting to his rote memories and behaviour patterns. (Though how these memories are going to accommodate the extravagant damage rendered to the ship by a howling, needle-toothed monster worm, and the giant corpse of same, is never explored.)

By now the Doctor has worked out what is going on, correctly discerning that they are inside a kind of ant farm or peep show. Jo is appalled that people are watching them just for kicks. The Doctor asks if she's ever been to a zoo, making a powerful point.

It turns out that the Doctor is familiar with miniscopes and regards them with disgust. So much so that he was instrumental in getting the Time Lords to ban the devices. It seems the Tardis has run afoul of one that escaped the prohibition or (in a possibility the story doesn't address) one that exists *before* the ban was imposed.

The adventures of the Doctor and the others inside the miniscope alternate with a subplot about Vorg and Shirna and the Minorians. Or, rather, a series of subplots, mostly undeveloped and none especially interesting. For instance, the Minorians decide that the living contents of the miniscope represent illegally imported livestock and set about to sterilise it (they fail). Then they decide that Vorg and Shirna might be spies and the miniscope some kind of spy transmitter, but nothing much comes of this either. The Minorians come across as paranoid and xenophobic, bureaucrats gone bad. The most substantial, and yet most nebulous, subplot concerns Kalik and Orum's conspiracy against their immediate superior Pletrac and their (unseen, offstage) President Zarb. (It can be seen that Holmes's alien names are generally quite exotic and imaginative, but occasionally a real cliché clunker like Zarb or Vorg does slip through, threatening to enmire us completely in the realm of B movie space opera.)

The main problem with the Minorian coup subplot is that it's underpowered and not especially interesting. It is further hampered by the difficulty the viewer has in differentiating the various factions of grey-faced Minorians, let alone identifying individuals and empathising with them. There is also a further suggestion that the oppressed Minorian underclass of Functionaries might be ripe for rebellion, but this too comes to nothing.

The Doctor escapes the miniscope through a panel in its base and, once he's outside, he quickly returns to his proper size in a scene that calls to mind the climax of *Fantastic Voyage*. He then stands up to the officious, bullying Minorians, behaving so fearlessly that they end up almost admiring his audacity, calling to mind the intimidated commanding officer in "The War Games." Indeed, the Doctor's unflinching bold assertiveness in the face of authority has now become one of the beloved riffs of the show.

Once free of both miniaturisation and alien bullying, the Doctor works out a way of linking the Tardis to the miniscope's circuitry and thereby returning all the specimens inside to their proper space-time coordinates, again rather like the resolution of "The War Games." The *SS Bernice* is sent back to the Indian Ocean to resume its interrupted voyage. Their experience in the miniscope has left no impression on the crew and passengers, except the kind of faint uneasiness that accompanies déjà vu: "It does seem to have been a long trip somehow."

"The Green Death" by Robert Sloman (and Barry Letts)

The planet the Doctor was actually trying to get to before going off course in "Carnival of Monsters" was Metebelis 3. At the end of Season 10, he actually managed to finally get there, in a story called "The Green Death." His visit to this strange blue world, however, is nothing more than a detour from a quite separate story. "The Green Death" is an eco-parable written by Robert Sloman and (uncredited because he was also producer at the time) Barry Letts. Sloman wrote three other *Doctor Who* adventures, all in collaboration with Letts: "Daemons," "Time Monster," and "Planet of the Spiders." In "The Green Death," the Doctor's companion is still Jo Grant (Katy Manning), who seems much fresher and more appealing than in "Carnival of Monsters." In fact, it almost seems like she is being played by a new actress, having been replaced in some kind of strange science fictional *Doctor Who* way. More likely, it's simply because this was Katy Manning's last story and the actress was aware of it, having chosen to leave and her energy levels were way up for her farewell performance.

When Jo reads about a charismatic young environmental protester called Professor Jones (Stewart Bevan) and his worthy activities in Wales, she is tempted to go and join him. The Doctor on the other hand wants her to accompany him on the long delayed visit to Metebelis 3. When Jo opts for the handsome eco-warrior instead (a move that neatly foreshadows their eventual and more final parting later in this story), the Doctor sulkily insists on going off to the planet by himself.

In Wales, we are introduced to the main plot and characters in a scene at a closed coalmine where out of work miners are protesting. This sort of gritty realism, and addressing of hot political issues, was refreshing and rather daring (for Doctor Who) at the time. At the disused mine a slick executive from Global Chemicals called Stevens (Jerome Willis) is trying to placate the miners. "I have in my hand a piece of paper," he says, in a rather explicit echo of Prime Minister Chamberlain's famous speech upon his return from having appeased Hitler in 1939 (the French called Chamberlain "J'aime Berlin"). The point of this is that it indicates Stevens is an oily political weasel who is steering us towards catastrophe. He is announcing a new refinery that will provide work in the valleys. The unemployed miners are not impressed. Also protesting against Stevens is the handsome long-haired Professor Jones (a rather anodyne name for such an engaging character), who opposes Global Chemicals because of the pollution they create.

While this is taking place on the surface, a miner stumbles through the disused mine tunnels below. He ascends from the pit, and we see that he has an unhealthy looking green mark on his hand, reminiscent of a similar stain in "Inferno," only this is a ridiculous luminous bright green that signals immediately that, despite the engrossing ideological drama unfolding above, we're basically in for a hokey science fiction adventure.

Like the Doctor, the Brigadier can't see the reason for Jo's interest in Professor Jones and his cause. Global Chemicals promises a new and cheaper method of processing oil. "Cheap petrol and lots of it," says the Brigadier. "Just what the world needs." Nonetheless, he gives Jo a ride down to Wales, where UNIT has business with Global Chemicals. Once they arrive in Llanfairfach (actually Deri), they learn that Professor Jones's commune is referred to disparagingly by the locals as "the Nut Hutch"—Jones prefers the Wholeweal. But Jo likes the place, and especially likes Professor Jones, who is busy trying to develop a fungus food source to feed the world and replace meat. This project still sounds fresh and contemporary today, not to mention pressingly required, and it is touches of environmental concern like this that make "The Green Death" still seem modern and relevant.

After his somewhat petulant solo visit to a strikingly photographed and forbiddingly beautiful blue planet (the film cameramen were Bill Matthews and Ken Lowe), the Doctor is soon speeding down to Wales in his little yellow car. The whole Metebelis 3 detour seems to have been to demonstrate that the production team could occasionally come up with a vivid and effective alien environment, but it also serves the purpose of supplying the Doctor with a souvenir blue crystal that will be handy later on for hypnotising people.

"The Green Death" is an interesting story. With its combination of paranoid conspiracy thriller, mining setting, and threat of profound ecological contamination, it echoes a non-*Doctor Who* television serial and one of the great BBC triumphs, Troy Kennedy Martin's 1986 masterpiece, *Edge of Darkness*. In *Edge of Darkness* the mine is called Northmoor and the deadly pollutant is plutonium. Kennedy Martin's marvellous script is borderline science fiction, and in its combination of SF with serious, adult, highly respected drama, it brings us full circle by echoing Nigel Kneale, the influence behind so many classic *Doctor Who* stories.

The Doctor is a little wary of Professor Jones and his influence on his female companion Jo. Perhaps he already senses that it will be Professor Jones who will split them apart. But the Doctor is affable enough, greeting the longhaired young scientist with some praise for his paper about DNA synthesis. "Quite remarkable for your age."

When Jones makes a sardonic reply about being a promising young fellow, the Doctor smiles and says, "No, I mean for the age you live in." Soon he and Jones discover they are kindred spirits, both anti-authoritarian and in favour of direct action. Jones leads a noisy, though sparsely populated (thanks to the budget) demonstration outside the main gates of Global Chemicals as a diversion while the Doctor breaks in. The Doctor soon runs afoul of some suspiciously sophisticated automated control systems. Guards are deployed and regard the Doctor with amusement, remarking that he's a bit old to be up to such tricks.

The Doctor, perhaps stung by this remark, replies that he's surprisingly spry for his age. He demonstrates this as he swiftly pulverises the entire team of guards using his martial arts skills. Unfortunately, he then has to spoil the moment with an unnecessary line about Venusian aikido. Yes, it's Venusian *aikido* this time. Quite why this particular giant superhot runaway greenhouse planet has been chosen as a mecca for martial arts is obscure, unless perhaps it was deemed slightly less ludicrous than Mars. In any case, it always lowers the story to the level of banal pulp SF.

The coalmine exteriors in "The Green Death" provide real production value and offer some great shots, but soon we are in an elevator shaft where motion is conveyed by some supremely phoney CSO work. Meanwhile the glowing, green slime on the face of the unfortunate miners does not get any better. It's the visual equivalent of Venusian aikido. But Jo looks great in mining gear, and in short order she is pluckily descending into the pit to investigate (once there, however, she will just whine to get out again).

Although his performance is flat compared to Troughton (Pertwee's genius was for comedy, not drama), the Doctor also looks great in mining gear as he goes down into the mine to, inevitably, rescue Jo. They are soon both ankle-deep in the giant maggots that exist in the mine in varying degrees of convincingness, as rendered by various forms of special effects (the visual effects are by Colin Mapson, Ron Oates and Richard Conway). Sometimes these maggots exist as enlarged documentary footage, shown in back projection. They're perfectly satisfactory, although the scene where Jo and the Doctor *move through them* on a mine cart are supremely phoney, with the colour separation overlay failing big-time and occasioning considerable laughter by the viewer. At other moments, the maggots are physical effects and are distinctly impressive. The squirming vermin actually have expressive, vicious little maws filled with tiny, threatening teeth.

Yet on other occasions, the physical maggots look flatly unconvincing. Nonetheless, they are vicious, threatening, and deadly enough to the touch. Sufficient reason for the Doctor to want to take an unhatched specimen back with him, of course.

Whereas "Inferno" had its brilliant secondary story about the alternate universe (or, if you prefer, its competent secondary story about the mining project and the monsters), "The Green Death" has what begins as a fairly ho-hum story about a sinister corporation (Stevens turns various underlings at Global Chemicals into hypnotised zombies). Stevens himself has to answer to a disembodied voice through a speaker. This too seems pretty ho-hum until we learn the voice belongs to a computer, BOSS or Biomorphic Organizational Systems Supervisor. BOSS has a nice line of waspish and menacingly avuncular dialogue that makes it a good character and one of the better villains in *Doctor Who*.

Jo and the Doctor eventually escape from the mine (with that vital maggot egg still intact and, for the moment, unhatched). They get out via a pipe, used by Global Chemicals for crude oil waste. One of the zombie underlings detects their presence and brutally decides to flush waste through the pipe to kill them. Once again this scene is echoed twenty years later in *Edge of Darkness* with the flooding of the mines when Jedburgh and Craven go in after the plutonium.

While the Doctor and Jo are dodging the waste in the pipe, the Brigadier and Stevens are drinking scotch in the boardroom. All our heroes survive to convene that evening in a pleasant, warm, expansive scene at a dinner party among the hippies at the commune. The Brigadier is at the table amongst these bohemians in full evening dress complete with black bow tie, urbanely smoking a cigar. The Doctor rather lowers the tone by telling hokey Venusian anecdotes. (Is this the only planet the man has been to?) Around them, like a group of counterculture poster people, the other commune members are playing a flute, sculpting a statue, and doing a rather undemanding yoga pose (not even a headstand).

Soon Jo and Professor Jones are alone in front of a roaring fire, and she is tearfully recalling what happened in the mine, the death of perky little Bert the miner who came in contact with the lethal industrial waste that glowed with a clichéd and unconvincing bright green glow. Professor Jones comforts her with some obvious metaphysical platitudes about the uniqueness of every life, and the next thing you know she's in his arms.

Their kiss is interrupted, of course, by both the Doctor and the Brigadier, who have whipped in as if they sensed Jo was about to have a good time. The Doctor, in particular, is a wet blanket as he insists on leading Professor Jones away for a scientific discussion. However, this does serve the purpose of leaving Jo all alone for the attack of the giant maggot that has hatched from the shell they brought back. (Who could have anticipated such a thing?)

Meanwhile, in a neat intertwining of subplots, Steven's strong-arm man arrives to also menace Jo. The two threats cancel each other out. The heavy falls afoul of the maggot (in a hilarious moment it jumps for his throat). Still, it was a close call and clearly there is a giant maggot threat. UNIT arrives in force and sets about doing what it does best, blowing things up. It blows up the mine containing the maggots and allows the Doctor to be exasperated once again with the military mentality. The Brigadier says they've seen the last of the crawling horrors, but his cheery pronouncement rings false even to himself. Soon the pesky mutants are back in forced, needle-fanged maws sneering at us. It seems they've tunnelled their way to the surface.

At this point, the Doctor offers the foreboding reminder that maggots are always some sort of larvae. They grow into a more developed form. This threat hangs over us quite effectively until late in the story when an unconvincing dragonfly-style insect finally turns up. It spits green goo feistily enough, but it's not a very successful effect and the Doctor downs it by the simple expedient of throwing his cape in front of it while it's in full flight.

The Doctor also infiltrates Global Chemicals dressed first as a Welsh milkman and then disguised as an old cleaning lady. Then at last, he is taken prisoner. But not before he meets Boss, the computer. Boss's snide, polished dialogue is one of the joys of the story. "Why should I want to talk to a machine?" says the Doctor. "Really Doctor, as far as I can gather from your computer record at UNIT, the difficult thing is to *stop* you talking." Such barbed epigrams also reveal something deeply sinister about Boss. It has the ability to reach other computers everywhere. Indeed, in this pre-Internet story Boss already has a *Forbin Project*-style ambition, to take over all the computers in the world, in fact to take over the world (*The Forbin Project* was a 1970 SF movie about malignant supercomputers, written by James Bridges from a novel by D. F. Jones). We would have been disappointed by anything else from such a suave and malignant artificial intelligence.

The Doctor manages to baffle Boss with a paradox similar to the elegant "This statement is false." Boss falls dangerously close to an infinite loop as it tries to parse this. Stevens interrupts and the spell is broken. The Doctor is taken prisoner, at last, and escapes, at last.

In a nearby subplot, Jo repairs her walkie-talkie and summarises the situation. She's on a slag heap with Professor Jones, he's injured, and they're surrounded by maggots. The Doctor rescues her. Professor Jones is now in a coma as a result of contact with the toxic slime, or maybe with the maggots. In any case, he's got the green death and is gradually succumbing to it, which breaks Jo's heart. The Doctor doses him with antibiotics, an oddly ineffectual course of action since we've already established the infection behaves like a virus, not a bacterium.

Serendipitously, the Doctor discovers that the meat-substitute fungus developed by Jones is toxic to the maggots. It will succeed where all of UNIT's armour-piercing ammunition and helicopter-deployed grenades and (most disturbing of all in such an ecologically aware story) pesticides have failed. Vegetarianism saves the world!

The Doctor drives through the black slag heaps, which are writhing with the white forms of the giant maggots. In the back of his car, Sergeant Benton (John Levene) is cheerfully dispensing fungus fragments. The maggots can't resist it. They devour it with their nasty little teeth.

The maggots vanquished, there is a final showdown with Boss, who consists of little more than a disembodied voice, some flashing lights and a spinning disc, and yet remains a classic *Doctor Who* villain. Boss is in an expansive mood as it takes over the world, paraphrasing Oscar Wilde, calling Stevens "my little superhuman" and humming a jolly tune. Stevens is now linked to the computer, and the Doctor can defeat it by freeing Stevens's mind, which he does. Boss has been stopped.

At the end of the story, Jo is paired off with Professor Jones, who proposes marriage. Obviously, the relationship must have been developing off screen to reach this advanced stage. When the wedding is announced, the whole commune begins to celebrate. The UNIT troops are there, jovial participants.

In fact, everyone is having a good time, except for the Doctor, who in a very moving moment leaves the celebrations behind and walks away alone into the night.

chapter 6

The Long Scarf

To many people the Fourth Doctor, as played by Tom Baker wearing his emblematic long scarf and eating Jelly Baby candies, *is* the Doctor, embodying the essence of the show. He was introduced in a story called "Robot" in 1974 with a splendid title sequence, predominantly in blue, that shows an awareness of the trippy hyperspace flight in Kubrick's *2001*. Baker would remain in the role for an unprecedented seven seasons and star in more than his share of classic stories.

The years 1974 to 1981 are the Tom Baker years. They were also marked by the following events: In August 1974, Richard Nixon finally resigned his embattled presidency. May 1975 saw the war in Vietnam (of which Nixon was one of the chief architects) end. On 19 September 1975, heiress Patty Hearst was arrested for assisting the Symbionese Liberation Army in robbing a San Francisco bank. Also in 1975, Jack Nicholson won an Oscar for *One Flew Over the Cuckoo's Nest*. On 21 June 1976, rioting began in the Soweto townships of South Africa. In July of that year young Romanian gymnast Nadia Comaneci dazzled the world at the Montreal Olympics. August 1976 saw more rioting, this time at the Notting Hill Carnival in London. In December 1976, the Sex Pistols cemented their fame by saying "fuck" live on television. In September 1977, singer Marc Bolan was killed in a car crash in southwest London. On 26 March 1978, the oil tanker *Amoco Cadiz* broke up off the coast of France, spilling nearly a quarter of a million tons of crude oil into the ocean and devastating wildlife. In July 1978, Louise Brown, the world's first test-tube baby, was born in Manchester. And in 1979, Martin Scorsese married Isabella Rossellini.

"The Seeds of Doom" by Robert Banks Stewart

"The Seeds of Doom" finds Tom Baker in his prime. It was the final story of his second season, first transmitted on 31 January 1976. It begins with good use of swirling snow to make a BBC studio set look like the Antarctic. Unexpectedly, the Tardis doesn't appear. Instead, we're among a group of British research scientists who have just dug something out of the permafrost. Something that looks like a seedpod.

"Seeds of Doom" immediately evokes pleasurable memories of Howard Hawks's *The Thing* (or, if you prefer its long title, *The Thing from Another World*). Nominally directed by Christian Nyby, this classic of cold war science fiction cinema was an intelligent and effective shocker and a high water mark for the genre. It was based on the classic SF chiller *Who Goes There?* by John W. Campbell and scripted by Charles Lederer and an uncredited, but inspired, Ben Hecht.

The remote, forbidding polar setting with its isolation and threat of death for the careless added immeasurably to *The Thing*, and it also pays dividends in "The Seeds of Doom." Once again, the sense of real people doing a real job—the scientists are fascinated by the seedpod—gives rise to a mood in the viewer and a welcome sense of involvement. It's well acted, and well written by Robert Banks Stewart.

Banks Stewart is a giant of British popular television writing, having worked on everything from *The Avengers* to *Adam Adamant* to *Robin Hood*. He also created the long running crime drama *Bergerac*. "The Seeds of Doom" is an excellent script, and if it has a flaw it's that it sometimes seems more like a straight action thriller rather than science fiction. It's full of fights and chases and guns and bombs and former mercenaries in the hire of interestingly demented millionaires. It is a style of story that descends from James Bond but has found its most complete and brilliant expression in the adventures of *Modesty Blaise* by Peter O'Donnell.

A science fiction aspect to the story kicks in when news of finding the gourd arrives in London and Dunbar. The head of the World Ecology Bureau and sponsor of the expedition is forced to call in the Doctor, representing UNIT who take a keen interest in such findings. Dunbar is dubious about this lanky eccentric figure playing with a yellow yo-yo. The Doctor gets the facts, then promptly sets off for the South Pole ("I've got my toothbrush," he says, brandishing it). He re-emphasises the need for caution to Dunbar in patronisingly simple terms, as though addressing a savage. "Remember. No touch pod."

Perhaps prompted by this insulting condescension, Dunbar goes to plant-loving (perhaps loving isn't strong enough a word) millionaire Mr Chase. In a departure from civil service protocol, Dunbar treacherously sells the news of the seedpod's existence. Chase is very interested in plants and is eager to collect such a rare specimen. This piece of private enterprise by Dunbar will have disastrous consequences for the scientists at the South Pole, and for the Doctor who has just gone to join them.

Arriving for some reason by conventional means, the Doctor reaches the research lab, stepping out of a helicopter in the company of his current companion, Sarah Jane Smith (Elisabeth Sladen). They are greeted by the scientist Moberley (Michael McStay) who observes that the Doctor doesn't seem to feel the cold. The Doctor is all business, brusque even, saying he hasn't come thousands of miles to discuss the weather. Maybe he's tetchy at having travelled in something so much more primitive than the Tardis.

Here in the Antarctic we find good actors, a convincing setting, good photography (the film cameraman is Keith Hopper, the studio lighting is by John Dixon) and some surprisingly impressive special effects of the pod splitting open to reveal a shoot that surges out to attack the sleeping scientist (visual effects for the story are by Richard Conway). It's a very effective sequence. The stricken scientist Winlett (John Gleeson) will end up with a silly green face (yet another one) to signify contamination by the alien, but you can't have everything.

Soon the green-faced man is covered with some marginally more convincing green growth all over his body. The Doctor examines some samples taken from the patient. "A human being whose blood is turning to vegetable soup." The condition looks critical, but the Doctor says it's more serious than mere death. The man is changing form. He goes out into the blizzard and digs up another pod. He knew it would be there because the things always travel in pairs.

The Doctor is brusque and no nonsense between wisecracks. He's also offhandedly godlike. "You've got to help yourselves," he tells the humans. Admittedly, this is an attempt to get out of amputating Winlett's arm. Or by this point maybe one should say *pruning*. Winlett has almost completed his transformation into a plant creature. The last glimpses of his tormented human face as it is swallowed by the vegetation of this new being is reminiscent of Richard Wordsworth in *The Quatermass Xperiment*.

Winlett goes on the rampage just as some unexpected visitors arrive. They claim their airplane has gone astray, but they were sent by Chase. The men, Keeler and Scorby (Mark Jones and John Challis), are a well delineated and differentiated pair of characters. Scorby is the former mercenary who will prove shockingly willing to use force.

Keeler is the botanist for hire whose conscience eventually kicks in. He is Scorby's reluctant helper. When he ties up the Doctor and the scientists, tellingly, he apologises to them. Scorby is Chase's enforcer and has been sent to collect the seedpod at any price, and he wants to know where it is. He menaces the Doctor with a gun, saying that he is not a patient man. The Doctor replies, "Your candour does you credit."

By now we know the seed-pods are from outer space, and the Doctor has identified them as Krynoids, a term that is also applied to the howling ambulatory plant beast (reminiscent of such comic book characters as Harry Stein's *The Heap* or Len Wein's *Swamp Thing*). The Krynoid does not look impressive. It is like a milder version of the giant rat we will encounter later in "The Talons of Weng-Chiang." Once again it inspires laughter, not terror. At least it *sounds* great, and scary, something the giant rat in "Talons" would never achieve.

The Antarctic research base is blown to smithereens by Scorby and all of its inhabitants, including the Doctor and Sarah Jane, left for dead. Back in England, meeting Chase in his cathedral-like greenhouse, Dunbar now realises the full cost of his treachery. The three scientists have all been killed, and he feels he has blood on his hands (in fairness, the Krynoid would have put paid to them anyway). The Doctor and Sarah Jane have survived and are back in London to be kidnapped by a chauffeur who draws a gun on them. The Doctor beats him up, and the whole scene plays out like something from *The Avengers*. There's not even the casual deployment of the sonic screwdriver. The Doctor comes on like an action hero, yet he never reminds us of Pertwee. Tom Baker has strange alien depths. After fending off the gunman, he and Sarah Jane find a good old-fashioned *clue* in the trunk of the car.

Like all good clues in all good detective stories, it introduces us to an interesting and nicely realized character. In this case, the clue is a painting of a flower and the character is the famous botanical painter, Amelia Ducat (Sylvia Coleridge). She is a charmingly absent-minded old lady. The Doctor wants to know if she can remember who sold her the painting they found in the trunk of the car (for some reason it's easier to trace the painting than the car itself). Miss Ducat remembers all right. "Harrison Chase the millionaire . . . Good lord. He never paid me."

The Doctor and Sarah Jane go to confront Chase in his mansion. Chase has, of course, by now set his uniformed armed guards, as well as Scorby, on them. Even with a gun to his head, the Doctor is not cowed. In fact, he behaves as if he has the upper hand, demanding that Chase hand over the pod. The first Krynoid was blown up in the Antarctic wastes, but he doesn't want the second one to get a chance to hatch.

Harrison Chase comes on like a traditional James Bond villain, giving his guests a guided tour of his stately home before he has them executed. Then he rises to the heights of Doctor Phibes when he starts playing electronic music on an organ in his greenhouse. "I could play all day in my green cathedral," he exults. "The music is terrible," says the Doctor, as if he'd bought a ticket for the performance. Actually the music is far from terrible in "The Seeds of Doom." The score is composed by Geoffrey Burgon and it's notably good.

The butler Hargeaves (Seymour Green) interrupts the recital with the news that the pod is hatching. The Doctor manages to escape, but Sarah Jane is forced to attend the hatching. Indeed her bare arm is pinioned and exposed so that the shoot from the pod can infect her. "I must know what happens when the Krynoid touches human flesh," as Chase puts it. His piece of gloating sadism is happily interrupted by the Doctor jumping in through the skylight. Once again, he's a conventional action hero here. He even holds a gun on the bad guys while Sarah Jane escapes. The pod opens on schedule and infects Keeler instead of its intended victim.

At six episodes, "The Seeds of Doom" frankly outstays its welcome. The repetitive capture and escape motif of the plot is devised to keep thrills going in a piece of serial fiction. But Thomas Hardy, for one, might argue that serial fiction should be capable of assembly into a single large, coherent work of art. In a single viewing, the formulaic thrills and near misses of "The Seeds of Doom" grow wearisome. Still, there are plenty of interesting characters and good touches, like the butler being appalled by Keeler's appearance as he begins to transform into a Krynoid. It's as if he's committed some unspeakable social gaffe. It shouldn't be shocking to us any more; in homage to *Quatermass*, *Doctor Who* stories were perpetually full of people mutating into monsters. There's also some excellent dialogue.

Also, less agreeably, there's a tendency towards dialogue like "Miss Smith will never get out of this place alive and neither will you." Or, "Why am I surrounded by idiots." Et cetera. At times like this one misses the kind of dialogue Robert Holmes wrote. Crisp, deft at conveying meaning, and highly original. We're seriously back in James

Bond territory with dialogue like, "Mr Chase . . . never wastes anything that could fertilise his plants." This accompanies, naturally, a
scene of the Doctor being introduced to a giant compost-grinding machine. "That's very commendable," says the Doctor. "Your death will
be agonising, Doctor, but mercifully quick . . . Within twenty-five
minutes you will be pumped into the garden to become part of nature's grand design."

Chase is an unabashed maniac and fanatic, watching avidly as poor
Keeler turns into a monster. While he is off indulging his megaloma-
niac fantasies of a green world, Sarah Jane tries to rescue the Doctor
from the great grinding jaws of the composting machine. He is being
inexorably conveyed into the blades by a moving floor and in a wonderful moment Sarah Jane at first hits the *wrong button*, accelerating
his progress instead of arresting it. She realises her mistake in time,
and he is soon safe and free. The Doctor and his companion escape
again.

Just when the plot seems to have degenerated into routine escapes
and captures and separations, Banks Stewart throws in a wonderful
curve ball. Miss Ducat, the dotty old flower painter turns up and
proves not to be so dotty. She's come to demand payment for that
painting she sold to Chase. Confronting the bemused millionaire maniac, she jacks the price up to a thousand pounds. Serious money in
those days. And, best of all, it turns out that she's snooping around on
behalf of the forces of good, in the shape of senior civil servant Sir
Colin Thackeray (Michael Barrington) and, looming behind him, the
military force of UNIT. The treacherous civil servant Dunbar is also
with them. He wants to redeem himself. When he attempts to infiltrate
Chase's estate, he falls victim to the Krynoid, now grown as large as a
garden shed.

It will eventually grow so large that it towers over Chase's mansion
(a very well-made model), and, at that extremity, against all odds, it
will still look pretty impressive. When it started out, as a shoot erupting from the split pod, it was similarly convincing. At this in-between
garden shed stage, the Krynoid is at its most ridiculous, with pathetic
floppy tentacles. Dunbar pumps bullets into it, to no avail. Scorby and
the guards turn up to pour in yet more useless bullets. The Doctor,
more sensibly, seizes an antique sword off the wall of the house.

When Scorby and the guards realise how dangerous the Krynoid is,
they sensibly make common cause with the Doctor. They all take
shelter in a small cottage together. The Krynoid is now at its best and
most effective, as an unseen menace, circling the cottage and making

eerie noises (the studio sound is by John Holmes), working on our imagination and exciting our fears.

The Krynoid is further redeemed by the revelation that it has the ability to influence plants all around it. A UNIT report tells of people within a mile of Chase's estate being murdered by their own gardens. This is a brilliant story development and anticipates Alan Moore's *Swamp Thing* comics by a decade. No one even has to mention a telegraph vine (an example of plant communication over distance in the real world).

UNIT moves in to fight the big green monster. Major Beresford's laser gun team proves as ineffectual as the earlier bad guys' bullets. Chase is cheering on his giant seedling. He envisions a silent and beautiful new world dominated by plants.

The Krynoid is influencing the ivy on the house. It writhes over the windows in an effective moment, smashing them. Chase is sitting cross-legged in the green house, talking to his plants. It's marvellous when they come to life to assist the Krynoid. They attack Sarah Jane, Scorby, and the butler as Chase looks on benignly. Then the Doctor and a UNIT Sergeant turn up, wielding spray guns fed by cylinders of super strength pesticide—defoliant. It's not a move Rachel Carson would have approved of, but it's effective. Chase examines the empty cylinders left behind afterwards and says "Filth." It's dismaying to find oneself agreeing with this madman on anything. He's a nasty piece of work, but convincing in his fanaticism. He knocks the UNIT sergeant unconscious and sticks him into the corpse-, sorry, the *compost*-grinder, as if to compensate for his disappointment over the Doctor escaping.

When Chase falls into the grinder himself it's a cliché, but a satisfying cliché. The Doctor reluctantly lets go of the vicious millionaire fanatic as he is dragged to his doom, noting that while he was trying to save Chase, Chase was trying to drag him in.

A UNIT air strike puts paid to the giant Krynoid before the gardens of England all rise in revolt (that would have been an *eight*-parter). It's quite refreshing for a simple lot of UNIT bombs to do the trick.

"The Robots of Death" by Chris Boucher

From "The Seeds of Doom" we move on to the following season's "The Robots of Death," first transmitted on 29 January 1977. This is from a classic era of *Doctor Who*, with Philip Hinchcliffe producing and Robert Holmes script editing, and it is a period haunted by menacing titles of a uniform pattern: "Seeds of Doom," "Robots of Death," "Planet of Evil," "Hand of Fear," "Face of Evil."

"The Robots of Death" features a new companion, and one of the best in the long history of the series. Called Leela and played by Louise Jameson, she seems to have been inspired by Nova (played by Linda Harrison) in *Beneath the Planet of the Apes*. Like Nova, Leela is the product of a once technologically advanced civilization which has declined into Stone Age tribalism. In the case of Leela, she belongs to the Sevateem—the descendants of the Survey Team from a crashed spaceship. She looks sexy, in her leather miniskirt, again reminiscent of Linda Harrison's Nova, and the gutter press salivated appropriately. "A sexy, space age cave girl" they called her—not entirely inaccurately.

Leela first appeared in the story "The Face of Evil," also written by Chris Boucher. Although Boucher had created her as a one-off, she showed the potential to become a running character. So, with the help of script editor Robert Holmes, Boucher began to develop Leela into a companion. She ended up leaving her tribe and her home world to join the Doctor on his travels. Clever girl.

In her first such adventure, "The Robots of Death," she's introduced using the Doctor's yellow yo-yo in what she believes to be an important piece of magic to keep the Tardis flying. The Doctor just wants to see if she has yo-yo skills.

According to *Doctor Who: The Seventies* by Howe, Stammers, and Walker, Robert Holmes phoned Chris Boucher up late one night with the inspired—or arguably demented—suggestion that Leela should have psychic powers inherited from a witch grandmother. This didn't appeal to Boucher, although a hint of it is retained in Leela's perceptiveness, an ability to see deeply into people that is perhaps more interestingly rooted in behavioural details such as body language than anything overtly psychic.

It is fascinating to see this character come to life in "The Robots of Death," and Boucher's emerging skill as writer, under Robert Holmes's guidance, is impressive. Chris Boucher started as a gag writer. His work on *Doctor Who* led to him being hired as script editor and writer on *Blake's 7*, another British science fiction classic with threadbare production values. He would later create and write *Star Cops* for the BBC, an unsuccessful attempt to introduce more adult and realistic science fiction—like Nigel Kneale, but fatally lacking the sense of ancient, cosmic horror—to a field dominated by space opera.

"The Robots of Death" begins with a reasonably well-made model of a giant vehicle moving through a reasonably convincing alien landscape. A sandstorm is whipping around the mechanical behemoth. We cut in for a close-up of the wide window of the control deck, to reveal tiny humans inside and thereby the scale of the vehicle. Unfortunately, the abrupt change of angle (with the concomitant impression that the vehicle—called a miner—has ground to a sudden halt) and a far less successful effects shot all add up to the momentary illusion of reality being shot to hell. We're no longer seeing an awesome giant vehicle on an alien planet. We're looking at a model in a set.

The robots in the story are very good though. They consist of actors wearing elegant ornamental masks with big eyes. Other than the robots masks, the costumes tend to a flamboyant and silly vision of the future. People working on an all business vehicle like the miner should perhaps have had blue-collar costumes like the crew in *Alien*. Such a realistic vision of the future was still years away. Perhaps there is a cultural explanation for the extraordinary "futuristic" flamboyance of these workers in the mobile miner, but disappointingly, the story never really addresses it.

The robot POV shots, however, as in the one dispassionately recording the fearful face of a human who is being strangled to death, are excellent. There is also a look of surprise on the face of the dying human—because he is being killed by what he believed was an obedient mechanical slave.

The sets (the designer is Kenneth Sharp) and music (by Dudley Sutton) are also assets in the story, which gradually reveals to us that the giant vehicle is harvesting minerals from the storm winds of this planet (a great concept). The Doctor explains to Leela that they're in a sand miner, in one of the scoops. This is the sort of thought-provoking detail that abounds in good science fiction. It conjures a vast and fascinating alien vista. The situation also highlights the Tardis's tendency to appear in less than convenient—even dangerous—places. The Doctor and Leela escape death from the screaming storm winds only to be taken into custody.

They have stumbled into a whodunit. Someone is committing murders, bumping off the crew members of the giant vehicle, and the survivors are annoyingly reluctant to accept what the Doctor and the audience know immediately, that a robot is the culprit. The Doctor points out that this entire civilization is founded on the use of robots and might crumble if these underlings cannot be trusted. (Which rather seems to ignore the history of slave rebellions in human culture that were stamped out before business continued as usual.) The Doctor and Leela are suspected of being murderers, or at the very least, ore-raiders.

The vast vehicle, with its part-human, part-robot crew is a fascinating milieu and an ideal setting for a murder mystery. Leela is a warrior woman, stalking the corridors of the miner with the Doctor, knife at the ready. The Doctor embraces tradition by separating from her and finding another dead body, in a hopper where he is almost buried alive in sand. A robot finds him and rescues him because it detected a high level of impurity in the ore. The impurity being the Doctor and the murdered man. The Doctor is naturally accused of this murder, too. As the crew remark, he is a stowaway, and what could be more suspicious than a stowaway?

"A dead stowaway," replies the Doctor. His being locked in the ore hopper was no accident. Someone intended to bury him alive. We also learn the interesting fact that the crew own shares in the valuable ore they're gathering. The fewer who survive, the bigger their shares. It's a good motive, but no one seems to have taken proper note of the fact that each murdered crew member has been found with a corpse marker, a red badge which, in a macabre and telling touch, is normally used to identify a deactivated robot.

Leela thinks the robots are "creepy mechanical men" and she's not wrong. There are three types of robot: the Dums that don't talk, the Vocs that do, and the Super Voc who is the head honcho. In an interesting and unexpected subplot, one of the robots D84, turns out to be an undercover robot detective, working on the murders. He reveals himself to Leela and cautions her, "Don't tell anyone." Since there are now corpses tumbling from every corner, Leela caustically remarks, "Is there anyone left to tell?" She's not only a knife-wielding warrior, she's also a wit. Later on the replacement commander, Toos (Pamela Salem), tries to explain how hard it is for the crew to imagine that a robot could be capable of murder. She says that robots can't harm humans. "It's the first principle."

"The second principle is that humans can't harm robots," says Leela with chagrin, having blunted her knife trying.

This fleet, witty talk is interspersed with good science fiction dialogue that conveys a ring of conviction. "Like a force 20 blow." "I never lost an orestream yet." This sense of the vehicle as a real, moving, place where people work helps immeasurably in creating suspense in the murder mystery. And it also adds a certain chilling relevance to lines like "Pressure on the hull is increasing," as the giant vehicle succumbs to sabotage and grinds to a halt, then starts sinking in the sand.

The interior of the vehicle is a series of good sets, generally well- and moodily-lit (the studio lighting is by Duncan Brown) as the robots are moved to homicidal revolt and begin tracking down the crew, Leela, and the Doctor. "Our controller has ordered the death of the remaining humans." In a chilling scene, the robots hand out corpse markers and specify who they are going to kill, so everyone can be dealt with in an orderly fashion. The Doctor finds the workshop and he discovers the tools used to modify the robots and make them into killers. We learn, very late in the story and only by the use of dialogue, that there is mad robot-building genius on the loose, and he has passed himself off as one of the crew.

This is less than deft plotting and the late, amorphous introduction of Taren Capel (a name that sounds as if Robert Holmes might have coined it) reduces the impact considerably. If he had been made a sinister offscreen presence in the first part of the story then his appearance here might have meant something.

Freed to kill by Taren Capel (David Bailie), the robots' murder spree has its disquieting moments. Their calm, gentle voices and flashing eyes give a bleak surrealism to some brutal scenes of assault. The whole sequence could have been terrifying but some ineffective moments prevent that.

Also introduced late in the story is robophobia, a psychological condition, an irrational dread of robots. The condition claims Poul (David Collings), the undercover detective (D84's human partner). Robophobia is also called "Grimwade's syndrome," an in-joke and allusion to Peter Grimwade, the *Doctor Who* production assistant who had an aversion to robots, at least the kind that appeared in the studio when shooting *Doctor Who*. Robophobia here is all about the sense of irretrievable alienness of the robots. They have no body language, so on a deep primal level they are disquieting to human beings. This is a great concept, but again it's very abstract. It needs to be properly dramatised in the story, and it never really is.

"The Robots of Death" has other flaws. Even at four episodes (concise by *Doctor Who* standards at this point), it begins to run out of

steam and out of plot. Eventually the surviving humans take refuge on
the control deck where the Doctor suggests building some magnetic
anti-robot bombs and then sneaks away through the dangerous corridors of the vessel, avoiding the robots on their killing spree. Taren
Capel is among them, dressed like a robot, his face made up to look
like one. He thinks they're his brothers. The mad scientist has gone
completely gaga.

He manages to trap the Doctor, strapping him to a table, James
Bond style, to await the attention of a laser in his brain. The Doctor
correctly identifies Taren Capel as "One of those boring maniacs
who's going to gloat. Are you going to tell me your plan for running
the universe?"

"No doctor," says Capel. "I'm going to burn out your brain, very
very slowly." Fortunately, the Doctor has concealed Leela behind an
arras. He has hit on the idea (it's a brilliant ruse from Boucher) of getting her to open a cylinder of helium. The gas effects Capel's voice,
and the robots, programmed for speech recognition, no longer accept
him as their commander. They turn on their master and Capel is defeated. From her place of confinement Leela says, "Will somebody let
me out?" She speaks in a squeaky helium voice and the Doctor grins
delightedly and says, "A mouse in the wainscoting!"

Tom Baker is perfect for the part of the Doctor. He seems effortlessly alien. He is sardonic, commanding, and strange. For charm, he
has a wonderful bug-eyed grin. However, his performance doesn't
have the warmth or tenderness or vulnerability that Troughton often
projected.

"The Talons of Weng-Chiang" by Robert Holmes

First broadcast on 26 February 1977, the six-part adventure "The Talons of Weng-Chiang" is one of the great *Doctor Who* stories, regarded
by many as the finest ever, and certainly one of the finest in colour.
Having said all that, it is also crucial to point out that it features a rat.
A giant rat. And that giant rat must rank as one of the weakest special
effects in the long history of the show and its weak special effects. To
watch "Talons," then, and appreciate its finer points requires even
more of a willing suspension of disbelief than normally required for
science fiction television in general, and *Doctor Who* in particular.

"Talons" is written by Robert Holmes, and in its quirky richness may well be his masterpiece. According to Howe and Walker, the script is based on an idea by Robert Banks Stewart called *The Foe from the Future*. Banks Stewart was unable to advance this idea beyond an outline before other commitments got the better of him. When Banks Stewart proved unavailable, Holmes suddenly found himself called upon to write a six-part adventure at extremely short notice. Virtually all the work on the script, and all the thinking behind it, was done by Holmes who retains sole screen credit.

The story that emerged is a kind of combination of Fu Manchu, *The Phantom of the Opera*, Sherlock Holmes, or any number of tales of sinister ventriloquist dummies and (in its futuristic elements) some of the colourful science fantasies of Michael Moorcock—his Jeremy Cornelius stories perhaps. Robert Holmes cheerfully acknowledged his debt to the Fu Manchu novels (by Sax Rohmer) and *Phantom of the Opera* (created by Gaston Leroux).

One guest character in the story, and the most active villain, is Li H'sen Chang (John Bennett) and to the apology for the giant rat must be added an apology for the presence in the story of a "Chinaman" who is a European actor with unconvincing eye makeup to suggest an epicanthic fold. Chang is the most active bad guy in the story, but not the principal one. This honour goes to the great and sinister Chinese deity Weng-Chiang himself. The Chang/Chiang confusion seems an unnecessary complication in a story where all the names are made up anyway, but it is soon dispensed with when we learn that Weng-Chiang is not a god at all but a ruthless time traveller from the future called Magnus Greel (Michael Spice).

Chang is a performer with a magic and hypnotism act in a Victorian music hall. He also does a ventriloquist turn with an unpleasant-looking masked dummy called Mr Sin (Deep Roy). We immediately assume Mr Sin is a little person in disguise, an assumption that is true enough as far as creating Mr Sin in the studio. In terms of the story, Mr Sin is in fact the Peking Homunculus, a semi-human hybrid from the distant future that is also part-machine and part-pig (this sort of thing is pure Robert Holmes).

Henry Jago (Christopher Benjamin), who runs the theatre, compliments the ventriloquist Chang, his top act. "Dashed clever the way you work the little fellow. Wires in the sleeves I dare say . . ." Outside in the foggy London night, beside the dark lapping waters of the Thames, the Tardis materialises. The Doctor emerges, looking suitably

Victorian and natty in a tweedy Sherlock Holmes outfit. Leela, cave girl of the future, is attired like a Victorian lad. "What is the name of the tribe here?" she asks, looking around at the dank cobbled streets. "Cockney," says the Doctor, and they walk off, straight into a murder being committed in the fog.

Soon there's a body being fished from the river, a gallery of Victorian grotesques in play, and a Chinese man under arrest at the local police station. The Doctor offers to help with his interrogation. "I speak Mandarin, Cantonese and all the dialects." But Chang arrives to act as an interpreter, and in the process slips the prisoner a poison pill so he can commit suicide. As the man drops dead, the Doctor identifies the toxin that killed him as scorpion venom, and the victim as a member of the black scorpion tong, who worship Weng-Chiang.

The Doctor insists on being present at the autopsy on the man and there he meets the delightful Professor Litefoot (Trevor Baxter), a pathologist who'll play Watson to the Doctor's Holmes. There is another body in the morgue that night, a man from the river who appears to have been mutilated by a giant rat. As evidence for an oversize rodent begins to build up, the Doctor notes that Weng-Chiang is the god of abundance. "He makes things grow."

Litefoot interrupts himself in a grisly cause-of-death discussion and suddenly registers the presence of a lady, or at least of Leela. He blanches at talking about such gruesome stuff in the presence of "the fair sex." But Leela knows even more about stab wounds than he does, having applied a fair few herself. "When aiming for the heart we were always taught to strike under the breast bone." Litefoot is duly astonished. The Doctor explains, inventing a new origin story for Leela, that she was a South American savage. "Found floating down the Amazon in a hatbox." Leela is soon saving the Doctor's life, using a poisoned thorn from a blowpipe to down an assassin (Chinese, with hatchet) who has been sent to dispatch him.

It transpires that Litefoot grew up in China, where his father died. "Fireworks at the funeral. Odd custom. Odd sort of people." Holmes's ear for terse, vivid, idiomatic dialogue is shown at full flower in "Talons."

Girls are disappearing off the streets of foggy London, Jack the Ripper fashion, because Magnus Greel requires them for his own survival. Chang does the dirty work for him. He tells Greel that the girls' life force will restore him to full health. The masked and mysterious Greel lurks in the basement of the theatre, *Phantom* style.

The Doctor and Leela descend into the sewers of London to pursue their investigation of the strange goings-on. Here we see plenty of normal-sized rats, and one shot of a normal-sized rat in a miniature sewer tunnel which is not only unconvincing, but actually makes the "giant" rat look kind of cute and appealing, instead of bloodcurdling. Worse is to come. The later shots of the rat will consist of what looks like a bloated glove puppet but is actually stuntman Stuart Fell in a giant rat suit. Seeing this apparition one wants to shout at the television to bring back the fake shots of the real rat.

In any case, a hint of this big, chubby, cute-looking, allegedly giant beast is enough to cause the Doctor and Leela to flee the sewers. "Ten feet from whisker to tail," says the Doctor as he seals the manhole cover. "You'd need a harpoon to stop that brute."

The phoniness of the rat is all the more lamentable because of the excellent, and entirely convincing, sewer tunnel sets. Along with the splendid sets of the dragon temple, which we'll see later in the story, the exemplary design here is one of the major assets of the story (the designer is Robert Murray-Leach).

Back at Litefoot's house, his housekeeper has provided a "cold collation" for his supper after working late at the morgue. It's a vast spread, a banquet of cold meat. To Litefoot's astonishment, Leela picks up a huge beef bone and begins to gnaw on it. Then Litefoot gets into the spirit of things and picks up a bone with his bare hands and begins to tuck in, too. While Leela and Litefoot are feasting, the Doctor is busy at the theatre where a ghostly apparition causes Henry Jago to faint. The Doctor greets it with delight, in a most Doctor-ish moment.

Back at Litefoot's house two subplots intersect so deftly that we hardly notice the high level of coincidence. Greel is searching for his "time cabinet," a device for temporal travel that is disguised as a Chinese heirloom. He can't get home without it and it just so happens that the cabinet is in Litefoot's house, among the artefacts brought back by his family from China. Chang sends in his henchmen, the Peking Homunculus, and Litefoot is ambushed and Leela finds herself confronting the knife-wielding inhuman dwarf. She's a no-nonsense sort of girl, though, and she throws a knife in his throat. The knife doesn't even slow him down, so she jumps out of a window. The Doctor's arrival disrupts Chang's plans, and he and his dwarf have to leave without the cabinet or "that Chinese puzzle box," as Litefoot calls it. The Doctor immediately identifies it as a piece of advanced technology. Litefoot says, "Weng-Chiang was one of the ancient Chinese gods." The Doctor says, "And he probably arrived in this contraption."

The Doctor decides he must venture down into the sewers again to look for Weng-Chiang. Of course, there is the small matter of that giant rat . . . "Professor, you don't happen to have an elephant gun?" asks the Doctor in a cherishable line. "I have a Chinese fowling piece," volunteers Litefoot.

As the Doctor and Litefoot prepare their foray and Leela pursues her own line of enquiry, there is still the matter of the disappearing street girls of London. Chang must continue to feed them to his master, who needs their life force to keep his own disintegration at bay. (It seems time travel in a primitive device like the one he used can have serious side effects.) Chang gathers two victims, drawn to him despite their will, by his strange hypnotic powers. (More strange hypnotic powers; more mesmerised dupes. In this case the hypnosis is accompanied by some ludicrous animated flashes of light that flicker over Chang's eyes.)

Leela finds one of the victims waiting and sees she's in a trance. "Spell of the shaman," Leela says, then she takes the woman's place. Chang breezes in with the other sacrificial victim, and urges the two women into the cellar. "You painted drabs. My master must feed." Leela's first encounter with Greel doesn't go to well, and she is forced to flee through the sewers, pursued by the bloated, fluffy rodent.

At the same time, the Doctor is probing through the sewers with the Chinese fowling piece he's borrowed from Litefoot (a serious piece of "hand artillery" as he describes it) to the accompaniment of some rather overemphatic music. He arrives just in time to rescue Leela, running away from the giant furry rat that waddles fatly through the dank tunnels after her. The Chinese fowling piece makes short work of the thing, fortunately. What is really unforgivable about this giant rat is that even the *sound* it makes is laughable instead of frightening.

It's a cosmic shame that a story as good as "Talons" suffers from such inadequate special effects, sub par even by *Doctor Who* standards. This is perhaps the ultimate example of the brilliantly scripted, well-acted story sabotaged by poor production. Even the Homunculus's mask is mediocre, which is patently unnecessary when you consider the vast range of striking Chinese traditional mask designs available. Only the fact that "Talons" is set in the Victorian period, a familiar and therefore bulletproof setting for BBC drama design, saves it from being a complete disaster visually.

The sets and props, however, are very good, with Roger Murray-Leach's imaginative set designs culminating in a wonderful temple with a statue of a giant gold dragon (it also shoots lasers from it eyes) that would be worthy of a modest but vivid Hammer film.

The characters are another great strength of "Talons," and Holmes interweaves them inventively. For example, when Jago finally meets Litefoot and they team up, the viewer is simply delighted. The two characters work so well together that there was even discussion at the time of giving them their own television series. Jago and Litefoot set about trying to help the Doctor but, of course, they bungle it, getting taken prisoner. (Refreshingly, neither the Doctor or the companion have been taken prisoner yet, though Leela voluntarily posed as one of Chang's captives.)

Weng-Chiang is finally unmasked as Magnus Greel, a war criminal, known as the "Butcher of Brisbane," on the run from the far future. In fact, with his regeneration plans and his (admittedly rudimentary) time machine, Magnus Greel is dangerously close to being a kind of low budget Time Lord.

The Doctor indicates that he knows the truth about his adversary's identity, but Greel doesn't believe him. "How can you in the nineteenth century know anything of the fifty-first?" The Doctor replies, "I was with the Filipino army at the final advance on Reykjavik." It's a great line, classic Robert Holmes, suggesting a whole turbulent future world—fascinating, bloody, and colourful. Again the breezy epic quality echoes the writings of Moorcock.

Magnus Greel realises the Doctor is a threat and, in the final episode of "Talons," he spoils a perfect record for the story by taking the Time Lord prisoner. Tom Baker as the Doctor is, as ever, witty and composed and effortlessly in control. He has mad eyes and a wonderful smile. He busts out by igniting the gas piped into the house's lamps (a ruse that would be reprised in 2005's Victorian story *The Unquiet Dead*).

Nothing can stop the Doctor, not even the laser beams from the eyes of the dragon statue, operated by the Homunculus. In fact, the Homunculus turns on his master and Greel falls victim to his own cruel technology and "cellular collapse." He ends up drained of life, like a pile of dry leaves.

The enemy defeated, the story concludes with one of the nicer clichés of Victorian London, the muffin man doing his rounds. "Come on," says the Doctor to Jago, Litefoot, and Leela. "I'll buy you some muffins."

"The Talons of Weng-Chiang" is overlong at six episodes and its weakness in several key areas (special effects, music, the dwarf's mask) have been amply noted. But Robert Holmes's script, with its wonderful dialogue and characterisation, the Victorian setting, an engaging companion, and a terrific cast led by Tom Baker, all manage to pull it out of the mire and make for a flawed but frequently brilliant classic.

"The Ribos Operation" by Robert Holmes

For the sixteenth season of the show, the producer of the show, Graham Williams, hit on the dangerously dull idea of linking all six stories with a unifying theme. He expanded on this notion in a lengthy memo dated 30 November 1976. One can only imagine the dismay someone might feel on receiving this three-page beauty. Reading the memo, as quoted in *Doctor Who: The Seventies*, one visualises script editor Anthony Read skipping through the scientific theorising, which makes up the bulk of the document (some gibberish about cosmic balance). He then hurries to the relevant bit: there was going to be a search for the six separated fragments to the "Key to Time," with the Doctor acquiring one piece in each story.

This uninspired concept—giving the whole series a story arc— would unfortunately resurface again dangerously close to my own era on the show, in Season 23 with "The Trial of the Time Lord," which admittedly makes the "Key to Time" look like *Citizen Kane*.

The first of the writers to have this unwelcome contrivance foisted upon them was Robert Holmes who had been working on a story called "The Galactic Conman." As the story was developed, script editor Anthony Read worked on integrating the Key to Time into the narrative. This is actually done rather cleverly. Holmes story involves a lump of a valuable mineral called jethrik. This is "the rarest and most valuable element in the galaxy" because it is essential for the warp drive of the starships (rather like the spice in Frank Herbert's *Dune*, although spice has a more intriguing psychic component to it). However, as to it being the most valuable element in the galaxy, Mavic Chen in "The Daleks' Master Plan" would tend to disagree.

In "The Ribos Operation," a four-part story first transmitted on 2 September 1978, two conmen called Garron (Iain Cuthbertson) and Unstoffe (Nigel Plaskitt) are galactic grifters who use this valuable ore in the same way that old time conmen used to seed dead mines on Earth, planting them with gold and silver. Garron and Unstoffe's trick is to plant the jethrik on some backwater planet and get some gullible rich person to buy, not the mine, but the entire planet. The sucker this time is a deposed ruler of another world, a tyrant in exile called the Graff (Paul Seed).

This all sounds like quite a good plot. But it doesn't allow for the problems of understanding a scam story—which is intended to be deliberately puzzling—in an alien environment that puts everybody's identity into question anyway. Con tricks mustn't be what they seem. If the viewer is floundering, trying to work out what the hell is going on, in a shadowy medieval world where everyone wears furs and the power structure and relationships aren't clear anyway, then there is a case for things needing to be exactly what they seem.

For instance, the audience has a lot of trouble understanding that the Graff and his entourage aren't natives, but instead alien visitors travelling incognito. This is only conveyed in some dialogue that is overwhelmed by the strangeness of this odd alien quasi-Russian world where everyone wears fur hats and the snow swirls over dark battlements. What was needed, and could probably never be permitted by the budget, was a scene of a spaceship landing with Graff and company.

Nonetheless, "The Ribos Operation" pleasantly evokes the science fiction of Jack Vance, with its alien world featuring a quasi-medieval castle with a dragon in residence. The dragon in this case is called a Shrivenzale—a lumbering foam rubber thing that was basically a costume worn by stuntman Stuart Fell, who at least here surpasses his incarnation as the giant rat in "The Talons of Weng-Chiang."

Worse than the rubbery dragon creature, "Ribos" suffers from the imposition of the Key to Time story. The worst aspect of this metastory was that it involved a new set of supreme beings, a power above the Time Lords. This consists of the Black Guardian and the White Guardian. Guess which one is the bad guy.

The Doctor is introduced to the White Guardian in a witty and effective scene written by script editor Anthony Read. He is summoned out of his Tardis by a bright light and a mellow voice. The White Guardian, in the sort of sardonic contrast delivered by science fiction writers like Robert Sheckley or Douglas Adams, turns out to look as though he might be sitting on the veranda at the Raffles. He's an affable imperial British gentleman sitting in a wicker chair sipping what could be green wine. He is cordially threatening and insists that the Doctor go off in search of the six missing sections of the key to time. The key is a McGuffin. In fact it's a meta-McGuffin.

The White Guardian is an agreeable enough character, but he's foisting an awfully tedious quest on the Doctor. The pieces of the key must be reunited to restore the cosmic balance, "before the universe is plunged into eternal chaos." Of course, there will be the Black Guardian to contend with along the way.

Gratifyingly enough, in a final twist in the saga, the genial White Guardian would eventually turn out to *be* the sinister Black Guardian. A small pleasure that does little to balance the tedium of the quest.

Worse than the quest itself is the whole concept of putting a power above the Time Lords. The Time Lords were bad enough, but just when the Doctor begins to cut them down to size—to allow himself once again to become the dominant mystery in his show—these jokers appear on the horizon. One can imagine a whole infinite regress of powerful mysterious entities, each trumping the last set of powerful mysterious entities as plot material is tediously flogged into the show. I once suggested to producer John Nathan-Turner that we could trump the whole process by suggesting that the Doctor is God, but he somewhat blanched at the notion. The point was that, on his own show, the Doctor should be top god—or dog.

"The Ribos Operation" begins with Tom Baker on the floor of the Tardis playing with K9, his robot dog (with a voice by John Leeson). K9 had joined the Tardis crew in a story called "The Invisible Enemy" in Season 15 (first transmitted 1 October 1977). He was the creation of writers Bob Baker and Dave Martin, and he had, like Leela, proved sufficiently popular to be written into the show on a regular basis. Unfortunately, Leela would not be returning because Louise Jameson had decided she didn't want to stay with the show. Her replacement was the beautiful, nubile, and statuesque Mary Tamm, who plays a lady Time Lord, or more coherently a Time Lady, pressed upon the Doctor by the White Guardian. Her name, once shortened to a convenient length, is Romana.

It has to be said that, lolling on the floor of the Tardis, Tom Baker shows a lot more affection for his robot dog K9 than he does for his new female companion. Indeed Baker sometimes seemed to be of the opinion that the Doctor doesn't really need a companion. The Doctor without a companion is an odd notion. He'd always be a strangeness imposed on other kinds of strangeness, with no down-to-earth characters as a reference point for the viewers.

Actually, Mary Tamm as Romana in her first adventure is anything but down-to-earth. She looks terrific in white furs but isn't given a great deal to do. She and the Doctor exchange brittle witticisms, which don't really give us a chance to warm to either of the characters in what is literally a cold story, set among the dark battlements of a winter castle.

In "The Ribos Operation," we learn that Romana did better than the Doctor at the Academy. It's a nice gag but it seriously diminishes the Doctor's stature. It's bad enough that a place called the Academy exists for Time Lords. The Doctor was just one more student there, a chump to be graded. Or, in this case, downgraded.

As they wander together through the shadows of the neo-Russian castle on the planet Ribos, the Doctor and Romana stumble on the two conmen who are seeking to sell Ribos to the Graff, the ruthless and rootless tyrant. The Graff and his entire entourage seem to think that Magellan (as in the Magellanic cluster) is pronounced with a hard "g." Someone should have explained to the actors that it is the name of a famous astronomer.

Romana falls afoul of the rubbery dragon, and the Doctor makes heavy weather of rescuing her. Still, it serves to bring them together, and Romana hugs the Doctor and he comforts her as a floppy foam rubber claw menaces them from under a door. The Shrivenzale would have been much more convincing purely as a sound effect.

The story unfolds slowly through dialogue among a lot of similar looking people in furry hats. It takes a while to realise that Garron, who as a conman is playing two roles, is not in fact two different people. Big furry hats and sudden changes of accent conceal an identity pretty well, and this confusion is to the detriment of continuity rather than to any delight of the viewer.

The Doctor hypnotises a guard. The Graff takes him prisoner, along with Romana—and Garron. They are believed to be accomplices to the conman. "The whole dirty gang of you will die together." The Doctor's feelings are hurt. "We're not a dirty gang, are we?"

"Of course not," says Romana. As the story unfolds in a leisurely fashion, in a fog of confusion, Romana is compelled to say, "We're looking for the first segment of the key to time." "Oh never mind that," says the Doctor echoing the audience's sentiments. Their immediate problem is freeing themselves. The Doctor uses a high-pitched whistle to summon K9. The robot dog pokes its snout out of the Tardis. "Master?" it says, in the voice of John Leeson.

K9 is coming to the rescue. It will take him an unconscionably long time, but that's only natural, considering how slowly the little automaton moves. While K9 is on his epic journey through the castle, we dwell endlessly on minor characters who may, like Binro the heretic (Timothy Bateson), be quite interesting in themselves but still tend to slow down what little plot there is and distract from the Doctor.

"The Ribos Operation" is a promising story, but it is awash with minor characters and has no properly thought-out role for the Doctor. Indeed, he stands around and does nothing when Binro the heretic is killed by Graff's ray gun wielding goons. Worse yet, he lets them murder an old shaman lady (Ann Tirard). Admittedly, Troughton stood around while people were being slaughtered in "Tomb of the Cybermen," but in neither of these cases does the viewer get the feeling that this is a deliberate story point. Rather, it's an example of poor plotting. It's not the only one. The two conmen have been using a giant lump of the precious mineral jethrik. By planting it for some dupe to find, they have managed to sell entire planets. Yet the Graff suggests the intrinsic value of the mineral is such that they could just cash it in and retire on the proceeds, never mind all this planet-selling business. Yet the two conmen seem unaware of this, even though the precious nature of the jethrik is at the very heart of their business. Maybe they're doing it for the love of the grift, but this point is never made.

Mary Tamm as Romana looks great, like a Czarist princess in white furs sweeping through the catacombs, which are the "home of the long dead and the ice gods." In fact, the catacombs don't amount to much. The Shrivenzale monster is cute and rather shiny rather than frightening. K9's slow humming movement provides a few amusing moments, though. By episode four, as Romana and K9 wander the catacombs, we have finally got our bearings and understand all the characters and relationships. Now the story is engrossing. But it's too late.

The Doctor has disguised himself as one of the Graff's guard. It is in this guise that he watches innocent people being killed without lifting a finger to help. In fact, he's altogether ineffectual throughout the story. What's worse, Romana, whose grand debut this is, also does nothing. They're notionally looking for that crucial fragment of the key to time. This seems to involve a lot of pointless wandering around. The plot does show some cleverness, though, in the notion that these fragments of the key can disguise themselves as other objects. This means that the lump of valuable jethrik ore turns out to also be the piece of the key we're looking for. This is a clever intertwining of the story's two McGuffins. Now we only have one of the damned things to worry about.

K9 proves to be even more of a deus ex machina than the sonic screwdriver, with beams shooting from his nose to stun guards and vaporise troublesome rubble. He gets considerably more to do than poor Romana, who should have been showcased in this, her debut story. The adventure as a whole also seems to have the production values of a Romanian soap opera.

At the end of the story, the Doctor has to explain verbally how he managed to switch the jethrik (or the key to time fragment, it is now the same thing) for a bomb. By cleverly doing this, he explains to us afterwards, he managed to get the fragment and blow up the Graff, whom nobody liked.

Getting the key fragment is notionally a victory, but at the end of this dull story, when the Doctor says, "Only five more to go," it is one of the most blood chilling lines ever uttered in Doctor Who.

"City of Death" by "David Agnew" (Douglas Adams and Graham Williams, based on material by David Fisher)

The seventeenth season of Doctor Who, with the "Key to Time" thankfully in the past, was Tom Baker's penultimate season. It featured as its second story (starting on 29 September 1979) "City of Death," which would win the highest ratings ever enjoyed by a Doctor Who adventure, reaching over sixteen million viewers. It should be said that at this time (October 1979), there were only three television channels in England and one of these, ITV, had just gone on strike. Nonetheless, "City of Death" is, by at least one objective standard, the most popular Doctor Who story ever transmitted.

Purportedly written by a pseudonymity called David Agnew, "City of Death" is the work of at least three writers. It began as a story by David Fisher, who wrote "The Stones of Blood," "The Androids of Tara," "The Creature from the Pit," and "The Leisure Hive" in Seasons 16, 17, and 18. According to Howe, Stammers, and Walker, David Fisher's original story featured a thick-headed detective who was intended as an affectionate parody of Bulldog Drummond, a jingoistic British action hero of the 1920s. It also crucially featured an alien trapped on Earth and trying to finance his attempts to get home (originally by rigged gambling at a casino).

These elements were heavily reworked by script editor Douglas Adams and producer Graham Williams into what became "City of Death." One factor motivating an extensive rewrite was the decision to do a story set in Paris—the first *Doctor Who* adventure ever filmed outside the United Kingdom. Interestingly, the location shoot was thanks to the characteristic financial acumen of production unit manager John Nathan-Turner, who would be promoted to producer by the time I joined the show, and who made this excursion possible.

"City of Death" begins with some very good special effects shots. We see the convincing landscape of a barren, alien planet (in fact, we'll later learn that it's Earth, though primordially ancient). Sitting in this landscape is a truly marvellous black spaceship consisting of three jointed legs attached to a spherical body. This superb model work by visual effects designer Ian Scoones can only be applauded. The same cannot be said of the very next shot, however, as we cut inside the spaceship to its alien pilot sitting at the controls. The cockpit of the ship is a poor set that doesn't convince for a moment. Much worse, though, is the creature sitting in it, a one-eyed alien called a Jagaroth with a face like a mass of worms. The original design sketches for the Jagaroth probably resembled one of the better and more horrifying aliens from an EC comic of the 1950s. What actually ended up on screen is so pitiful that it quite destroys the sense of wonder engendered by those opening shots. The creature, and its environment, are so lamentable that they might as well not have bothered with the painstaking work on the planet background or the spaceship model. It all goes for naught. After we see this roiling heap of rubber, the spaceship explodes, not a moment too soon.

From this shaky but at least science fictional beginning we cut to cherry blossoms. We are in Paris in the present day (1979) where the Doctor and Romana (now recast as Lalla Ward) are larking around on holiday. They peer down from the Eiffel Tower. They hurry across Parisian streets and ride a train in the Metro. It's a boon that these sequences are shot on film, and the novelty of the Paris locations lasts for a few seconds, but tedium rapidly sets in as the viewer senses that, while the production team might have had a nice holiday, the story is going nowhere. We are eventually introduced to the villain, Count Scarlioni (Julian Glover). We know he's the villain because of some thunderous bad-guy music that accompanies the establishing shots of his domicile. In his basement, the Count has a genuine mad scientist laboratory (badly designed), complete with hired scientist Professor Kerensky (David Graham). The Count amusingly bemoans the high price of mad science (the humorous dialogue is the chief, perhaps only, strength of the story). "The Gainsborough didn't fetch very much," he says. It looks like they will have to sell one of the bibles. Gutenberg bibles, that is.

While this goes on the Doctor and Romana (dressed as an English schoolgirl) sit in a café where the Doctor experiences the déjà vu sensation of time looping back on itself. It's as if time "jumped a groove," a metaphor that will become increasingly cryptic as people cease playing vinyl. Then it's off to the Louvre (another uninspired studio set) where Romana wants to know why the Mona Lisa has no eyebrows and the Doctor suffers another time loop.

The plot is by now at last lurching into motion, albeit at a leisurely pace. Plotting was never Douglas Adams's forte (a prime example being *Dirk Gently's Holistic Detective Agency*, a novel that recycled another, abortive *Doctor Who* script called "Shada"), and it's tempting to attribute some of the story problems of "City of Death" to that late, great writer's preference for clever dialogue over robust plot. Despite the novel distraction of seeing the Doctor and Romana in genuine Paris locations, "City" is a dull story and overlong at a mere four episodes. Nor does it help that Tom Baker seems to be totally on autopilot in this, his sixth series as the Doctor.

Finally, a conspiracy to steal the Da Vinci masterpiece hoves into view. The theft seems to involve some suspiciously advanced technology. Romana underlines the point, "You mean an alien's trying to steal the Mona Lisa?" The Doctor says, as if by way of explanation, "It is a very pretty painting."

The Doctor and Romana join forces with Duggan (Tom Chadbon), a blundering English detective investigating art theft. Someone has been selling masterpieces of uncertain provenance (to put it mildly), and the Count is under suspicion. However, the Count is much more than just an aristocratic thief, as we discover at the end of episode one when he takes off his human face which proves to be a mask. Underneath it, he is another one of those ludicrous worm-faced aliens, a Jagaroth called Scaroth.

The Doctor and Romana are snooping around and end up getting dragged before the Count's wife (Catherine Schell) and his manservant; at least we get some whimsical dialogue. "What a wonderful butler," says the Doctor. "So violent." The Countess has a rare and precious Chinese puzzle box, but it's a fraction of the size of the one in "The Talons of Weng-Chiang," and Romana makes short work of it.

The Doctor is clowning as they are taken prisoner, which makes the whole thing seem inconsequential—and it is. As they're locked in the cellar the Doctor reveals that this is exactly what he wanted and takes out the sonic screwdriver, which sets them free. The Doctor studies the basement laboratory. "I've been through two timeslips and I think this might have something to do with it," he says as he studies the cheap-looking equipment.

Some more melodramatic music accompanies Professor Kerensky as he uses his apparatus to change an egg into a chicken. "Which came first," says the Doctor, looming over his shoulder. He then reverses the polarity (that old chestnut) and turns the chicken back into an egg. This sort of messing with the natural flow of time is an expensive business, and the Count and Countess are planning to steal the Mona Lisa to fund it. In the first real flash of interest in the story, we learn that the Count intends to sell the stolen painting not once, but at least six times. The Doctor works this out when he finds another six copies of the painting sealed in a room in the cellar. They are perfect copies but, in an ingenious touch, the Count must still steal the one in the Louvre to create buyers on the black market. Presumably he believes he can keep the various buyers unaware of each other for long enough to pull off the con.

The other interesting aspect of this scam is that the other Mona Lisas have been walled up in this cellar for centuries, and all of them are authentic—insofar as they have all been painted by Leonardo Da Vinci (the Doctor knows enough about his work to authenticate them). To find out just what the hell is going on (and, in fairness to Douglas Adams et al., the viewer is probably now also quite intrigued), the Doctor decides to pay a visit to Leonardo, an old friend of his. He returns to the Tardis, which is parked in a little gallery of modern art, looking like just one more baffling modern exhibit.

When he arrives in Leonardo's studio in Florence in 1505, the Doctor finds that the painter is absent (we never do get to meet him); instead he does meet an exact double of the Count. What is even more disturbing is the fact that this sixteenth century double seems to know exactly everything the twentieth century Count knows. In fact, he seems to be in constant mental communication with him. We gradually piece together that when Scaroth's spaceship exploded, he was split into a number of separate but still linked entities in different eras. "My problem is very simple," says the Count in one of the script's most mischievously amusing lines, "I was in the warp control cabin and when the explosion occurred I was flung into the time vortex and split into twelve different parts." The central conceit of the plot is that his twelve different selves have been working throughout history to advance the human race to the point where he can acquire the technology to take him home. This recalls "The Krotons," but it's different enough to qualify as a good plot in its own right, and it's only a pity that "City of Death" doesn't deploy it less shambolically and with more conviction.

The notion of this corporate entity, simultaneously sharing its experience throughout time, is somewhat reminiscent of Kurt Vonnegut's *Slaughterhouse Five* where Billy Pilgrim becomes "unstuck in time." Nevertheless, it's also one of the better concepts in "City of Death," and it's neatly presented by cutting back and forth between the modern day Count and his "ancestors" and showing them sharing dialogue and experience.

"I'm the last of the Jagaroth," he tells the Doctor. "I'm the saviour of the Jagaroth." The Doctor replies, "If you're the last, there can't be many left to save." The sixteenth century Count has forced Leonardo to paint six copies of the Mona Lisa, which he will brick up for nearly 500 years as a capital investment. He hopes it will pay for the final technological push he needs to achieve his goal. "Soon the centuries that divide me shall be undone," he cries. "I don't like the sound of that," says the Doctor.

The Countess doesn't know about the Count's little secret (he's clearly never removed his mask in her presence), but she must have had some doubts. All it takes is for the Doctor to sow a tiny seed of doubt in her mind—by telling her that her husband has a green face and one eye in the middle of his forehead.

Romana has provided the Count with the final technological fix he needs to complete the device in his basement. Now he can fulfil his plans to go back in time and prevent his spaceship blowing up. Romana isn't to be blamed too much for giving in to his pressure. He's been threatening to blow up Paris if she won't cooperate. He reiterates his threat to the Doctor, demanding that he also help with the time machine. "If you do not, it will be so much the worse for you, for this young lady, and for thousands of other people I could mention if I happened to have the Paris telephone directory on my person." This kind of spaced-out wit is one of the redeeming features of the script, and it is probably Douglas Adams's dialogue, since it sounds like pure *The Hitchhiker's Guide to the Galaxy*.

Meanwhile the Doctor's remarks have brought the Countess's doubts to a head (as it were), and she pulls a gun on her husband, thereby instigating a classic horror movie moment as he unmasks himself, to reveal that rubber monster mask. Having thus put his domestic affairs in order, the Count travels back to the dawn of time to stop his spaceship blowing up. The Doctor, Romana, and Duggan follow, to stop him stopping it. If the Count interferes with history in this way, he will cause untold damage, not the least of which is preventing life arising on Earth; another one of the clever grace notes of this story is that the exploding spaceship provided the pulse of energy needed to invigorate the primordial soup.

The Doctor and the others appear in the world of 400 million years ago (an uncharacteristic slip for Douglas Adams, who usually knew his science. The best estimates of the origin of life on Earth put it around four *billion* years ago). They look around at the barren primitive landscape and the Doctor explains, "This will be the middle of the Atlantic Ocean." The easily puzzled Duggan says, "We're standing on land."

Romana wittily observes, "He's out of his depth." Then the Count arrives and Duggan stops him with a simple blow to the (writhing, wormy, green) head. This is Duggan's sole vital contribution to the whole story, and it could as easily have been provided by the Doctor or, in a world of equal rights, by Romana. Still, the Doctor calls it "Possibly the most important punch in history."

That's the end of the story, but the most endearing and memorable moment came earlier, in a kind of premature coda. When the Doctor and the others hurry into the Tardis it is still parked in the little gallery of modern art. Two pretentious culture vultures (played by John Cleese and Eleanor Bron) are busy studying this blue police box. They continue to watch it, unfazed, as it disappears with the traditional Tardis dematerialisation roar. "Exquisite," says Eleanor Bron. "Absolutely exquisite."

The same cannot be said of "City of Death" as a whole. The rewrite of the original David Fisher script was reportedly an eleventh-hour marathon by Douglas Adams and Graham Williams, working flat out day and night. This might excuse some of the weaknesses in the script, but the fact remains that it's a story that has been seriously distorted to accommodate a Paris setting, when in fact Paris is utterly irrelevant. The Mona Lisa, as an iconic art treasure, has a certain pertinence but not enough to justify the boring and feckless Parisian scenes that litter the piece. The clever dialogue doesn't compensate for a frustratingly weak story—all the more frustrating because there are some interesting and vivid ideas buried in it. Superior production values might have saved the day, but once we glimpse that Jagaroth mask, everyone may as well have stayed at home.

chapter 7

An Ordinary Guy

John Nathan-Turner, the resourceful production manager who had enabled "City of Death" to be shot on location in Paris, was promoted to producer of *Doctor Who* for Season 18, Tom Baker's last stint on the show. For the duration of that season, Barry Letts returned to the show as executive producer, to oversee John. For Season 19 Letts departed and John Nathan-Turner really began to make his mark on *Doctor Who*. Tom Baker had now bowed out, and John was able to recast the part of the Doctor with an actor who was more to his liking, Peter Davison, whom John knew from his work as the vet Tristan in the BBC's *All Creatures Great and Small*. As we'll see, Davison would be a very different kind of Doctor.

"Mawdryn Undead" by Peter Grimwade

"Mawdryn Undead" is the third story of Davison's second season as the Doctor. Written by former *Doctor Who* production assistant Peter Grimwade (immortalised in the reference to Grimwade's syndrome in "The Robots of Death"), it was a four-parter that began transmission on 1 February 1983. The story sees the return of the Black Guardian (Valentine Dyall), who is now intervening in the affairs of Earth in an attempt to have the Doctor assassinated. Specifically he seeks to achieve this through the unusual expedient of asking an English public schoolboy to help him.

The schoolboy is called Turlough (Mark Strickson) and he's a mature, slightly sinister figure. There's more to him than meets the eye. He is an alien trying to make his way home. This is why he is willing to help the Black Guardian, who appears in a blaze of hokey video effects when Turlough is knocked unconscious after crashing a vintage car in a rather well staged sequence (the director of "Mawdryn" is

Peter Moffatt). The Black Guardian is like the devil brokering a deal, offering a world beyond the Earth to Turlough.

As the car crashed it forced another vehicle off the road, and that vehicle was driven by our old friend the Brigadier. It's great to see Nicolas Courtney again in the guise of the Brigadier, a kind of corrective to the sigh of bored dismay that greeted the recurrence of the Black Guardian.

Meanwhile the Doctor seems to have wandered into a sitcom, or perhaps a soap opera, as two attractive women wander in and out of a brightly lit set while he tampers with what are supposed to be the control panels on his strange inter-dimensional ship. The Doctor has now acquired these two attractive, young female companions (Nyssa played by Sarah Sutton and Tegan played by Janet Fielding), and they have been given—perhaps for reasons of family viewing—their own rooms on board. The Tardis has begun to seem less like a spaceship, or a time machine, and more like a hotel. Or perhaps the Crossroads motel. Certainly some basic sense of wonder had drained away. We're not excited being in the Tardis.

When the Tardis lands on a spaceship, it's a great huge flying hotel of a spaceship, too. There's no science fiction thrills to be had here, either, although interest rallies when we discover that the ship has a transmat—what *Star Trek* would call a teleporter—and is in contact with the school and therefore the subplot where Turlough lurks.

Turlough slips into the Tardis, and there is a Doctor-ish moment when the Doctor races back in and finds him there—and he doesn't pay Turlough any attention. Just for a moment. Then he reacts and it's back to routine plotting.

The Black Guardian flashes back into the narrative, a swarming halo of cheap psychedelia flashing around his head. "In the name of all that is evil," says the Black Guardian, then going on to refer to himself in the third person, he insists that Turlough keep his part of the bargain and bump off the Doctor. With a rock to his head. Instead of being brained, the Doctor runs into his old friend the Brigadier. The Brigadier doesn't recognise him, but of course this is business as usual since the Doctor has now regenerated into Peter Davison, a clean-cut leading man with an engaging manner, who has replaced the Tom Baker Doctor.

Naturally the Brigadier doesn't recognise him, but there is something deeper here than just the usual confusion. That also applies to the subplot where Nyssa and Tegan have discovered a badly burned man (Mawdryn played by David Collings). For no apparent reason, they have jumped to the conclusion that he is the Doctor, being horribly deformed after an accident with the transmat. The man bears no resemblance to the Doctor whatsoever, so this assumption by Tegan and Nyssa seems arbitrary, to say the least.

For his part, the Brigadier is experiencing some form of mind block that prevents him remembering about the Doctor or indeed about his experiences with UNIT. In a neat and moody—and witty—little scene, the Doctor recites a string of old and familiar names. The Brigadier looks troubled and says, "Someone just walked over my grave." The Doctor responds, "Maybe it was a Yeti."

The Brigadier is affectionately presented by Peter Grimwade, and "Mawdryn" is an interesting script. However, it loses itself in abstractions and complexities that weaken the story. Nyssa and Tegan are rationalising the fact that the burned man looks nothing like the Doctor. "The transmat process induced a regeneration." In other words, just about anyone could turn up at any time, not looking like the Doctor but pretending to be him, and they would be honour bound to believe said person. The drawbacks of this policy are demonstrated when the burned man turns out to be the eponymous Mawdryn, who is an alien with the top of his head cut off and his brain squirming inside. Mawdryn succeeds in being quite gruesome on first appearance, and is intermittently an agreeably horrible presence thereafter, but he is also occasionally laughable, particularly in his choice of vestments.

Turlough also makes a vivid impression, so much so that he will be asked to join the Doctor—another presence in the already overloaded Tardis, another companion. At this stage in the show's history, the Doctor didn't need another companion; what he needed was to become a more vivid presence himself. In *The Television Companion*, Howe and Walker state that John Nathan-Turner was unhappy with Tom Baker's portrayal of the Doctor because his "assured and flippant interpretation made the character seem too dominant and invulnerable." While there is certainly a case to be made for Tom Baker being rather too flippant, especially in his later years, it seems that with Peter Davidson in the role, the character of the Doctor has gone too far the other way. Not that he is humourless or anything like that. But if Baker was too dominant and invulnerable, the Davidson Doctor is marginalised, a victim of fate. Peter Davison is an excellent actor, and he is handsome, confident, and likeable. Physically, and in his dress, he is also very normal . . . an ordinary guy. It's as if, again in reaction to Tom Baker, all eccentricity in the character has been eradicated. But the Doctor is anything but an ordinary guy and portraying him as such is a dangerous course of action.

A more appropriate choice for the role of the Doctor might have been Mark Strickson, who plays Turlough in "Mawdryn Undead." Although he's cast as a teenage boy here, Strickson was actually old enough to have played the Doctor and, crucially, he reveals an introverted alien quality that might have been right for the part. There is something enigmatic and not entirely reassuring about his onscreen persona, and that's just what Doctor Who needs. But Peter Davison was John's choice for the Doctor, and in "Mawdryn" he was in the middle of his three-year run in the role. (Having spent years working together with John Nathan-Turner on Doctor Who, it seems a trifle artificial and officious for me to insist on always calling him by his last name. Now that he's beginning to take centre stage in the book, I'll mostly refer to him as John.)

Meanwhile, back in the Tardis, Nyssa and Tegan are having their own crisis about the Doctor's identity. They are in agreement that they can't be certain if the mysterious burned guy is the Doctor or not. It never seems to occur to them that a simple expedient might be to ask him some questions. Meanwhile the Doctor and the Brigadier have taken the transmat, a nifty device involving a giant, silver sphere with a luxury lounge interior that fails to evoke an alien environment.

In a highly theoretical subplot, the luxury liner in space turns out to have had some Time Lord technology on board. It seems that the crew of sliced-skulled, open-brained mutants, Mawdryn and his shipmates, had been tampering with this Time Lord regeneration device in an attempt to make themselves immortal. "It all went disastrously wrong," says the Doctor. "They're immortal?" asks Tegan. "For what it's worth," says the Doctor.

Another, younger version of the Brigadier has wandered aboard the Tardis, which Nyssa and Tegan have taken back in time to the school six years earlier. Then the Brigadier, who was once such a man of action, had been reduced to teaching mathematics in some backwater public school. With both the Tardis and the transmat in play, we have two ways of getting back to the boring luxury liner in space. Soon we have two Brigadiers wandering around.

The old chestnut about not ever letting anyone meet themselves is invoked (cf. "Inferno," which had two different Brigadiers in two different dimensions), and the alert viewer who is willing to get excited about this admittedly rather abstract and theoretical, threat will eventually be disappointed. When the Brigadier meets himself, there is not the promised apocalyptic explosion but rather a beneficial flash of energy that solves all the Doctor's problems. End of story.

"Mawdryn Undead" is a story full of dark and intriguing ideas, it is also full of theory and talk about things that will or might happen, but nothing much actually does happen. In a ruse that will be repeated with Peri in "The Caves of Androzani," the attractive young female companions will come down with a debilitating, not to mention deforming, disease. This overworked motif of the female companions undergoing repugnant physical change would also recur in a weird scene in "Vengeance on Varos."

"The Caves of Androzani" by Robert Holmes

"The Caves of Androzani," which concluded Peter Davison's third and final season as the Doctor, started transmission on 8 March 1984, is a much more interesting proposition. It's exceptionally well directed, by Graeme Harper, who stages some great gunfights. It is also well designed (by John Hurst) and excellently cast. It benefits from a Robert Holmes script, full of vivid ideas and well wrought characters. It bows out the smooth leading man style Peter Davison Doctor and introduces what promises to be a more acerbic and quirky character, in the shape of the Colin Baker Doctor.

It also completely misses the mark.

One early failure that throws "The Caves of Androzani" seriously off course is the first appearance of the magma creature. The magma creature is basically a guy in a dragon suit with a head like a crocodile. In fact, the creature's face is terribly reminiscent of the demon that appears at the end of the classic horror film *The Night of the Demon*, (to catastrophically negate and deflate the atmospheric, suspenseful direction by Jacques Tourneur and an outstanding script by Charles Bennett and Hal E. Chester, from an M. R. James story). Similarly, "The Caves of Androzani" is a strong and intelligent science fiction adventure derailed in its first five minutes by the appearance of the silliest Chinese New Year's dragon you ever saw attacking a miner in a cave tunnel.

When I first started working on *Doctor Who*, the producer John Nathan-Turner gave me a tape of "Androzani." It was, he said, one of the best stories he'd worked on. This was true, and it was a good choice. In many ways "Androzani" is a top piece of television science fiction. Robert Holmes had handed in a well paced, rich, and coherent script with plenty of gothic menace, and the production team had risen to the occasion. However, John had also said, "You'll like the monster. The monster's good."

The monster, however, was not good and hasn't improved in the intervening years. It seriously diminishes the story right at the outset. Why show the monster in the first five minutes of a story, anyway? Even with the greatest special effects in history, you should still try and save the monster for the *last* five minutes.

"The Caves of Androzani" would be improved dramatically by the simple expedient of cutting out all the shots of the magma beast altogether. I can imagine John resisting any such suggestions. Without the magma creature, "Androzani" just becomes a story about guys in military uniforms running around tunnels with guns. There's a brief sequence in a spaceship, true, and the villain has a suitable science fictional mask concealing his hideously deformed face. But that wasn't enough. John always liked a monster in the story. He insisted on us inserting some token monsters in "Ghost Light" in Season 26, an exceptionally good and subtle story that didn't benefit from the imposition of such shambling and unconvincing critters. John felt *Doctor Who* required a monster, that the viewers expected it, that it was a vital part of the mix.

While the inclusion of a magma creature, and a derisorily bad one at that, did mark "The Caves of Androzani" out as typical *Doctor Who*, the story had in just about every other important particular ceased to be *Doctor Who*.

In many ways, Peter Davison was *too* likeable a leading man. He was amiable, confident, and clean cut, as none of the previous Doctors had been. Indeed, according to *Doctor Who: The 80s*, Peter Ling, who had written "Mind Robber" for Troughton, regarded the new actor playing the Doctor as a "juvenile lead." This seems a little unfair. In character, Davison could be assured and knowledgeable, but he offered little to suggest the essential alienness of the character. All the previous Doctors had managed to convey this; they had been in some way quirky or offbeat.

In "The Caves of Androzani," this lack of distinctiveness combines with a story that marginalises the Doctor to such effect that it might as well not be a *Doctor Who* adventure at all. The Doctor isn't crucial or instrumental. In fact, he's a combination bystander and victim throughout. Like the magma beast, you could remove him from the story and merely improve it as a result.

It's Holmes's great skill as a writer that allows him to pay homage to *The Phantom of the Opera* yet again, and to set the story on an alien world that is the antithesis of space opera. Despite the characters exotic names, these people move in a realistic and believable world. That's one of the great strengths of "Androzani." Despite the gothic excesses of Sharaz Jek (Christopher Gable), a madman in his underground lair, "The Caves of Androzani" has a sense of real people and real institutions operating in a real society.

The Doctor arrives on Androzani Minor, a desert world riddled with caves. He is accompanied by Peri (Nicola Bryant), a nubile, allegedly American young woman in culottes. "Oh wow!" she says as she steps out of the Tardis to look at this alien world. The Doctor discourses knowledgeably about caves and the risk of sudden lethal mud floods in them. Of course, into the caves he goes. "Is this wise I ask myself?" says Peri.

The Doctor and Peri have a good rapport and Holmes's breezy, witty dialogue helps. Soon they have stumbled on gunrunners in the caves and been arrested by government troops. The Doctor will now spend the rest of the story as the prisoner of one party or another. Occasionally, for variety's sake, Peri and the Doctor will be prisoners of separate parties. Neither of them will have much to do with the colourful and well-mounted action-adventure story that is unfolding around them.

"We're the fall guys," says Peri, not inaccurately. The Doctor replies, "Try and speak English," a line that might have sounded right coming from crusty William Hartnell or donnish Patrick Troughton but echoes oddly from this amiable, modern young guy. Soon enough Peri and the Doctor are scheduled for execution. Peri whimpers a lot about this, but then she's only just joined the Doctor in the Tardis (having been introduced in the previous story, "Planet of Fire" by Peter Grimwade). She doesn't yet realise that being taken prisoner and sentenced to execution is part of the job description for the Doctor's companion.

The Doctor and Peri are rescued by Sharaz Jek, the Phantom of the Opera character, lurking in the deep tunnels. Jek is an android maker, and he has whipped up Doctor and Peri androids at amazingly short notice, having only ever seen the Doctor and Peri on screens in his underground lair. In any case, his replacement androids fool the firing squad, and the viewer, into thinking at least momentarily that the Doctor and his companion have been gunned down. The thing is, Jek has fallen in love with Peri, although he is realist enough to sense that his hideously deformed face, concealed by a groovy black and white mask, might prove an obstacle in his pursuit of her.

The reason that Jek is down here in his underground cavern is that this place is the source of spectrox, the most valuable substance in the universe. While one heaves a sigh at hearing this old cliché again, spectrox is rather more interesting than some of the other most valuable substances in the universe. It's a drug derived from organic matter associated with creatures living in the cave, and it can be used to make what Morgus (the real villain of the piece, played by John Normington) calls "a wonderful restorative." It at least doubles the life span of human beings who take it. No wonder, "The public want their spectrox."

Sharaz Jek puts it in traditional mad genius fashion, "It's mine. All of it." The Doctor and Peri have also been exposed to rather too much of it. They blundered into something reminiscent of a cobweb when they first entered the cave. This was a spectrox nest, the substance in its raw form. It's deadly to humans and also to the Doctor. That's why the androids are required (neat bit of plotting), to harvest the spectrox that, for living creatures, would be poisonous to the touch.

Peri and the Doctor start to slowly succumb to the poison that can only be cured by the use of the milk of the queen bat who lives deep in the cave system. One looks forward to a quest in search of the giant cave bat's milk, but it's a vain wish because the budget of the story can't accommodate it. Indeed, in the final episode the Doctor's quest to get the milk and save Peri (and himself) is reduced to such a truncated and schematic venture that it's almost like something in an experimental theatre production.

The black and white masked Sharaz Jek can create androids who are exact doubles of human beings, but for his foot soldiers he uses faceless droids with shiny helmets that only feature one eye-type scanner. Like Jek's mask, these android helmets are a simple solution to a special effects challenge, and they work well, making the androids' seem inhuman.

Amidst all this exotica, the Doctor is just too normal. He's just a likeable, regular guy standing around. Robert Holmes does his best to build the Doctor up in dialogue. Jek is about to dismiss the Doctor as a fool, but he reconsiders and says, "Your eyes tell a different story." Unfortunately, eyes, or dialogue about eyes, don't sufficiently convey to the audience the feeling that they're on an adventure in the company of an unearthly and extraordinary fellow, which is really what *Doctor Who* is all about.

We are reminded about the Doctor's special alien nature. Jek's android guards are programmed to shoot human beings on sight. However, the Doctor with his two hearts doesn't register as being a target. "What a clever little android you are," he tells it, as he slips past unharmed. Somehow the Doctor seems too nice and ordinary a guy for any of this alien stuff to stick. Soon he is being slapped around with impunity by Sharaz Jek and then being tortured by his androids.

The vicious yet pathetic Sharaz Jek is a fascinating, wily guerrilla fighter, waging war against great forces in a battle for control of the life-giving spectrox. He is much more interesting a character than the Doctor or Peri. Notionally this story should in some sense be about Peri, showcasing or featuring her, since it's her first venture with the Doctor. But she's lost in the background of the story, only really making an impact when it looks like she might die of spectrox poisoning, and we have lots of close ups of her feverish face.

Like "The Ribos Operation," "The Caves of Androzani" is a Robert Holmes story told in an intriguing and coherent alien world. It's full of fascinating characters and ideas, and there's enough action to keep things bowling along. Like "Ribos," "Caves" sidelines the Doctor and his new companion in a story in which they're almost totally irrelevant. At least in "The Ribos Operation," Tom Baker had sufficient towering spookiness to remain a dominating presence. In "The Caves of Androzani," the Davison Doctor is just one amongst a group of interesting and engaging characters. It is no longer his show.

At the end of episode three of "Androzani," the Doctor suddenly shows signs of life. Having been taken prisoner by gun-running mercenaries, after having already been taken prisoner by every one else in the story, the Doctor actually manages to turn the tables and takes control of the mercenaries' spaceship, a better than average model (the visual effects for this story were provided by Jim Francis and Stuart Brisdon). The Doctor is in a race against time to save Peri. Sharaz Jek has rescued Peri from the military who had taken her prisoner after she managed to escape from Jek who had taken her prisoner after the military had taken her prisoner in the first place. By now Peri is succumbing to the poison in her blood. She is wilting in Jek's arms as he says, "I have lived so long in these caves alone . . . Now I can feast my eyes on your delicacy."

As the story reaches its climax, Sharaz Jek begins to emerge as a memorable and tragic figure. He heroically defends his inner sanctum as he is overrun by the military. Then, unmasked, he faces his beloved Peri who, seeing him for the first time, screams and screams and screams. Jek flees from her as though mortally wounded by her reaction.

The story is rich with memorable characters. Even the evil Morgus's slavey of a secretary (Barbara Kinghorn) suddenly turns on him, draining his clandestine bank accounts before he can tap them, as he becomes a wanted man. It's all great stuff, but it's not about the Doctor.

Eventually the Doctor does, in a sense, save the day. Peri is on death's door, so the Doctor descends into the depths of the cave in search of the giant queen bat and her milk, the only thing that can cure her. This odd quest turns out to be almost a purely symbolic, expressionist venture with the Doctor climbing up and down strange sets to return triumphantly with a little glass bottle of bat's milk which he pours into Peri's fevered lips as they stumble through the door of the Tardis. He gives her all the bat's milk, despite needing some himself to cure the deadly poison.

The Doctor reckons he might have another way of throwing off the poison. He is about to regenerate. This regeneration actually takes place with the Doctor lying on the Tardis floor while faces from his past spin around him and spout dialogue at him. It's like something from *The Wizard of Oz*, and then after a blaze of tacky special effects, Peter Davison transforms into Colin Baker and there is a new Doctor staring out at us. There is something deranged and acerbic about this new character, not entirely likeable, that suggests he might be a more vividly alien and memorable Doctor.

"The Caves of Androzani" is an intelligent and surprisingly adult science fiction adventure, exceptionally well directed and treated with seriousness and respect by a first-rate cast. Had it been part of an anthology series of new science fiction stories, or if it had been a stand-alone adventure, it might well have been some kind of classic.

As a *Doctor Who* story it doesn't hold a candle to earlier, more vivid adventures. The problem with the show was that there hadn't been a truly Doctor-ish Doctor since Tom Baker relinquished the role. After working with Tom Baker for a number of years, the notion of a less convincingly, madly alien of a Doctor may well have seemed like a good notion. However, the more likeable and average-Joe in character one made the Doctor the more diminished he tended to become.

Of course, it was possible to compensate for this, to enhance the alienness and essential mystery of the Doctor through the scripts that gave him life. Such stories would need to be conceived *around* the Doctor. This was a different proposition from creating a steady flow of science fiction adventure stories in which the Doctor was basically a walk-on character. *Doctor Who* could get away quite successfully with such stories when the Doctor was a sufficiently weird and vivid character, as in "The Ribos Operation." Tom Baker was the tent pole for the whole notion of *Doctor Who*, stories about a strange time traveller who takes us on scary cosmic adventures.

The concept is more problematical with his two immediate successors. In "Mawdryn Undead," Peter Davison impresses as a nice, down-to-earth guy lost in a parade of weirdness. In "The Caves of Androzani," he's a likeable chap who stumbles into a dark science fictional adventure.

In "Vengeance on Varos," we will find that Colin Baker's Doctor is a more acerbic and abrasive creation, but basically he's still a normal guy lost in the background in a bleak, violent dystopia.

"Vengeance on Varos" by Philip Martin

"Vengeance on Varos" began transmission on 19 January 1985. It was a two-part adventure, because the BBC was now experimenting with *Doctor Who* in a forty-five minute rather than twenty-five minute format (an experiment that would be repeated, with great success, in the 2005 season). It is the second story in Colin Baker's first season as the Doctor (following a Cybermen adventure), and it was written by Philip Martin who wrote the classic BBC underworld thriller *Gangsters* (1976), which had deservedly enjoyed a huge critical and popular success. Philip Martin's *Doctor Who* script, which eventually became "Vengeance on Varos," had been in the system for some years and had undergone several changes on its way to the screen. It concerned a human colony in space, one that had originated as a prison planet. John Nathan-Turner and his script editor Eric Saward wanted the writer to address such then topical issues as "video nasties" and snuff movies, so Philip Martin duly added these to the mix. He also had to write blind in early drafts, since he didn't know who would be cast as the Doctor or even as the companion. To add to the challenges, "Vengeance" went from being four twenty-five minute scripts to two forty-five minute episodes.

As it finally saw the light of day, "Vengeance on Varos" has some impressive aspects. Some of the acting is solidly convincing; there is an exotic and evil villain, and visually it's above average. Some evocative noirish photography, with coloured lights, roving spots, and smoke drifting across the set suggest an awareness of *Alien.* When sympathetically lit, the sets suggest a grim concrete reality.

There are less laudable aspects to "Vengeance." The story opens with a fairly well accomplished alien landscape, the sky perhaps a little too obviously artificial, the domes somewhat obviously models, but nonetheless fairly convincing. We then cut into one of the domes—the Punishment Dome—and find Jason Connery, a juvenile lead if ever there was one, being tortured with his shirt off. Whatever the visual appeal of this scene for some (John used to have a framed still from it up in his office wall), it's fairly nasty and gets nastier still as the story widens to take in the grim and squalid Orwell's *1984*–style environment and social structure. A middle-aged couple sit passively viewing a large screen that shows them the torture of Connery *fils* and will later show them other disturbing images of executions and various trials and humiliations throughout the story.

As they watch, the couple make sardonic comments, serving to illustrate the debased nature of life in this world and generally act as a Greek chorus. This was Martin's solution to the challenge of working in the video nasty/snuff movie angle. It's not particularly well integrated. The couple really need to develop as characters and serve some kind of function, even if the Doctor only ends up running through their living room some time before the story ends. He doesn't, and they don't.

According to Howe, Stammers, and Walker, Philip Martin's original concept was that the video-watching couple shouldn't even speak, but script editor Eric Saward encouraged him to give them some dialogue. This does lead to one effective moment at the very end when they are told their supply of sordid video titillation is being switched off. The couple have no idea what they are going to do with their lives now there is nothing to watch, and the screen goes black.

For the most part the watchers, though anticipating some of the murkier aspects of today's reality TV, are a tedious device that only serves to alienate us further from a not very engaging story. There is also a serious lack of chemistry between the Doctor and Peri, and Peri seems stridently phoney in her role as a young American woman (Nicola Bryant was actually a native of Surrey). Both Doctor and companion are dressed in terrible costumes. (The Doctor's gaudy and tasteless outfit was a particular eyesore and would remain a distraction and annoyance throughout his tenure, stacking the odds against poor Colin Baker.)

However, Nabil Shaban as Sil is extremely good value, despite some less than ideal makeup. In fact, he is one of the few truly effective *Doctor Who* monsters. While events unfold around him and the Governor of Varos (well played by Martin Jarvis), we are introduced to a dark and evil world where public executions are recorded in the Punishment Dome. "We sell tapes of what happens there. . . . They entertain as well as instruct."

While this is taking place, the Doctor is sidelined in a desperately tired subplot about the Tardis malfunctioning. As it eventually develops, he needs a vital substance to stop the Tardis breaking down. This ruse, in one form or another, dates back to "The Daleks" in 1963 (the second ever *Doctor Who* story) and is wheeled out again, but only after a cringingly bad scene in which Peri hauls out a giant prop book that obviously weighs nothing and we're told it's the Tardis manual. It even says so on the cover. Any sense of the Tardis as an awesome, shadowy, mysterious creation is long since past. Ditto the Doctor.

It seems the Doctor, and the Tardis, need a rare element called zeiton 7. Finally, the two stories intersect, because Varos is a mining planet where they have zeiton 7. So the Doctor shuffles wearily there in pursuit of this dull McGuffin. A more hackneyed plot device would be hard to find, and it's a real shame. Varos is such a sink of iniquity that it would have been great to send the Doctor there deliberately, like the Lone Ranger riding in to clean up the town.

But no, the Doctor bumbles in by accident and continues to bumble. He is a clown, or at least so his costume shouts, preventing any chance of Colin Baker's character developing stature. He might as well wear a "kick me" sign. As he is bundled through the dark smoky sets where terrible things are happening, it no longer seems like *Doctor Who*. When a giant fake fly turns up, it's a momentary relief. For an instant, we feel we're back in the show we know.

Colin Baker strives to make the Doctor thoughtful and unusual, but he doesn't quite click. He's just a clean-cut young guy in a silly costume. His cherubic face is unmarked by trouble or experience. The

hints of anarchy and malice and biting wit never quite pay off. The
Doctor is just another character in the story, and a victim to boot.
When he shows some sudden activity, it isn't pleasant.

At one point, we are supposed to believe that the Doctor is dead.
He is taken into the room where they dispose of dead bodies in an
acid bath. Two guards chuck a body bag into the bilious fluid. Then
the Doctor, who is lying on the next slab, gets up, and one of the
guards is so shocked he falls into the acid. The Doctor then manoeu-
vres the other guard into the acid bath. He doesn't actually push him
in, but he sure as hell doesn't try and stop him. Then, in a devastat-
ingly dreadful moment that harks back to the Bond films and echoes
forward to Schwarzenegger's screen persona, he watches the melting
bodies in the acid and quips, "Forgive me if I don't join you."

It's a new low for the show. At this point all sense of the Doctor is
lost altogether. At the same time Peri's phoney accent grates, and the
story is as depressing and brutal as the video feed to the Varosian couple. After failing to execute the Doctor with a laser, there is, perhaps
purely for variety's sake, a staged hanging complete with double gal-
lows, masked hangman, and monks in robes. This is followed, for our
titillation, by Peri and another attractive young woman being converted into semi animal mutants in a chamber called the transmogri-
fier. The plenitude of humiliation and brutality in the story are
presumably intended to make it dark and adult but merely serve to
make it distasteful. No one involved seems unduly aware of the irony
that "Vengeance on Varos" offers precisely the same sort of dubiously
nasty entertainment that it condemns. Tom Baker might have survived
it, and perhaps even redeemed it a little by adding his alien presence
to make it all seem more like a fable. With Colin Baker it just
seems relentlessly negative. "I want to hear them scream until I'm deaf
with pleasure," says the Governor's scar-faced enforcer (Nicholas
Chagrin).

*　　*　　*

One person not screaming with pleasure was BBC controller Michael Grade who would cancel the show soon after "Vengeance on
Varos" was broadcast. In some ways it's an understandable action. The
show had, for some seasons, been drifting away from its original
uniqueness and charm. The problem was that unless the Doctor was
perfectly cast, the whole tone of the show could rapidly go south.

During John Nathan-Turner's tenure as producer, attempts had certainly been made to invest the new Doctors with some traditional and necessary strangeness. It was odd having breezy young Peter Davison come on like a crusty curmudgeon, reprimanding his pneumatic, scantily attired companion about grammar, behaviour that might have better suited Patrick Troughton. It was equally strange watching Colin Baker deliver lines that could have been written for William Hartnell. He seems positively crotchety with Peri on occasion. For Hartnell, crotchety was fine. He was a insect-frail, silver-haired old man. But Colin Baker's Doctor was young, virile, full of life. Such lines sat oddly with him. Like Davison, he was an average-Joe overwhelmed by the weird and menacing drama that swirled around him.

The irony of this is that John Nathan-Turner, the producer during the Davison and Colin Baker era, had a very clear handle on the notion of the Doctor's essential engaging strangeness. Or at least he had evolved one by the time I arrived to work as script editor. He called it being Doctor-ish. Yet John presided over some of the least Doctor-ish presentations of the Doctor's character.

Certainly something essential about *Doctor Who* seemed to have been lost during this era. It had lost a quality that made some of the show's darker moments less forgivable. The violent shenanigans of "Seeds of Doom" or "Weng-Chiang" seemed entirely forgivable as they took place off in some fantasy realm. In any case Tom Baker himself was enough of a disclaimer. He was convincingly alien and remote and conferred on us the necessary insulating distance of fantasy.

Peter Davison and Colin Baker, for all their sallies at quirkiness remained normal guys, others like ourselves. So as they were swept up in the gritty combat and high body count of their stories from the nineteenth to the twenty-third season, Davison and Colin Baker could at best hope to prevail as a kind of anodyne action hero, like so many others available elsewhere on television.

This loss of specialness, of the essential Doctor-ish quality might have been a factor in the show's cancellation. In fact, *Doctor Who* was banished from the screens only from March 1985 to September 1986, hardly a dramatic hiatus considering what was to follow.

The man generally regarded as chief engineer of this dramatic cancellation was Michael Grade, a scheduler of some genius. Grade, above all people, understood how to move programs around in the schedule to get best advantage of them. He may well have resented *Doctor Who*'s traditional, indeed iconic presence on Saturday evenings, at a cultural crossroads of the week, clogging up the prime time. Grade may have had his own ideas about what a Saturday night on BBC1, showcase for the nation, should look like.

Certainly the show was suffering from criticism of its high-level of violence. When I was being interviewed for the job of script editor on *Doctor Who*'s twenty-fourth season, Jonathan Powell, the head of BBC drama, told me in no uncertain terms that *Doctor Who* was for children. I smiled mendaciously and pretended to agree.

I got the job and, with great good fortune, joined the show at the same time it saw the return of the Doctor-ish Doctor par excellence, in the shape of Sylvester McCoy.

chapter 8

A Doctor-ish Doctor

In January 1986 I began work as the new script editor of *Doctor Who*. London was in the grip of the coldest winter in living memory. Half the BBC was missing in action. John Nathan-Turner turned up at the cold, deserted office where I was waiting at noon. We spent the afternoon watching VHS cassettes of an actor, a prospective candidate to play the new Doctor, in the tiny video room choking on John's cigarette smoke. As I wrote in my diary, "The tapes are fascinating. The actor is a perky little Scottish elf called Sylvester McCoy. He's full of mischief and charm and anarchy . . ."

We invited Sylvester to the screen tests we were shooting for the new Doctor. He turned up with a straw hat and a wicker basket and a huge wide US Air Force insignia tie. Again my diary records the occasion. "Sylvester McCoy comes on like a cross between Bugs Bunny and Richard Burton. He blows the other candidates off the screen. Janet Fielding (who played Tegan) is reading in for [the companion]. She's responding to Sylvester, rising to the occasion, working with him on bits of business, rehearsing with him at every pause in the recording. Their leave-taking scene puts a lump in my throat."

Sylvester got the part and became the seventh Doctor. Soon I was out on location with him and working in the studio. In "Time and the Rani," his powerful voice echoed across the quarry that stood in for an alien planet (of course it was a quarry, it was *Doctor Who*). In "Paradise Towers," he stepped out of the Tardis into a scene of squalid urban decay and a tall, skeletal metal pump. He took off his hat and greeted the pump. "Well, you never know," he explained to his companion. This was a pure Sylvester McCoy ad lib, and it was wonderful. On "Delta and the Bannermen," he devised a bit of business that involved him *listening* to an apple at the start of every take. It was clear from the start that Sylvester was going to be great in the role, and amply Doctor-ish.

The question then became to cast a companion who was the ideal foil for him. In the end, a young actress called Sophie Aldred was chosen to play Ace, a wonderful anarchic streetwise teenager. In my diary, I recorded her rehearsing a scene for "Remembrance of the Daleks." "Sophie in a black tee shirt and black gym trousers swinging a baseball bat at a Dalek. "All in a day's work," says Sophie, and strikes a pose with the bat. "All the Daleks are actually little silver haired old geezers."

By the time Sylvester McCoy and Sophie Aldred appeared in the final story we filmed, "Ghost Light," they had both, as I've written elsewhere, "evolved seamlessly into their roles and both their characters were well rounded, intelligent and likeable. The Doctor had his humour and mystery and core of immense strength. Ace was gutsy, had her own street level wit and humour and, above all, she was intelligent. Unlike other companions, she didn't have to receive constant words-of-one-syllable explanations. Instead, she's always guessing, anticipating, meeting the Doctor half way."

"Ghost Light" is one of Sylvester's best performances, masterfully assured and underplayed. It's heartbreaking to think of what a great Doctor he could have been once he reached this point. As I've said elsewhere, it's a great shame that the financial minds of the BBC pulled the plug on us at this point. Sylvester was just gearing up to greatness with stories like "Ghost Light" and "Remembrance of the Daleks."

In this chapter, I'm discussing stories that I script edited. Apart from referring to Sylvester and Sophie as "Sylvester and Sophie" (it would seem strange to call them anything else), I'll try and treat these stories as dispassionately as any of the others in this book.

"Remembrance of the Daleks" by Ben Aaronovitch

Ben Aaronovitch's "Remembrance of the Daleks" was the first story transmitted in Sylvester's second season as the Doctor (the first episode being broadcast on 5 October 1988). It begins with a pre-title sequence (a rarity in *Doctor Who*), featuring a shot of the planet Earth in space, with voice-over fragments of radio broadcasts featuring President Kennedy and other luminaries to establish the period (1963).

Then a large and rather well made spaceship moves, somewhat jerkily, into view . . .

Wasting no time we cut to the seventh Doctor (Sylvester McCoy) and his new companion Ace (Sophie Aldred) outside a London school where they are watched by a rather spooky schoolgirl (played by Jasmine Breaks). These sequences are well shot by director Andrew Morgan and "Remembrance" is immediately a promising story.

It transpires that it's not just any school, either, but Coal Hill, the setting for the first ever episode of *Doctor Who* where Barbara and Ian were teachers and that "unearthly child" Susan was a pupil. Barbara, Ian, and Susan are all gone now, though, the Doctor having looped back in time to a point after their departure (I trust that's clear).

Ace is dressed in an unflatteringly baggy bomber jacket and her hair is severely scraped back. Indeed, her entire appearance seems specifically designed to minimise Sophie's considerable beauty. It doesn't matter though. It's clear even from the earliest moments that she is one of the best companions in years, paired with one of the finest Doctors. The portable stereo Ace balances on her shoulder, though, is laughably huge even for 1988, the year "Remembrance" was filmed.

Sylvester McCoy as the Doctor is agreeably Doctor-ish, scrambling up onto a strange van parked outside the school, examining scorch marks in the playground, then returning to the van and letting himself in. The van contains a load of high tech monitoring equipment and a lady scientist called Professor Rachel Jensen (Pamela Salem), and the Doctor quickly makes himself at home with both. He is assured, active, decisive. A far cry from the amiably passive victim so often featured in the past. The Sylvester McCoy Doctor is also likeable and has a gift for physical comedy combined with an authoritative burr of a voice. Altogether, he is the strongest and most distinctive Doctor since (according to one's taste) Tom Baker or Patrick Troughton. From the start of the story, he is nosing around, interfering, taking charge—just the way the Doctor should.

The story also benefits from a lack of *faux* science fiction trappings. The solid authenticity of the period setting and a military presence in the shape of Group Captain Gilmore (Simon Williams) and his men, as usual, serves to strengthen the enterprise. The Doctor is soon at loggerheads with Gilmore, who is a straightforward army officer quite unprepared for the unearthly predations of the Daleks. "I don't think you realise what you're dealing with here," says the Doctor, possibly experiencing a strong sense of déjà vu. Indeed, he makes the telling slip of calling the Group Captain "Brigadier."

Soon Gilmore is forced to accept that he's out of his depth as a Dalek arrives, gun blazing, and starts to wipe out his men. It's an impressive first appearance for the Dalek, emerging from the wreckage of a burning shed, with a bit of flaming debris still attached to it. Unfortunately, the Dalek also *wobbles*, a problem that will afflict all the location-shoot Daleks in the story (those shot on the smooth studio floors proved to be no problem). This annoying flaw is one of the few exceptions in a story featuring laudable special effects (by Stuart Brisdon) and outstanding design (by Martin Collins).

The Doctor is gutsy and brave and full of initiative. He lures the Dalek into an explosion that destroys it. Ace is no shrinking violet either. In a refreshing departure from recent companions, she's something of a teenage anarchist and a connoisseur of explosives. "Unsophisticated but impressive," she says of the military pyrotechnics. She is also smart, not passive, and capable of putting two and two together.

The Doctor and Ace requisition the van and go speeding through the streets of London while Ace (and the audience) are given a potted history of the Daleks. Ben Aaronovitch's dialogue is unfailingly good throughout the story, elliptical, strong, suggestive, and witty. Even this somewhat didactic scene is interesting and lively. It also features a cherishably Doctor-ish moment as Ace, who is complaining about driving, is mysteriously supplanted by the Doctor, ending up in the passenger seat with a look of puzzlement on her face after they drive through a tunnel. The Doctor continues lecturing to her as *he* drives.

After four tall actors playing the Doctor, Sylvester McCoy is relatively diminutive. Indeed, the Doctor and Ace are both about the same height, making for an interesting visual and helping to evoke our sympathy for this pair in their battles against cosmic dangers.

"Remembrance of the Daleks" features *Quatermass*-style realistic scientists ("I want a direct line to Jodrell Bank," says the Doctor) caught up with an equally realistic military. Indeed, there's an affectionate homage to *Quatermass* in Ben Aaronovitch's dialogue. "I wish Bernard was here," says the professor's assistant, Allison (Karen Gledhill). "The British Rocket Group's got its own problems," replies Rachel. Bernard is, of course, Bernard Quatermass and the British Rocket Group is his pet project.

Poking around in the cellar of Coal Hill School, the Doctor and Ace discover a transmat—a Dalek teleportation device. A Dalek begins to materialise on it, in a well realised video effect that shows the soft organic innards of the creature appear first, followed by its metallic shell. The Doctor rewires the device and destroys the new arrival. "Dangerous things, transmats," says the Doctor happily. Then a Dalek sentry turns up and pursues him up the cellar stairs. In a classic *Doctor Who* cliff-hanger, we see the Dalek closing in on him, hovering upwards on a flickering red beam, shrieking "Exterminate."

"Remembrance of the Daleks" is an intelligent and perceptive script, but it is also a fast-moving adventure story full of enjoyable mayhem. Having escaped the Dalek on the stairs, the Doctor is delighted to find a military consignment of antitank rockets turning up at the school. The soldier delivering them says he'll have to sign for them, as the Doctor absconds with the weaponry. Ace uses one of the ATRs (acronyms are infectious) to blow the head off the Dalek, which is raging through the school. "Did you do that?" says Mike (Dursely McLinden), the personable young sergeant who has an eye for Ace. He stares at the flaming wreckage of the Dalek. "Makes a lot of smoke, doesn't it?" says Ace modestly.

We begin to learn that the Doctor's presence here is not merely fortuitous, nor is that of the Daleks. In fact, the Doctor is up to something. "I'm beginning to wish I'd never started all this," he says, leaving the others behind as he wanders off to contemplate the elaborate strategy he's set in motion. He arrives in a lonely late night café. As the forlorn cry of foghorns haunt the night, he chats with John (Joseph Marcell) the West Indian proprietor of the café. A bowl of sugar on the counter prompts an intriguing philosophical discussion. John reflects that his great grandfather would never have been taken into slavery "if this sugar thing had never started," and his own life would be very different. "Every great decision creates ripples," says the Doctor, meditating on the ripples he will soon be creating himself.

The moodiness of the story continues as the Doctor visits an undertaker where a very large and very creepy looking casket is waiting for collection. The undertaker's assistant is glad to get the thing off his hands, though he can't help recalling that the Doctor who left it there was "an old geezer with white hair." The Doctor, in the shape not of William Hartnell but Sylvester McCoy is now left alone with the casket. He commands it to open, and an eerie glow and dry ice fog lurks inside, shrouding something very intriguing. We will gradually learn that the coffin contains the Hand of Omega, a dangerously powerful piece of Time Lord technology.

Yes, it's a McGuffin, but it's more interesting and more sparingly used than the majority of them. It also provides a nice scene when the Doctor walks out of the undertakers accompanied by the grim, scarred, metal casket, which floats along behind him, following like an obedient pet. The Doctor seems mysterious and powerful now—verging on the awesome—which is the way he always should have been.

What better place for a coffin than a cemetery? So the Doctor escorts the floating casket to a churchyard and a newly dug grave which he has ordered. "Your pall bearers are very quiet," says the blind vicar who is conducting the burial service. "Silent as ghosts, really."

Ace is temporarily cooling her heels in the rooming house run by Mike's mother. When Mike is summoned by the Group Captain, he is given specific instructions that Ace should stay put. "Back at six," he tells her as he leaves. "Have dinner ready." "Toerag," is Ace's post feminist response.

This awareness of culture clash, the contrast of attitudes from different periods, is one of the gratifying aspects of "Remembrance of the Daleks." Ben Aaronovitch's writing also deftly showcases political and racial issues. The Daleks' genocidal policy of racial supremacy is neatly paralleled with the behaviour of a group of 1963 British fascists led by Ratcliffe (George Sewell) who is working for the aliens. Ratcliffe laments that he fought on the wrong side in the last war. His half-seen Dalek boss advises him that he'll be fighting on the right side in this war.

Ratcliffe may be a bad guy, but he is a well realised and well rounded character. He has a coherent and plausible point of view, saying that people require a firm hand, and that they are more comfortable under a strong leader. Just then a burst of Dalek gunfire alerts him to the fact that his Dalek masters are rather *too* firm and strong.

The racial theme is picked up again at the boarding house where Ace discovers a hand-lettered sign on the window that reads "No Coloureds." The expression on her face says it all, but just in case it doesn't, she announces to Mike's mother that she is going out "for a breath of fresh air."

"Remembrance" is a complex story—we gradually realise that there are two competing Dalek factions (neatly colour coded as white and grey) caught up in the Doctor's machinations. The plot is rooted in such strong characters and vivid situations that it remains clear, or at the very least compelling, throughout.

Meanwhile the Doctor has forgotten about the transmat in the cellar at Coal Hill (he's had a lot on his mind), and Daleks are pouring into the school. His omission, however, sets the stage for a great running battle between Ace and the Daleks. She has a souped-up baseball bat provided for her by the Doctor, and she uses it to great effect as a weapon. Nonetheless, she soon needs rescuing by the Doctor who has jury-rigged a Dalek-baffling device (in a delightful scene, he is as surprised as everyone else when it actually works).

Now we cut to a scene on the bridge of the Dalek mother ship in a "powered geo-stationary orbit" above the Earth. This is the first full-blown science fiction set in the story, and it is superb. Designer Martin Collins has done a marvellous job of suggesting a great deal with very little. It's a minimal, skeletal piece of design in which darkness, shadow, and empty space count as much as hardware. Long, elegant neon tubes rise upwards in graceful arcs, hinting at the huge space of the ship. (When we were shooting these scenes in the studio, no one could find the plugs to power up these neon tubes and, with the clock ticking inexorably away as it always did on *Doctor Who*, there was a danger of shooting the bridge without them. Luckily, Martin Collins stood his ground and insisted that the correct plugs be found. Finally, they were and the neon tubes were switched on for the shot.) The mother ship bridge is a terrific piece of design and, when compared to something like the cockpit of the Jagaroth ship in "City of Death," it begins to look like an out and out masterpiece.

The Daleks (which here were the work of Stuart Brisdon and his special effects team) also look impressive—the odd wobble notwithstanding. They feature some interesting variants on the standard Dalek design. One of these is Ratcliffe's unseen master, who appears to be a Davros-style hybrid (i.e., humanoid from the waist up, sitting in a Dalek shell). Another is the Emperor Dalek, which commands the mother ship bridge and possesses a giant golf ball-style head. In a clever twist, the Emperor Dalek hatches open to reveal a concealed Davros while the Davros-style Dalek spins around to reveal the sinister little girl at the controls. The latter, particularly, is a memorable moment though it's somewhat undermined when the girl stops talking in a synthesised, sinister Dalek voice and instead begins to say things like "The time controller has been disabled" in her own cultured, childish tones.

A more serious handicap is Davros himself. The mask that is supposed to make him look inhuman unfortunately looks just like a mask and is the first completely dud visual in the story.

By now "Remembrance" has built up sufficient momentum that it can survive such setbacks. We learn that the Hand of Omega is a "remote stellar manipulator" and of course, the Daleks want to obtain it. "I will transform Skaro's sun into a source of unimaginable power," shrills Davros. "We shall become all powerful." The Doctor finishes his tirade for him. "Crush the lesser races. Conquer the galaxy. Unimaginable power. Unlimited rice pudding." He is deliberately antagonising Davros, whose Dalek troops have now acquired the Hand for him. Davros activates the device.

But the Hand of Omega is a poisoned chalice, and Davros has to bail out in an escape pod (for further adventures) as the mother ship is blown up, a small side effect of the destruction of Skaro's sun and Skaro itself. The whole thing was an elaborate trap set by the Doctor.

It's a major triumph, but the story has a downbeat ending. Mike has been killed and, though he turned out to be a crypto-Fascist and a Dalek stooge, his passing is observed with an elaborate funeral service attended by all the surviving major characters. The Doctor and Ace duck out at the church door, heading for further adventures. Who can blame them? Everybody hates funerals.

"The Curse of Fenric" by Ian Briggs

"The Curse of Fenric" was first transmitted (25 October 1989) in Sylvester's third and final season as the Doctor, Season 26 of the show. The first thing that needs to be said about "The Curse of Fenric" is that, for a vampire story, it suffers from the unfair handicap of being shot entirely in daylight for its exterior scenes. The practise of occasionally wafting some smoke across the shot to suggest a menacing shroud of fog in no way compensates for the lack of night shooting. However, night shooting was a luxury we just couldn't afford on our budget.

"Fenric" is also the story of an ancient Viking curse, and the choice of setting is doubly felicitous—the North Yorkshire coast being the site of routine Viking invasions, as well as the spot where Bram Stoker's novel *Dracula* first docked in England. The first episode begins with some fairly ineffectual underwater photography of the wreck of a Viking ship's prow. (These underwater sequences will grow less effectual when we see the menacing intrusion of some monster's talons—a very obvious rubber glove.) Then we cut to the Doctor and Ace arriving at a top secret military base. The time is late in the Second World War, and the music score (by Mark Ayres) quotes wittily from some popular tunes of the day while both the Doctor and Ace are in appropriate period costume. In Ace's case, this is a minor disaster since there could hardly have been a less flattering costume chosen for such a lovely actress. Sophie Aldred also, like most of the rest of the female cast, has to contend against a brutally ugly period hairstyle.

They've hardly arrived at the base when they're surrounded by armed guards pointing their weapons at the pair. Thankfully, instead of being taken prisoner, the Doctor barks orders at the guards and slips away. This apparent homage to earlier Doctors (cf. Troughton pretending to be an inspector of military prisons in "War Games") is in fact an example of parallel evolution since neither Ian Briggs nor I had seen these earlier stories at the time. Sylvester McCoy as the seventh Doctor adds a new wrinkle to this walk-in-and-take-charge ploy by borrowing a typewriter and some stationery. He types an official letter to explain his presence and signs it simultaneously and ambidextrously—while crossing his wrists (the latter bit of ingenious comic business being added by Sylvester)—with the signatures of the prime minister and the head of the secret service. Having thus established their credentials, the Doctor and Ace plunge into an unusually rich and complex story.

Stationed at the base is a civilian academic called Dr Judson (Dinsdale Landen), a mathematician and code expert, who is using an early supercomputer called the Ultima machine in an attempt to crack the German U-boat ciphers. "They're using six rotors instead of five," exclaims Judson happily, as he presides over the whirling calculations of the Ultima machine. The Ultima was, of course, our version of the real-life Enigma machine and, as Ian Briggs puts it, "Dr Judson was a riff on Alan Turing."

"Fenric" is a script full of ambitious ideas, some of them confusingly presented on screen. The first shot of the senior officer at the base, Commander Millington (Alfred Lynch), finds him in an office full of Nazi paraphernalia. The perplexed viewer thinks we must have suddenly cut to Berlin or something; Alfie Lynch's Hitler-style moustache certainly doesn't help.

Having introduced themselves to Judson, an embittered obsessive in a wheelchair, the Doctor and Ace do some more poking around at the base and sneak into Millington's office. Now, at last we get an explanation. "A perfect replica of the German naval cipher room in Berlin," the Doctor tells us. "Commander Millington's a spy?" asks Ace, embodying the audience's confusion. No, the Doctor explains, he is merely trying to get inside the mind of the enemy. It's a nice touch, but for purposes of clarity the shot of Millington in his office would have been better *following* this explanation than preceding it. The Doctor looks at an oil painting of Hitler on the wall and says, "That dreadful man."

Meanwhile some unseen nastiness—its origins hinted at by the underwater shots—is attacking and killing members of a clandestine party of Russian troops who have landed on the beach near the base. One of the casualties drops a vital packet of papers that the Doctor and Ace later find on the beach. A visit to a nearby church, St Jude's, yields a further discovery. Some ancient Norse carvings eerily echo the Russian documents—the Viking crew was slain in the same way that the Soviet troops are being picked off. It's our first hint of the eponymous Viking curse.

Judson is studying the runes, which to him present an intriguing code-breaking puzzle. He is accompanied by Nurse Crane (Anne Reid). The combative relationship between the invalid and his nurse is deftly and sardonically evoked by Ian Briggs. It may be Crane's job to look after Judson, but she draws the line at sitting around in the damp cellar of a church and hauls him off before he's finished with the inscription. Judson curses feverishly in protest, and Nurse Crane calmly replies, "Language, Dr Judson. There's a lady present." Meaning herself.

At the end of episode one the Doctor and Ace are taken prisoner by the Russian troops, but thankfully only briefly, and the diverse strands of this fascinating story soon begin to dovetail. Commander Millington is in charge of a chemical weapons program and a secret chamber under the church is a source of a virulent, naturally occurring lethal toxin (the sort of poisoned wellspring which might well have been featured in Norse legends) that he uses as the payload in his bombs. He intends to employ these chemical weapons against the enemy—but the enemy isn't the Germans. Millington is aware that the Russians are conspiring to steal the Ultima machine, and he wants them to do exactly that. Anticipating a postwar political climate in which the Soviets are once again the enemy, the Ultima machine will be equipped with a deadly poison bomb that can be triggered by the British at will. All they have to do is send a coded message containing a certain word, and when the Russians try to decode it with their stolen machine, goodbye Kremlin. In a darkly evocative touch, the trigger word is "love." "What else?" says Millington.

In effect, the Ultima machine gambit is similar to the use of the Hand of Omega in "Remembrance of the Daleks," with the crucial difference that the Doctor isn't behind it and that, in the end, it doesn't come off.

Ace is mistaken for one of the teenage girls, like Phyllis (Joanne Bell) and Jean (Joann Kenny), who have been evacuated from bomb-torn London and rehoused in the area. Phyllis and Jean have had the misfortune to end up under the roof of the formidable spinster Miss Hardakre (Janet Henfrey who was immortalised as the scary school-teacher in the BBC production of Dennis Potter's *The Singing Detective*). She forbids the girls to go into the dangerous waters at Maidens Point. "Just because you've never been swimming!" they say to her. It's clear that swimming and water are metaphors for sexual experience, not the sort of thing one necessarily expects to find in a *Doctor Who* adventure.

"The Curse of Fenric" is a sophisticated and intelligent piece of writing, but it shows signs of being severely cut in postproduction. Despite the scripts having been timed as being, if anything, somewhat under-length, "Fenric" overran lavishly, and it had to be seriously truncated to fit its time slot of four twenty-five minute episodes. The DVD release affords viewers the luxury of seeing the story in its entirety, but the original transmission version remains a damaged work. Occasionally it is so swift in its transitions and so brief in its scenes that it drifts towards incoherence. The sequence where Phyllis and Jean abruptly plunge into the sea and suddenly transform into vampires is a good (or bad) example. Nevertheless, Ian Briggs's excellent dialogue and intriguing, well rounded characters serve to compensate.

The second major weakness of "Fenric" has already been touched upon, the necessity for daylight shooting of exteriors. The scene where the vampire girls close in on the local vicar, Mr. Wainwright (Nicholas Parsons) in the graveyard amply demonstrates why smoke can't replace night shooting in a tale of suspense. Lapses like these are nothing compared to the third and final flaw in "Fenric," the cadre of floppy rubber monsters who eventually emerge dripping from the sea, to terrorise the characters in the story while merely inviting ridicule from viewers.

The monsters are called *haemovores*, a word coined by Ian Briggs when our producer John Nathan-Turner objected to doing a script about vampires. Ian and I simply substituted haemovore for vampire in the script, and John was mollified. His original objection was that a vampire story would be too frightening. Looking at the monsters' costumes, it's clear he need not have worried.

As in "Remembrance," there is an intelligent alertness to the culture clash that time travel can create. Here Ace is admiring a baby that belongs to one of the women who works on the base, Kathleen Dudman (Cory Pulmnan), and she implies, in all innocence, that Kathleen might be an unmarried mother. A perfectly acceptable thing to be in the 1980s, but not in the 1940s, as Kathleen's reaction makes clear.

The haemovores attack the church where the Doctor and Ace are taking refuge, and Mark Ayres's music works hard to convince us that our heroes are being threatened by horrifying creatures, but the patently phoney rubber masks inspire embarrassed laughter rather than fear. Laughable or not, they are soon getting the best of Ace and menacing her with their floppy mandibles. Luckily, the Russian soldiers arrive in time to rescue her. "Try a little Cossack blood," says the dashing Captain Sorin (Tomek Bork) before dispatching the latex fiends.

Sylvester McCoy, however, is as impressive as the monsters are risible. His haggard face and expressive, intelligent eyes that hint at hidden depths make him perfect for the Doctor. In a notable scene, he looks genuinely formidable as he concentrates on creating a psychic barrier to keep the haemovores at bay. He explains later that vampires—sorry, haemovores—are phobic to religious faith and any deeply held beliefs. Hence, the efficacy of crucifixes and other religious symbols, in the right hands. Ian Briggs makes skilful use of this concept throughout "The Curse of Fenric," as in the scene where Captain Sorin drives the bloodsuckers off by brandishing a Soviet red star badge and concentrating on his faith in the Revolution. Conversely, the Reverend Mr. Wainwright fatally fails to hold the haemovores at bay when his faith proves wanting. He goes down impotently clutching his Bible.

Ace has a less ethereal approach to dealing with the vampire threat. She plants some explosives and warns the Russian troops to take cover in characteristic fashion. "Five seconds and you're yesterday's breakfast, sunbeam." Although the presence of the haemovores in broad daylight is a bad joke, they are fairly effective when pursuing our heroes down the darkened tunnel that connects the church to the base.

When they are, briefly, safe again, Ace confronts the Doctor. "You know what's going on, don't you?" she demands. "You always know. You just can't be bothered to tell anyone." "The Curse of Fenric" was the second to last story transmitted in the Sylvester McCoy era, before a seven-year absence from television screens. By this time, the Doctor is presented as a powerful, shadowy, and manipulative entity, bearing little resemblance to the marginal figure who was such a plaything of fate in some of his earlier incarnations.

Ace begins to show hidden depths, too. When the Russian Sorin is captured by British troops (a refreshing departure, for someone besides the Doctor or his companion to be taken prisoner), she offers to distract the guard. "How?" says the Doctor. "I'm not a little girl," says Ace, and she proceeds to seduce the soldier away from his post.

Finally, Fenric himself enters the story, by taking possession of one of the humans at the base. Commander Millington announces Fenric's arrival by suddenly beginning to speak in some rather effective Norse-sounding blank verse. "The dead man's ship has slipped its moorings," he says. Naturally, we think that the Commander is going to be the new incarnation of Fenric. However, in a neat piece of misdirection, it turns out to be Judson instead, no longer crippled, rising to his feet with coloured contact lenses to suggest his lost humanity. Dinsdale Landen is terrific in the role of Fenric—grinning cheerily as his servants kill Nurse Crane—and his minimal makeup serves much better than the swathes of latex on the haemovores. Similarly, the vampiric Phyllis and Jean work well with just eyes and talons to suggest their new form.

However, the motley crowd of haemovores prove to be merely a warm-up act. Not only is Fenric now with us, but rising from the ocean depths comes the Ancient One (Raymond Trickett), the big daddy of all haemovores. The Ancient One is an altogether more impressive article than his minion monsters. His face might just be a rubber mask, but it's a distinctly superior one. Ken Trew's costume design is exemplary, alien, and potentially quite scary. Unfortunately, for most of the story it's unsympathetically lit or clumsily manipulated, letting down a potentially classic *Doctor Who* creature.

We learn that the Ancient One is actually the denizen of a distant future Earth, brought back to the twentieth century by Fenric. The

Ancient One's world has been catastrophically poisoned by the pollution of earlier generations. The Doctor will ultimately make use of this fact to turn him against Fenric.

As events swirl to an apocalyptic finale, the Doctor faces a firing squad (again an inadvertent echo of "The War Games"). Haemovores menace Ace while thunder and lightning crashes (providing some effective atmosphere at last). Millington and Fenric are working together to try and deploy the arsenal of chemical weapons stockpiled at the base. There is a chilling topicality (more so now than in 1989) to the threatened atrocities of chemical weapons.

Meanwhile, in a gratifying moment, one of the Russian soldiers shoots down the crazed Commander Millington. In the face of the end of the world, the Russian and British troops are joining forces. "Fenric" is a story about elaborate games—logic games, ciphers, decoding machines, runic puzzles, chess problems, the Doctor and Fenric's master strategies—and the Russian soldier explains his new allegiance in these terms. "War—a game played by politicians. We were just pawns in the game. But the pawns are fighting together now."

The Doctor and the Ancient One are also fighting on the same side. In an attempt to avert the poisoned world of the future, the haemovore uses the toxic weaponry to put paid to Fenric—and himself.

"The Curse of Fenric" is a flawed masterpiece. As Ian Briggs has observed, the eleven-day shoot yielded enough footage to make an entire feature film, complete with elaborate effects shots and underwater photography. So it's not surprising, perhaps, that the pressure of a short budget and a tight schedule shows on screen. Some of the more ambitious elements of the script may not have reached the screen intact. Nevertheless, it remains one of the most intelligent, compelling, and deep (not to mention dark) *Doctor Who* adventures ever made.

More to the point, the special uncut edition of the story that features on the DVD release is a real gem. Suddenly, the correct pace of the material is reinstated, and this has a profound effect. Mood, character, and plot are all immeasurably deepened and strengthened. Suddenly everything *works* and the hectic cutting style imposed on the broadcast version is shown, in retrospect, to have been a disastrous mistake.

The problem is that, when confronted with too much material, John Nathan-Turner and director Nic Mallett tried to keep all of the different story strands, by paring each one down to the bare minimum. Indeed, *beyond* the bare minimum, as is made clear when you compare the broadcast episodes to the uncut version. All of the story strands are still there, all right. However, they have been so seriously cut that they become breathless and foreshortened and no longer work dramatically. With the advantage of hindsight, it's clear that what we should have done is lose some of the subplots altogether, thereby allowing more important parts of the story to remain in at their full length. That way we would have had lost some of the material, but what remained would have been fully effective. Instead, we got a sampling of everything, and none of it works.

For example, we should have ruthlessly cut the Reverend Wainwright and Miss Hardakre material. This would have allowed the rest of the story the necessary breathing space. Of course, John Nathan-Turner would never have countenanced such an action; it would have meant losing some of the guest stars, and John loved his guest stars.

In any case, the uncut version of "Fenric" is the one to watch.

"Ghost Light" by Marc Platt

First broadcast on 4 October 1989, "Ghost Light" commences very promisingly, with exterior shots of a rather spooky looking old Victorian mansion called Gabriel Chase (actually footage grabbed on location in Dorset while we were shooting "Survival"). We then cut to a scene inside the house where the maids are delivering dinner on a tray to some strange creature in the cellar. Not just dinner, but also a copy of the *Times*. Right away, it's clear that we're in for a witty and bizarre adventure.

Upstairs we see the house in more detail, and it's a splendid environment, even more promising than the exterior. It's a terrific set (designed by Nick Somerville), intricately detailed and moodily lit (by Henry Barber) and beautifully shot with an incisive and observant moving camera by the director Alan Wareing. The talent behind "Ghost Light" represents one of the finest teams ever to work on *Doctor Who*.

The Tardis appears in an upstairs room, amusingly too near the wall so that Ace and the Doctor have to edge out, as if from a badly parked car. Ace is, at last, given an attractive costume (by Ken Trew) and flattering hairstyle (courtesy of makeup designer Joan Stribling), allowing Sophie Aldred's natural beauty to shine through. It shines through a little too clearly for some the Victorian denizens of the house. "Young lady, you're hardly dressed," says Redvers Fenn-Cooper (Michael Cochrane), while the Reverend Ernest Matthews (played by John Nettleton, all muttonchop sideburns and wobbling, scandalised jowls) declares that she is a shameless wanton. Just as Ben Aaronovitch did in "Remembrance of the Daleks" and Ian Briggs in "The Curse of Fenric," Marc Platt has grasped and exploited the culture clash potential of time travel.

Redvers Fenn-Cooper is an explorer who, having braved darkest Africa, has somehow managed to get lost in the shadows of this strange rambling house. He has been driven mad by the terrible, alien things he's seen. One souvenir of these events is his snuffbox which sizzles with radiation when the Doctor points his Geiger counter at it. Indeed, Redvers himself is radioactive. The Doctor points the Geiger counter at him and it buzzes fiercely. "Damned tsetse flies," says Redvers. "He's a headcase," opines Ace. "His mind has snapped," says the Doctor, speculating that Redvers has seen something that his time and culture left him utterly unequipped to deal with.

The story that now unfolds is fast moving, witty, intriguing, and beautifully mounted. We meet Nimrod, a butler with a suspiciously Neanderthal brow. The Doctor recognises him for what he is and hands him a cave bear's tooth, a powerful totem of his people. We also encounter Reverend Matthews who has arrived from some bastion of religious ignorance to confront the owner of the house about his heretical beliefs, specifically the blasphemous theory of evolution. "You're a worse scoundrel than Darwin," he says at one point.

Like the chemical weapons in "Fenric," the preoccupation of "Ghost Light" with "the unholy theories of evolution" seems oddly keen in its enduring topicality. Reverend Matthews might personalise the forces of organised religious ignorance even now mobilised to bury scientific knowledge. He comes to an agreeably ignominious end. In the very act of denying man was ever an ape, he finds his own hands sprouting huge simian patches of hair, as he peels a banana and commences making "oop" noises.

The parameters of the story are swiftly established—radiation, evolution, madness, and sinister Victorian trappings. Sylvester McCoy proves uncommonly relaxed and confident in this bizarre milieu (maybe thanks to the solid reality of Nick Somerville's beautiful, atmospheric set). Sylvester is playful and witty, at the top of his game as the Doctor. He has a wonderful speech, courtesy of Marc Platt, about the thing he hates most. The list includes burnt toast, depressing bus

stations, unrequited love, and tyranny and cruelty. "Too right," agrees
Ace. In this story, Ace is affecting, tough, and vulnerable by turns, and
Sophie Aldred has never looked better. Marc Platt's writing is elo-
quent and clever throughout with exceptionally able dialogue, equally
comfortable in its handling of Victorian vernacular and Ace's street-
wise idiom of a century later.

The sinister Victorian aspects of the story begin to accelerate as the
creepy housekeeper Mrs Pritchard (Sylvia Sims, all dressed in black)
applies chloroform to a lace handkerchief and holds it over the face
of Reverend Matthews, that meddling religious bigot. Meanwhile the
psychotic young lady of the house, Gwendoline (Katharine Schle-
singer) is merrily playing the piano. We will eventually learn that Mrs
Pritchard and Gwendoline are actually mother and daughter, though
poignantly they no longer remember this fact. Their new role as amne-
siac, homicidal pawns was assigned to them by the master of the
house, the grandly named Josiah Samuel Smith (Ian Hogg), whom the
Doctor immediately spots as an alien interloper (after all, he knows a
thing or two about alien interloping)—a cuckoo in the nest.

Josiah blusters, "I'm as human as you are." The Doctor cheerfully
agrees.

The script is eccentric, witty, erudite, and allusive. "Let's go down
the rabbit hole," says the Doctor, noting the Alice in Wonderland
quality of the proceedings as he forces Josiah to accompany him to the
cellar where they will meet Control (the excellent Sharon Duce), a sort
of extraterrestrial Eliza Doolittle, who is hell-bent on evolving into a
proper lady (or "lady-like" as she calls it).

During my time as script editor on *Doctor Who,* I deliberately
strived to avoid the usual clichés of the show. I banned scenarios
which routinely contrived a prolonged separation of the Doctor and
the companion. Such separations allowed for lazy plotting and prevented any real interaction of the Doctor and the companion. Only
through such interaction, I reasoned, could the two establish an interesting and convincing relationship and become well rounded characters. I also tried to ban, or at least reduce the use of, McGuffins, and
"Ghost Light" is a fairly McGuffin-free story. My attempts to pro-
scribe dodgy monsters, however, proved rather less successful.

The producer John Nathan-Turner, while aware of the qualities of
the script of "Ghost Light" and alert to its offbeat brilliance, insisted
that we chuck in a couple of conventional monsters. Under protest,
Marc Platt and I did so. Hence the "husks" at the end of the first epi-

sode of "Ghost Light." These were intended to be hideous hybrids with human bodies and monsters' heads. They work to the extent that a monster in Victorian evening clothes is quite a nice idea. The heads themselves (a reptile and an insect), though nicely sculpted by Mike Tucker, remain utterly unconvincing. When the husks come shuffling towards Ace, they make for a feeble cliff-hanger and fumbling resolution at the beginning of episode two. Still, the cellar corridor set is amazingly good and beautifully lit—shadowy and menacing—and altogether deserving of a better monster. Mark Ayres's music is atmospheric and sinister, possessing some of the propulsive menace of Michael Kamen and Eric Clapton's classic score for "Edge of Darkness."

Victorian men's evening suits prove not only to be suitable for monsters. When she's ordered to change into something less revealing than her 1980s garb, Ace opts for just such a gent's suit. For a lark, Gwendoline dresses up in one, too. They both look great, especially Ace, although another opinion is that she is "dressed like a music hall trollop." This is a reference to the tradition of female Victorian entertainers dressing up like men on stage, a practise that would later provide the plot for Andrew Davies's BBC drama *Tipping the Velvet* (2002), from the novel by Sarah Waters, a modern television masterpiece directed by Geoffrey Sax, whom we'll meet in the next chapter.

Ace and Gwendoline also indulge in a number of enjoyable catfights. In the climactic one of these, Ace is now wearing a Victorian lady's dress (and very fetching she looks in it). In a wonderful moment, Gwendoline throws Ace down on a bed (prefatory to dispatching her with chloroform), and Ace's legs go up in the air in a foam of corsets, revealing that under all that Victorian lace she's still wearing her Doc Marten boots.

Night is falling at Gabriel Chase, and the Doctor is getting to the bottom of the mystery. There is a spaceship in the basement. Sleeping inside it is the ship's owner. The Doctor is determined to wake him, or it. Ace is less certain. "Maybe it should be left alone . . . just this once." The Doctor is by no means certain she's wrong. "To catch a wolf I may have unleashed a tiger," he says, as he wakes up Light (John Hallam), who appears in the form of an avenging angel. We discover that he is a kind of alien Darwin on an intergalactic *Beagle*, searching out and exhaustively cataloguing every new life form he finds. It's a mind bogglingly complex task. No sooner has he finished making his list than the life forms start changing. Or, more accurately, go on evolving. "That's life," says the Doctor sardonically.

Light approves of Nimrod because at least the Neanderthals knew when to stop evolving. He decides it would be nice if all life on Earth was similarly arrested. In other words, he's going to wipe out all life here. By the most circuitous and enjoyable route imaginable, we have arrived at an old *Doctor Who* staple, the sinister alien who is going to destroy the world. He begins by eliminating an annoying policeman, Inspector Mackenzie (superbly played by Frank Windsor), turning him into a liquid slush of his constituent molecules—literally "primordial soup." The Doctor cautions Ace not to have the soup when they sit down to dinner, and there is subsequently a tasteless but brilliant joke about Mackenzie being "the cream of Scotland Yard."

Moving from the specific to the general, Light sets about wiping out life on Earth. No more evolution, no more perpetual amendments to that unending catalogue. As he is poised to trigger the apocalypse, the Doctor distracts him with a list of mythical beasts who have escaped Light's catalogue. Soon he has him so baffled by the impossibility of escaping change that Light freezes into a catatonic trance before melting down altogether and disappearing in a burst of . . . well, you know.

Once again, as in "Remembrance of the Daleks," the Doctor has triumphed by talking the enemy into defeating himself.

"Ghost Light" has the reputation, entirely undeserved I think, for being one of the most complex (not to mention complicated) *Doctor Who* stories ever made. Some say that it can only be understood after repeated viewings. Others maintain it resists all attempts at deciphering. Fortunately, there is an equally strong consensus that it is also one of the *best Doctor Who* stories ever made.

To address the issue of the complexity of "Ghost Light" and its alleged obscurity, I have to say that I think it's a perfectly straightforward narrative. Just to hammer home the point, let me summarize the story. An alien spaceship and its crew have been travelling through the cosmos on a mission to gather specimens and record data about life forms (as I said, a kind of interplanetary version of Darwin's voyage on the *Beagle*). The commander of the ship is a being known as Light, and he is, not surprisingly, an obsessively cataloguing kind of intelligence. On each new planet he visits, he conducts an experiment. This involves using two of the crew members, beings who have the chameleon-like ability to adapt to their surroundings and mimic the local life forms. One of the creatures leaves the spaceship and evolves into an example of the dominant life form on the planet. The other crew member stays on the ship and remains in its original form. It's what is known as an experimental control (hence the name Control). The specimen that left the ship (for simplicity's sake, let's call it Josiah) returns once it has assumed its new form and is compared and contrasted with the Control, thereby providing an accurate picture of the dominant local fauna. Then the spaceship moves on to another planet. This mission has been going on for a long time. (As the Doctor says, "It's very, very old. Maybe even older.") Dissension is growing amongst the crew. There is a mutiny and, while Light is in a state of suspended animation between planets, Josiah takes over the ship and returns it to the Earth, a world for which he has conceived an affection. Back on Earth, it's the Victorian era and Josiah duly evolves into what he regards as the highest form of life—an English gentleman (of course). He moves into Gabriel Chase, killing off the man of the house and taking his place. He corrupts and subjugates the dead man's wife and daughter and generally has the run of the place. Meanwhile Light sleeps in the spaceship (in the cellar) unaware of what is happening, and Control is locked up, longing for her own chance to finally evolve into a dominant life form. This is the situation when the Doctor and Ace arrive.

What could be simpler?

The very last scene shot for "Ghost Light" was also the last scene of *Doctor Who* for a very, very long time (perhaps even longer). It was recorded on 3 August 1989, and it was the sequence in which Light puts paid to Gwendoline and Mrs. Pritchard, freezing them into a stone-like state of total immobility. There is a certain eerie poetic aptness in this being the last scene, since *Doctor Who* was itself about to be petrified into a state of suspended animation.

It would next thaw out, briefly, seven years later.

chapter 9

The Movie

While *Doctor Who* was in hibernation at the BBC, it remained a much sought after project elsewhere. Philip Segal, an English producer working at Spielberg's Amblin Productions, acquired the property in 1994. Segal was reportedly a fan of the show, in particular of the period exemplified by the writing of Terrance Dicks. However, the script that ended up being filmed was scripted by another English writer, one who already had a track record in American television, Mathew Jacobs.

Stylishly shot in Vancouver, the *Doctor Who* movie had the benefit of one of the most talented directors to ever work on the show, Geoffrey Sax. Sax is a British director whose CV also includes *White Noise*, another techno horror fantasy shot in Vancouver, although his finest work to date is probably Andrew Davies's BBC drama *Tipping the Velvet*.

Despite these advantages, the television film, simply entitled *Doctor Who*, bore little resemblance to *Doctor Who* in any form. It opens with a rather ponderous new arrangement of the classic *Doctor Who* theme by Ron Grainer reworked by John Debney (*End of Days*, *Sin City*) and John Sponsler. Nonetheless, Philip Segal is to be congratulated on his insistence on using the original music at all. Other crucial trappings of the show are firmly in place. The Tardis is a mysterious and impressive space. The Doctor behaves in some fairly Doctor-ish ways (sometimes too Doctor-ish, dispensing jelly babies as if this were a comprehensible gesture).

The tone of the movie is uncertain and sometimes ruinously comic, with a traffic jam scene that involves chickens hopping around, having been freed from a crashed vehicle, because that's the sort of thing you have in broad comedy. Chickens.

The story also doesn't benefit from a confusing voice-over at the beginning that tries to explain to us that the Doctor is transporting the ashes of his old archenemy, the Master. From what one can piece together, the Master has been killed by the Daleks on Skaro. This immediately sets up a longing that the Daleks were involved in the story, not the Master, an evil Time Lord who first appeared (in the guise of Roger Delgado) as a foil to Jon Pertwee back in 1971. The Master is, I think, a distinctly second rate *Doctor Who* villain and a sinking feeling greets the news that this is going to be a story about him.

The *Doctor Who* movie actually begins beautifully, with Sylvester McCoy portraying the Doctor in a memorable farewell appearance. The moodily lit set of the Tardis is weird and wonderful, and the photography (Glen MacPherson) and design (Richard Hudolin) are triumphantly good. It's a pleasure to see Sylvester in these sumptuous and mysterious surroundings, sitting comfortably reading *The Time Machine* by H. G. Wells, eating grapes, and listening to a torch singer on an old-fashioned record player. The record sticks on the word "time."

It's a terrific opening sequence, and it's reprised at the end with the Paul McGann incarnation of the Doctor in place of Sylvester. Both times, it's a very nice sequence—witty, atmospheric, and evocative. These admirable moments catch much of the spirit of *Doctor Who*, and they are evoked with a budget unmatched by anything in the entire previous history of the show.

Book-ended between these scenes is a story which, although it might have been developed into a recognisable *Doctor Who* adventure, wasn't. While Sylvester is peacefully reading, the Master's ashes commence behaving strangely in the urn where they are stored. Yes, the ashes are coming back to life. Suddenly, and quite capriciously, it seems the Master has acquired some of the attributes of Dracula. Indeed, for the length of the movie, the Master seems to be a kind of all-purpose villain who has arbitrary, strange powers that can be wheeled on without explanation. To start with, he escapes from his funeral urn in the form of a slithering morphing blob. This is intelligent use of the technology of the time, playing to the strengths of CGI, which had just developed the technology to make films like *Terminator 2*. But the Master's character and motivation seem as piecemeal and arbitrary as his strange powers, as he vanishes into the superstructure of the Tardis, like a blob of mercury fatally invading an airliner.

The Tardis makes an emergency landing in San Francisco (an attractively shot Vancouver) in 1999—still somewhat futuristic in the years when the movie was first broadcast (1996). The choice of the year is a deliberate plot point, with it being December 30 and the dawn of a new millennium imminent. The script makes some ineffectual gestures towards evoking millennial panic, but this aspect of the movie mostly just serves to give the story a very short shelf life.

The Tardis arrives in an alley in the middle of a gun battle between punks in rival Chinatown gangs. The sequence has the feel of an American cop show, but in its combination of gritty, urban crime and the arrival of a time traveller, it is also reminiscent of *The Terminator*, a movie that seems to have shaped much of the thinking here. James Cameron's film is a science fiction masterpiece, but it's not the sort of science fiction that the makers of *Doctor Who* should have been admiring. *The Terminator* is a story driven by its villain and ordinary people—even the soldier from the future is an average-Joe. Making *Doctor Who* conform to this template means the Doctor is marginalised in the story, something that had happened often enough in the past but never had he been becalmed in a setting so unlike *Doctor Who*.

The Doctor steps out of the Tardis and promptly gets gunned down by the cross fire of the Chinatown gangs. One of the young hoods, Lee (Yee Jee Tso), seems to have at least some rudimentary conscience and accompanies the Doctor in an ambulance to the hospital. In a good moment for the fans, he fills in the patient's name as John Smith (though Lee doesn't know it, this is the pseudonym the Doctor has frequently adopted in past adventures).

The film's producer, Philip Segal, is avowedly a big fan of Terrance Dick's *Horror of Fang Rock*, but the *Doctor Who* movie is actually more reminiscent of Robert Holmes's "Spearhead from Space." In "Spearhead," the Doctor had already regenerated before he is rushed into hospital but otherwise the stories run a similar course ("Two hearts," says a nurse, looking at his x-ray), with the Doctor even filching his new clothes from the physician's locker room. When Jon Pertwee did this, he ended up in some Edwardian dandy's jacket, a fact accounted for by the eccentricity of the surgeon who owned the clothes. In the movie, Paul McGann ends up dressed rather like Pertwee, and the explanation is that the hospital is having a fancy dress party to usher in the new millennium.

Meanwhile the Master, in the shape of a semi transparent blob (well rendered by the new special effects available in the mid-1990s), is slithering around like a snake. Indeed, he is beginning to look like a snake. For a fellow whose death was posited in the pre-titles voice-over, he is moving with surprising alacrity.

At the hospital, Sylvester McCoy, who has not yet regenerated into Paul McGann, is being treated for gunshot wounds. The Doctor is about to encounter his new companion, Dr. Grace Holloway (Daphne Ashbrook), a surgeon who is being summoned to perform an emergency operation on his bullet-riddled chest. This world, where a top surgeon is summoned in on her night off to operate on a John Doe gunshot wound, must be some kind of alternative dimension, though a more benign one than in "Inferno."

Grace is introduced to us inauspiciously, shedding tears in the audience at the opera and then running towards the camera in slow motion. At the hospital, she is hurried into her surgical garb and strides into the operating theatre to save the Doctor. She is observed from above by the hospital's bigwigs. Then, in what seems like a missed opportunity, the Doctor does *not* regenerate during surgery.

Instead, he is mistaken for dead and wheeled into the hospital's morgue.

Elsewhere the vagueness of the story is manifested when we see a woman in a darkened bedroom. Is it Grace? It might be. Beside her snores a man. Is he someone we saw earlier? Possibly. Finally, we get our bearings when we see the paramedic's uniform lying on the chair. It's the ambulance guy we met earlier, Bruce (Eric Roberts). The slithering, semitransparent snake which constitutes the Master has somehow been hiding in Bruce's uniform. Now it slithers out and takes possession of his body, another surprising new power of the Master's that has manifested itself with numbing arbitrariness.

He's not the only one suffering from this condition. In the hospital morgue, the Doctor suddenly smashes through a steel door, knocking it off its hinges with his bare hands. It makes for a dramatic entrance but suddenly he might as well be Superman. There seems to be a strange uncertainty about just what kind of hero the Doctor is, as he strides through the door he smashed down, now in the shape of Paul McGann, causing the morgue attendant to faint in a clumsy gag. Again, there is the fatal uncertainty of tone. Is this supposed to be a funny story, and if so how funny should it be? Soon the Doctor is letting us know that he suffers from amnesia, screaming, "Who am I?" as a thunderstorm echoes and crashes around a strangely deserted wing of the hospital.

By now the story is seriously off the rails and a long way from being anything recognisable as *Doctor Who*. Why didn't the Doctor *talk* his way out of the sealed morgue room? It might have been scarier, and funnier, and then maybe the guy fainting might have worked. But the Master turns up in shades and a leather jacket, behaving in a robotic manner, and again it seems that we're more in the world of *The Terminator* than *Doctor Who*.

Yet the Paul McGann Doctor is agreeably Doctor-ish. Grace might be shrill and undeveloped as a companion, but at least she's a real American, unlike Peri. What's more, the Tardis looks great and spooky as Lee lets himself in with the key he stole from the Doctor at the hospital. Then we find that the Master is already waiting there for him (how did he get in?). While McGann is finding his feet as the Doctor, Eric Roberts is saddled with a character who is an all-purpose, all–powerful, yet oddly anonymous villain.

The Master is paired off with the Chinatown teen hoodlum, Lee, and the Doctor with the beautiful lady surgeon Grace. However, we don't care much about any of these characters. By the time the Doctor begins dancing in the park and reminiscing about his childhood on Gallifrey, his specialness and mystery diminishing with every word, we don't even care much about him. About halfway through the story the Doctor gets his memory back and remembers the subplot. There's some guff about needing to get hold of an atomic clock for one of its components. This so bad that it's almost good, harking back to William Hartnell going off ostensibly to get some mercury when what he's really up to is wanting to meet the Daleks. There's nothing ostensible about the McGann Doctor's McGuffin. If he doesn't get hold of it, the Earth will be destroyed because the Master has been messing with the Eye of Harmony (the what?) in the Tardis's cloister room (the where?).

The Eye of Harmony is actually a sort of über-McGuffin from the Robert Holmes story "The Deadly Assassin." It has no business being in the Tardis. The cloister room previously featured in the stories "Logopolis" and "Castrovalva." But one shouldn't need to know these things. Indeed, knowing them in no way improves the shambolic plot.

The Tardis continues to look impressive throughout the story, though with its sweeping staircase it begins to feel like a sinister castle, not a vehicle. This is a problem that also cropped up when it began to feel like a hotel during the Peter Davison era, with everybody having their own bedroom on board. Like Davison, McGann is a very young Doctor. Unlike Davidson he escapes the average guy image. Despite being given weak material, McGann is convincingly the Doctor, offbeat, alien, yet likeable. Between the bouts of shouting required of him by the script (competing with the shrieking Grace), McGann handles some extremely difficult dialogue with aplomb and vividly conveys the sense of a stranger in a strange land.

Ironically, the filmmakers, having cleverly cast a Doctor who doesn't look like a conventional leading man, then insist on making him behave like one. When he gets his memory back, he kisses the beautiful Grace. Who wouldn't?

The Doctor wouldn't.

The abstract threat about the Eye of Harmony destroying the world (how? why?) continues, and the Doctor has to get hold of that vital component from the atomic clock, which is being unveiled at a millennial ceremony (of course). The Master is also after this McGuffin and has now acquired yet another unprecedented and deadeningly convenient power—the ability to slime people with some odd secretion that seems to paralyse or kill them. Or maybe it allows him to take possession of them later on, as he will do with Grace, who is spattered by some of the slime on her forearm.

The Doctor gets the component. He and Grace escape from a balcony, climbing athletically down a length of fire hose as the soundtrack music references the Indiana Jones movies. Later the Doctor uses a fire extinguisher to confound the Master (perhaps in a nod to "Inferno," or perhaps continuing the tradition of making novel use of fire fighting equipment). Then in a ridiculous scene, as those escaped chickens circulate in the background, the Doctor hijacks a traffic cop's motorcycle. Soon he is roaring around on the bike with Grace clinging to him and we're back in *The Terminator*.

There is an amusing scene where a motorcycle cop, in pursuit of the Doctor, drives into the Tardis and hastily back out again, retreating in confusion. But soon it's back to that abstract and meaningless story about the Eye of Harmony. Grace becomes possessed by the Master and looks rather striking and fetching with her unearthly black eyes. Finally, the Doctor is taken prisoner—at last, briefly, it seems like *Doctor Who*, though not great, or even good, *Doctor Who*. There is also a great deal of business about the Eye of Harmony opening or closing or something. The Master is now wearing an oriental cloak which would do credit to Marvel Comics' Doctor Strange, and he socks Grace, who is no longer possessed. She has been scrabbling around and rewiring the Tardis control panel as if this were suddenly her forte, rather than thoracic surgery. Indeed, she is operating the Tardis like an old hand. The Doctor is so incensed about the Master hitting Grace that he escapes from the contraption he has been tied up in. Literally, with one bound he is free. The Master's head begins to wobble like something out of *Jacob's Ladder.* There is a countdown to the millennial midnight, but the good guys triumph, mainly thanks to Grace's sudden skills as a Tardis mechanic. There is an interminable coda, millennium fireworks, and another kiss between Grace and the Doctor . . .

The *Doctor Who* movie possessed production values that were, at the time, the best ever for *Doctor Who*, yet the story was weak and barely comprehensible, the characters undeveloped. It was particularly ill-suited to attracting a large new audience unfamiliar with the show. The *Doctor Who* television movie failed in the American market and, in 1997, the rights reverted to the BBC.

Eight years later, *Doctor Who* was back on screen.

chapter 10

Resurrection

In late February 2005, the *Guardian* journalist Gareth MacLean was interviewing Russell T. Davies. Davies, a highly regarded television writer and producer was cursing as he tried to operate the VCR in his west London hotel room. In the event, the VCR failed to cooperate, and the two men were forced to view a tape without the benefit of synchronised sound. This event reads like a mild version of a familiar curse, because the tape consisted of the first episode of *Doctor Who* to be made by the BBC since Sylvester McCoy bowed out in 1989.

After sixteen years in the wilderness, the show was finally back on screens as a regular series, with the full backing of the BBC (reportedly to the tune of £10 million). The man behind the comeback was Davies, one of a generation of television professionals who had grown up as devoted fans of the show. Best known for *Queer as Folk* (1999) and *The Second Coming* (2004, a religious drama whose SF, fantasy, and horror elements foreshadowed the new *Doctor Who*), Davies had quietly and politely been pressuring the BBC for years to let him take a crack at reviving the series. In 2003 Lorraine Heggessey, controller of BBC1, had unexpectedly told him to go ahead. It must have been like knocking on a door for so long that you've forgotten why you're doing so . . . and then it opens so suddenly that you fall through.

Davies himself was unsure what motivated the BBC's decision. "I don't know why it happened," he wrote in *Time Out* magazine on the eve of the show's transmission. "I still haven't asked why they decided to bring it back. I don't want to analyse it too much." Amusingly he adds, like a man crossing his fingers, "And I don't want them to analyse it too much. Let's just do it."

The new series stars Christopher Eccleston, a respected British actor with starring roles in films like Michael Winterbottom's *Jude* to his credit. He had also starred in Davies's *The Second Coming* as Steve, the new messiah. However, playing the son of God was going to seem distinctly second fiddle compared to his new role . . .

When I read that Eccleston had been cast as the Doctor, I thought it was an intriguing choice. The actor has a dour, authoritative quality, and a gaunt brooding look that could suggest the alien. When I heard that the young British pop singer Billie Piper had been chosen as the new companion, however, I immediately thought it was a master-stroke of casting. Piper was the perfect choice, so right that in retrospect she seemed inevitable. She was a coup not only because of her persona but also in terms of the rich harvest of publicity she instantly brought to the production. The late John Nathan-Turner, an accomplished manipulator of the media in his time as producer of the show, must have been smiling in *Doctor Who* heaven at the announcement.

With Eccleston and Piper in the lead roles, the new series would consist of fourteen forty-five minute episodes, including three two-part stories. Russell T. Davies was writing the bulk of the episodes as well as serving as executive producer. The producer of the series was Phil Collinson and the script editors were Elwen Rowlands and Helen Raynor.

"Rose" by Russell T. Davies

First broadcast on 26 March 2005, "Rose" begins with shots of the Earth in space, zooming in to the planet to select the British Isles, England, London, and then a close-up of a ringing alarm clock as the working day begins for Rose Tyler (Billie Piper). We're introduced to Rose and her mother Jackie (Camille Coduri) on the fly as Rose dashes off to the department store where she's employed. At a furious pace, we're presented with the store (a variation on Harrods called Henriks) and various London tourist sites as Rose plunges into her daily routine, flirting with her boyfriend Mickey Smith (Noel Clarke) on her lunch break in Trafalgar Square. They're a photogenic interracial couple in an equally photogenic, multicultural London. The London location photography is a notable strength of "Rose" (the director of photography is Ernie Vincze).

The preliminaries over, the story really begins with the end of Rose's workday as the store empties and she descends into the basement on an errand. The basement is shadowy, eerie, and populated with mannequins waiting for their big chance in the shop windows.

Anyone familiar with the history of the show might now discern the general contours what is about to happen, because "Rose" features the return of one of *Doctor Who*'s most successfully scary villains short of the Daleks. As discussed in the Jon Pertwee chapter, the Autons were the creation of Robert Holmes and first appeared in "Spearhead from Space" (1970), Pertwee's debut, and returned the following year in "The Terror of the Autons." The Autons themselves are just mindless cat's-paws, manipulated by the Nestene, a disembodied consciousness from outer space with a particular gift for animating plastic. This ability memorably manifests itself in bringing to life store window dummies that then march forth like murderous zombie hordes.

Rose's first brush with the Autons takes place in the store's basement. The scene is suspenseful and creepy, but events at the time of the first broadcast served to somewhat undermine it. As Rose made her way quietly among the blandly menacing mannequins, there was a sudden, inexplicable burst of applause on the soundtrack. Then, as the sinister dummies began to come to life, the silence was obliterated by the cheery shouts of a game show host yelling encouragement to his contestants. It was some kind of technical glitch, cutting in the wrong sound feed during the first really dramatic moment in the first new episode of *Doctor Who* to be broadcast since the 1980s.

It was enough to make older fans feel nostalgic. After all, power cuts had played havoc with the transmission of the first ever episode in 1963.

Minor technical quibbles aside, "Rose" was an immediate winner. Just as the Autons surround Rose, the Doctor arrives to rescue her. As he drags her off, she theorises that the sinister mannequins were actually "students"—the only people with the leisure and the inclination for dressing up and behaving in such a ridiculous fashion. The Doctor allows that it's a good theory, but fundamentally incorrect. He chases Rose out of the store as he plants an explosive device to blow the place sky high.

As she flees, Rose passes the Tardis stationed discretely on a darkened street. She looks back and sees flames lick from the windows of the exploding store. End of Auton threat. At least, that's the Doctor's theory . . .

Of course, it's not that simple. The next day Rose is twiddling her thumbs at home—no job now that the Doctor has blown up her place of employment—when the mysterious stranger turns up again. In a great comic moment, Rose discovers him peering in through the cat flap. The Doctor is tracking down a rogue Auton mannequin limb, which is soon menacing Rose and himself. The Doctor and Rose battle with the murderous plastic arm while Rose's mother sits under a howling hairdryer, oblivious. This threat pales in significance compared with the burgeoning chemistry between Rose and the Doctor.

The humorously written and well-observed urban reality of Rose's life, her mother, her boyfriend, her council estate (i.e., housing project) flat all honourably recall Rona Munro's script, "Survival," for the Sylvester McCoy Doctor. The earlier script filled out the background of the companion Ace, another young female streetwise Londoner, in a similarly authentic urban milieu evoked with an agreeable blend of gritty authenticity and humour.

Here the bewildered Rose insists that the Doctor has to tell her what is going on. "No, I don't," is the characteristic response of this dark, witty, imposing new Doctor. Although still finding his feet in this most elusive and demanding of roles, Christopher Eccleston makes a strong impression in his first outing as the Doctor.

This made it all the more regrettable that, mere days after the broadcast of this opening episode, Eccleston announced he was leaving the show. He would not be returning for a second season.

This departure was so abrupt, and followed so close on his debut, that it put one in mind of the old Marx Brothers' song, "Hello, I Must be Going."

Back in the first episode, though, Rose is fully focused on the Doctor and insistent on finding out what his story is. Even his blunt insistence that she forget about him and his mysterious abrupt disappearance in the Tardis are not enough to discourage her. In her attempts to track down and identify this mysterious stranger, Rose has a new resource, one unavailable to any companion in any previous adventure—the Internet.

She googles the Doctor and his blue police box and ends up in contact with conspiracy theorist Clive (Mark Benton). Clive fills her in on what little he knows about this enigmatic figure who has cropped up throughout history at crucial junctures. (Clive's theory to account for the Doctor's longevity is that it's a role handed down from father to son—like Lee Falk's apparently immortal comic strip crime fighter *The Phantom*). Unfortunately, the evidence on offer is a notably unconvincing photograph of Eccleston supposedly standing in the crowd on the day of JFK's assassination. Quibbles about photo-doctoring (or Doctoring) aside, this sequence is another typically well written piece by Davies, blending character, humour, and plot, with Rose's boyfriend Mickey waiting fretfully for Rose outside in the car, in case Clive—the Internet nut—turns out to be some kind of axe murderer. As a matter of fact, Clive is an ideal suburban father with a pretty wife. In a nice moment, the wife Caroline (Elli Garnett) registers surprise that Clive's visitor (and presumably fellow conspiracy theorist) is a woman. This is a witty touch, echoing the fact that the *Doctor Who* fan base is predominantly male.

Waiting outside in the car, it turns out that it's Mickey who is in jeopardy. He is drawn from his vehicle by the odd movements of a plastic garbage can. Mickey thinks there's a child inside the can, but of course it's possessed by the Autons and, in one of the best special effects in the episode, the black plastic morphs and attacks Mickey, sticking to him like the tar to Brer Rabbit. After the garbage can swallows him, it belches loudly, its lid flapping.

Using the captive Mickey as a template, the Autons fashion a walking, talking, plastic simulacrum of him and leave it in his place. It speaks volumes about the inadequacy of their relationship that Rose doesn't notice the switch until much later. In a hilarious scene in a restaurant, the synthetic Mickey sits across the table from Rose and gets his voice stuck in a kind of tape loop of insincere endearments—"sugar, baby, sweetheart." Once again Davies's writing resonates with the real world, and the plastic Mickey, spouting mendacious blandishments, could be read as a symbol for any number of low rent lotharios taking advantage of vulnerable women.

Luckily, the Doctor turns up in time to expose Mickey, who tears the restaurant apart in a chaotic fight scene that involves the plastic Mickey's head being ripped from his shoulders. (When this happens, in another typical Davies touch, it is a *man* among the restaurant diners who screams at the gruesome sight.) Rose and the Doctor sensibly flee, and this time they flee into the Tardis, where we share Rose's awe at her first glimpse of the new interior of this time ship.

One of the few strengths of the Paul McGann *Doctor Who* movie was the Tardis interior. The environment there was huge and detailed, but it ended up falling into the trap of making the Tardis seem less of a vehicle and more of a place—an exotic hotel interior. The new BBC Tardis avoids this pitfall and easily outclasses all earlier versions of the interior. An exemplary piece of work by production designer Edward Thomas, it's vast (a domed structure twenty-one feet high) and looks alien and almost organic, with something of the radial symmetry of a jellyfish. Indeed, in the *Radio Times*, Edward Thomas stated, "Coral came to mind, and glass, and superior technology. Natural organic things." The set decorator who worked with Thomas on the Tardis interior was Peter Walpole, who has also worked on the second Star Wars trilogy.

Rose's first reaction to the awesome sight is, of course, the classic observation that its larger on the inside than the outside, but this is followed up by some refreshingly intelligent leaps of logic. Based on what she's seen, she concludes that the Tardis must be an example of alien technology and therefore the Doctor, too, must be alien. He looks at her and, in a touching and amusing moment, asks her if that's all right with her.

The Doctor also reassures Rose that they are safe from the plastic Mickey here in the Tardis. He tells her that there's no way the Auton could get through the Tardis door; in fact, all the hordes of Genghis Khan couldn't break in. They've tried.

Still obsessing on the Doctor's alien nature, Rose wants to know if he comes from another planet, why does he have an accent that hails from the north (of England; Eccleston grew up in Salford). In a much-quoted line, Davies has him tell the Anglo centric Rose that Earth isn't the only planet with a north. On the other hand, he could have just left the whole thing a mystery (after all, Sylvester McCoy had a Scottish burr).

The judicious and striking use of London locations continues with the Tardis appearing on the nocturnal Embankment beside the river Thames in central London. This occasions another memorable and witty moment where the Doctor tells Rose that the Nestene consciousness needs to send out a transmission to remotely control the Autons who, like plastic Mickey, who are shambling around the city.

In fact, he concludes, it must be using some kind of gigantic circular metal structure as a transmitter. The Doctor tells us all this as he stands there on the riverbank with the gigantic circular metal structure of the London Eye haloing his head.

It's a fantastic shot and a great gag. The splendid night shooting continues as the Doctor and Rose race to the south bank across Westminster Bridge (Rose having finally convinced the Doctor to look over his shoulder) with double-decker London night buses sweeping past them. Meanwhile, Murray Gold's music kicks in with some atmospheric vocal effects.

We are now sweeping to the climax of the story. Full-blown Auton attacks will soon be erupting around London in the grand Robert Holmes tradition with mannequins coming to life and bursting out of shop windows and shooting at innocent passers-by with the integral guns in their forearms which are revealed by their hinging plastic hands.

First, we discover, in its sinister underground lair beneath the London Eye, the Nestene consciousness. The Nestene turns out to be another highly effective piece of computer-generated visual effects, a giant seething vat of what looks like molten steel, a mass of flaring red and orange flame. It has noble antecedents in other writhing alien blobs in films like *Quatermass II* or *X the Unknown*—a far cry from the first Nestene blob, the thing in a fish tank that Jon Pertwee wrestled with (although that blob too, in its own modest way, was a convincing piece of special effects magic).

The living, human original of Mickey is safe and sound here in the Nestene lair, cowering, as he will continue to do figuratively and literally for the rest of the story. For all Rose's stated concern for her missing boyfriend there is a lack of warmth between the couple that will give logic to Rose's decision to ultimately leave Mickey and go journeying with the Doctor. Mickey is not a tremendously appealing figure, relegated with characteristic Davies irony to the role usually reserved for terrified helpless females in earlier *Doctor Who* stories.

The Doctor too is passive—too passive—in the climactic scenes, witty but ineffectual. He tries talking with the Nestene, although he's also brought along a kind of chemical weapon, should negotiation fail. The Doctor announces that he is negotiating under the auspices of something groovily called the Shadow Proclamation. The Nestene isn't having any of it and mannequins seize the Doctor. At this moment of supreme tension, Davies characteristically modulates into the comic and domestic, with Rose's mother calling her on her cell phone.

Rose's mother has the misfortune to be shopping in a mall that is one of the scenes of the mannequins coming murderously to life. Davies has the savvy to include, among the innocent passers-by, some characters we have met and in whom we're emotionally invested. Chief among these is Rose's mother, but also included is the Internet conspiracy theorist Clive, his wife and their son. Clive suffers the traditional fate of the sympathetic minor character in television who isn't required to turn up again in future episodes. He becomes cannon- or Auton-fodder, gunned down by the zombie mannequins.

Rose's mother, a more major character who will be turning up throughout the series, merely suffers a lot of threat and menace. Across town, the Doctor and Rose are contending with some threat and menace of their own. The Doctor is pinioned by the Autons, and it is left to Rose to save the day. The Doctor is rather too helpless in his first new adventure, but Rose is allowed a strong introduction as the new companion. She swings on a chain like Errol Flynn, knocks the Autons over, and rescues the Doctor. There's a great moment when the Doctor observes, with a note of delight in his voice, that they're really in trouble now. Basically the Doctor and Rose triumph over the Nestene and its Auton foot soldiers, while Mickey cowers some more, clinging to Rose.

It's not surprising that she opts to go with the Doctor, running in slow motion, into the Tardis to join him. She's smiling. It's a great smile and augurs well for the future of the show.

*   *   *

When we were making "Ghost Light," the last of the Sylvester McCoy stories, we concluded two things. Firstly, historical stories are the best and most foolproof kind of dramas to be presented as *Doctor Who*. While you might be blessed with a designer of the stamp of, say, Raymond Cusick or Geoff Powell, who could handle alien or futuristic settings with imagination and flair, there was always the danger that you might instead get someone who looked on such material with incomprehension (or contempt) and provided work that was clichéd or ludicrous. The same was true of costumes and makeup.

But with stories set in genuine historical settings, ones that could be researched and recreated, the BBC production teams would inevitably come up trumps. The first lesson we learned from "Ghost Light" was that historical stories were the best bet, in design terms, for *Doctor Who*.

The Victorian era represents the second lesson *Ghost Light* taught us. Perhaps because it was a period teetering on the verge of the modern world (with Darwin and the industrial revolution already making their influence felt) but also hidebound, ancient, and exotically strange with its repressive, conservative attitudes, the Victorian era allowed for particularly striking contrasts and was therefore the ideal setting for a science fictional historical tale. (It was also the era in which science fiction, as we know it, was born.)

In short, give me a *Doctor Who* story set in Victorian times . . .

That is exactly what "The Unquiet Dead" delivers.

"The Unquiet Dead" by Mark Gatiss

First broadcast on 9 April 2005, "The Unquiet Dead" is written by Mark Gatiss, who is famous in Britain as a writer and actor in the quirky comedy ensemble *The League of Gentlemen* (kind of a darker and more gothic Monty Python), this story takes our heroes to cobbled streets draped in snow. The Doctor, having taken Rose to Earth's far future now decides to show her the recent past, steering the Tardis for Naples in 1860. He ends up in Cardiff in 1869, not bad going, all things considered.

The plot actually begins in a funeral parlour belonging to one Gabriel Sneed, a name worthy of Dickens—which, as it transpires, is highly appropriate. Sneed, played by Alan David, discovers that one of his clientele, the corpse of an old lady on show in a handsome coffin lined with purple velvet, has come to life. What's more, she's throttled the young mourner who has come to pay his respects. The undertaker's reaction is more mournful than terrified, and he merely says that they've got another one. Another what? We'll learn soon enough in this entertaining story. Sneed goes and fetches his servant girl Gwyneth (Eve Myles) and tells her that the corpses are moving around again.

The old (dead) lady, now fully ambulatory, is wandering the snow-clad streets. Sneed readies the hearse and tells Gwyneth to get ready for a spot of body-snatching.

Meanwhile, the Doctor and Rose have arrived in the Tardis. It's been a bumpy ride and they're lying on their backs laughing, like two kids having a lark. The Doctor reflects on the utter freedom of his existence, at liberty to wander time and space. He allows that it isn't a bad life. In a warm and resonant line, Rose suggests that it might be an even better life for two together instead of one on his own.

As Sneed and Gwyneth search the streets in their hearse, we learn that Gwyneth has psychic powers, which will be of invaluable help in locating their zombie. This sudden revelation, coming so quickly on the heels of the reanimated corpse, might be in danger of overloading the story with macabre detail. But it works, and such density of plot revelation is inevitable in a story that consists of one forty-five minute episode. ("Ghost Light," by contrast, had three episodes of twenty-five minutes each to develop its plot.) What's more, the subplots of Gwyneth's psychic talents and the macabre awakening of the dead will be neatly dovetailed later in the story.

The Victorian setting is engaging and attractive from the moment the episode begins, but it really starts to pay dividends when we find ourselves backstage, in the dressing room of a theatre, with Charles Dickens, beautifully played by Simon Callow. It transpires that the roving cadaver of the old woman still has some vestiges of memory in her dead brain. Specifically, she remembers that she had made a booking to see Dickens give a talk on stage, and she isn't going to miss it for the world—this one, or the next . . .

The zombie woman takes her seat in the theatre and sits, attentive and well behaved, for Dickens's initial peroration. Things begin to go awry when strange, luminous, swirling entities start pouring out of her and flying around the theatre, in a manner reminiscent of the avenging spirits at the climax of *Raiders of the Lost Ark*.

The Doctor and Rose, who is now wearing garb appropriate for a young Victorian lady, are wandering the Cardiff streets and pass the theatre just as the ectoplasm hits the fan. They hear the screaming and rush in to investigate, in time to see the theatre emptying, except for Dickens on the stage and the old, dead, lady in her seat. Even the swirling phantoms vanish, disappearing into the gas lamps that illuminate the theatre. "Gas!" says the Doctor, already beginning to piece together the situation.

Sneed the undertaker arrives with Gwyneth and retrieve the old lady. With the wraiths out of her body, she has reverted to the sort of reassuring stillness one normally associates with a corpse, and they don't have any trouble sticking her in the hearse. Rose is snooping around as they do so, and she gets chloroformed by Sneed (a notably villainous undertaker) and abducted for her trouble.

The Doctor realises what's happened and takes off in pursuit, commandeering Dickens's coach in a wonderful sequence. The Doctor orders the driver to follow the hearse. The driver asks Dickens if he wants this intruder ejected, but by now the Doctor has realised who Dickens is, and launches into a comprehensive, though somewhat mischievous, appreciation of the great man's work. He explains to Dickens that he is a huge fan, and then of course has to explain that fan means fanatic. He's full of praise, particularly for Dickens's classic ghost story, "The Signalman." Dickens responds in much the way any writer would, his hostility transforming into pleasure, and when the coach driver persists in asking whether his master wants the interloper ejected, he tells the man instead to lay on the whip and pursue that hearse.

Back at the funeral home, we're treated to some great dialogue courtesy of Mark Gattis. Sneed is bemoaning the ghostly doings that beset his business. He reminisces about doing the bishop a favour by making his nephew look presentable despite the boy being under water for two weeks, and he wonders if the bishop will return the favour by providing him with a cheap exorcism.

Then Dickens and the Doctor arrive, with the writer delightfully reversing the old cliché of "What the Dickens?" by instead invoking the name of Shakespeare. Rose wakes up from her chloroform swoon and finds herself locked in the viewing room with two corpses, both of whom are coming to life. The script, however, has already come to life, and it's fast, funny, and creepy in equal measure. As the baleful cadavers inexorably close in on her, Rose is still spunky enough to chuck a vase at them, but she's also freaking out, and who can blame her? The shambling Victorian zombies are terrifically good value, supplemented by the swirling luminous mist, CGI effects that are all the better for being simple.

The Doctor intervenes to rescue Rose, and then the story takes a breather and we're granted a moment of repose. Callow is terrific as Dickens and quite riveting. He can steal a scene just by sitting silently, listening. The script features some tiny deft touches like Gwyneth, the psychic servant, knowing the Doctor takes two sugars in his tea. Sneed explains that the dwelling where he's installed his funeral business has a reputation for ghosts. There are tales going back for decades. That's why the place was so cheap. This notion of supernatural evil with its roots in the distant past is pleasantly reminiscent of the writings of Nigel Kneale, and indeed Gattis is a knowledgeable fan of Kneale's work.

Dickens feels compelled to put the rationalist point of view. He assumes that there must be some mechanical explanation for what he's seen and begins poking around the funeral parlour in search of apparatus, while Rose and Gwyneth pair off in the larder. This latter scene is also a little gem, exploring the culture clash of nineteenth and twenty-first century girls through neat, witty dialogue. When Rose expresses astonishment that Gwyneth is being paid eight pounds a year, Gwyneth quickly agrees that it's surprising and says she would have been content with six. Rose wants to know if she went to school, and Gwyneth says, of course, she did—every Sunday. Rose soon gets onto the subject of boys, enumerating the virtues she seeks in a man, chiefly a good smile and pert buttocks. Gwyneth is suitably scandalised. This isn't just good, amusing dialogue; it's motivated by keen social observation and a lively awareness of the Victorian mentality. Gwyneth assumes that (despite her shocking talk) Rose must be a lady with many servants of her own.

The Doctor has been making progress working out what is going on. The house is sited on "the rift," a tear in the fabric of time and space. Gwyneth's psychic abilities are a crucial element in what's happening. She grew up in the rift and is intimately connected to it. He then proposes a séance.

Dickens agrees to attend the séance, with the Doctor, Sneed, Gwyneth, and Rose—but under protest. In a classic piece of dialogue, he declares that this is just the sort of fraud he strives to expose. Gattis is writing great lines and the actors love them.

As these five characters sit around the table, waiting for the spirits to arrive, it becomes clear that one of the virtues of "The Unquiet Dead" is that it's a small ensemble piece, restrained in its use of locations and even more so in its deployment of characters. Possibly the discipline of writing for the comedy series *The League of Gentlemen* has benefited Gattis in showing him how to use a small cast to telling effect. Whatever the reason, "The Unquiet Dead" is a beautifully constructed piece.

The story also benefits from some excellent special effects, as we see when the phantoms arrive—although it turns out that rather than ghosts they're aliens. Sneed thinks they're phantoms from the *other side*. The Doctor corrects him by saying that they come from the other side, all right—the other side of the universe. The aliens are called the Gelth, and they're a collective entity (played by Zoe Thorne).

The Gelth are aliens who can only enter our world by possessing dead bodies. Rose is shocked and disgusted by this notion, but the Doctor has a more philosophical view of it, amusingly comparing it to recycling. Still he acknowledges that there is a problem to be addressed here. Specifically, he needs access to the rift. The undertaker's house is built on a weak spot and, of course, the precise locus of the weak spot turns out to be downstairs, in the morgue, a dark place full of gruesome undertaker's tools. The Doctor, surveying the place, makes a nice wisecrack about *Bleak House*.

Gwyneth opens a portal for the Gelth—who by now are presented as benign and in need of help—and they abruptly pour through with dismaying force. The Doctor observes that things are beginning to get out of hand, in a nice bit of understatement. The next thing you know

these sinister gaseous beings (if nothing else, this story offers a collo-
quium on how to pronounce the word gaseous) are bringing back to
life every cadaver in sight, including the just-killed Sneed. There are
suddenly Victorian zombies everywhere (ah, so that was why it took
place in the *morgue*). The Doctor and Rose are trapped (though at
least they're trapped together) behind a barred door while Charles
Dickens runs around the house, saving the day, helpfully explicating
to a modern audience what he's doing with the gas lamps—turning up
the gas while turning off the flames.

Ultimately, it is Gwyneth who is the key to putting paid to the
Gelth predations. She sacrifices herself by psychically holding the
alien invaders at bay while the others flee to safety and the house fills
with gas. Then she strikes the match that will destroy the Gelth—and
herself.

The house goes up in an abbreviated but satisfying display of pyrotechnics. The villains are thwarted. Rose, the Doctor, and Dickens survive, thanks to Gwyneth. As Rose observes, a servant girl has saved
the world, and no one will even know of her sacrifice.

If I wanted to be ruthless about this story, I could easily make the
argument that the Doctor is marginalised at the end, leaving all conse-
quential action to other hands . . . and not even to the hands of the
companion. I don't mean in the scenes where Dickens gets the bright
idea about the gas. The Dickens character is great, and if you're going
to go to the trouble of having Charles Dickens in your story, you
damned well better let him have a significant effect on the drama. In
addition, his inspiration to use gas to defeat the Gelth arises naturally
out of the kind of lively, resourceful, rational mind we've seen at work
throughout the story.

Yet after this, having awarded the major portion of the denouement
to Dickens, the rest is given not to the Doctor but to Gwyneth.
There's nothing wrong with her being left to nobly sacrifice herself
for mankind (she could have done with a touch more fleshing out first,
but the dialogue scenes with Rose were pretty damned good). The
problem is that the Doctor doesn't even strike the match to ignite the
gas.

One can see why. If he'd struck the match, he would have been directly responsible for Gwyneth's death. So I suspect that somewhere
in the process of script development, it was decided to let Gwyneth
light the match and ignite her own immolation. Yet there's dialogue at
the end about Gwyneth already being dead before the explosion but

remaining alive because she's a kind of zombie conduit to the Gelth. This seems suspiciously like a get-out clause included to exonerate the Doctor in an earlier draft where he *did* strike the match.

These are minor quibbles. "The Unquiet Dead" is classic *Doctor Who*, beautifully written by Mark Gattis and expertly directed by Euros Lyn.

If the new *Doctor Who* is going to sell in the USA, it won't be because it's a fast-paced science fiction/fantasy adventure with good-looking young stars and some amusing wise cracks. They already have a surfeit of shows just like that. If the Americans go for *Doctor Who*, I suspect it will be on the basis of episodes like "The Unquiet Dead." If anything appeals to American audiences about the show, it will be its uniquely English eccentric nature. After all, distinctive English nuttiness is what set *The Avengers* above any number of other polished action-adventure series of the 1960s and enabled it to actually get a network slot on American television, an almost unprecedented feat.

"The Long Game" by Russell T. Davies

First broadcast on 7 May 2005, Russell T. Davies's "The Long Game" opens with another playful scene presenting the sense of wonder inherent in travelling in the Tardis. The novice now, though, is no longer Rose but supplementary companion Adam (Bruno Langley) who came on board at the end of the last episode. The Doctor cues Rose about where they have arrived, on a space station in the year (more or less) AD 200,000. The technology on hand, however, looks more like the near future instead of the unimaginable horizon of hundreds of thousands of years hence, and nothing in the episode alters this view. Despite the advanced science we see, there isn't anything to suggest that we're much more than, say, a century away.

This is in sharp contrast to another Davies episode "The End of the World" where the sense of the far future is perfectly evoked, with another space station orbiting around the Earth to observe the planet's final destruction, as it is swallowed by the fiery wash of an expanding sun. The feel of that episode was agreeably reminiscent of science fiction like Michael Moorcock's *Dancers at the End of Time* or indeed Douglas Adams's *Restaurant at the End of the Universe*. It also had the spirit, though not the detail, of Jack Vance's *Dying Earth* fantasy stories, with the ageing sun shining its last rays on a decadent world.

In the "Long Game," though, there is the feeling that the Doctor might have got his dates wrong, as is his wont. When you consider the leap in science and technology from the late nineteenth to the late twentieth century (from steam locomotives and the telegraph to the space shuttle and the Internet), it seems reasonable to imagine that space stations, interstellar travel, and microchips in people's brains could be artefacts of the twenty-second or twenty-third century. Even when we see in this episode a stream of information being beamed directly into someone's brain through a gaping hole in their forehead, such development seems pretty much just around the corner, a mere step beyond the mobile phone.

This minor caveat is just a prelude to saying that "The Long Game," directed by Brian Gant, is one of the best and most enjoyable episodes of the new series. The space station where the Doctor, Rose, and Bruno have arrived turns out to be a giant news gathering and broadcasting system, transmitting 600 channels. It's called Satellite 5, possibly in homage to Britain's Channel Five, which began life as a tabloid station subject to much satire and ridicule before becoming a classier act. The space station sets are good (not surprising since Edward Thomas is the production designer), and the lighting and use of colour are excellent (the director of photography is Ernie Vincze and the colourist is Kai van Beers). Murray Gold's music is also notably good.

There's a nice scene early in the episode when the apparently dormant space station suddenly bursts to life, becoming a hive of activity as lunch hour dawns for the workers on board. The Doctor is busy poking around, and he's given some good quirky dialogue, as we've come to expect from Davies. Rose is as fine as ever, and Bruno Langley is improving by leaps and bounds.

It doesn't take us long to identify the villain of the piece, a sinister senior corporation figure simply called the Editor (Simon Pegg) who keeps the Doctor and the other new arrivals under close observation as they fall in with Cathica (Christine Adams) who explains about promotion in this media hive. It seems that everyone aspires to get promoted to the 500th floor, but once there no one ever returns. Much to her chagrin, Cathica is not among the chosen few and instead her subordinate Suki (Anna Maxwell-Martin) is invited up to 500, ostensibly for promotion but actually because she has caught the Editor's attention . . . he senses a subversive personality.

Floor 500, when we arrive there with Suki, turns out to be agreeably strange. There's snow on the floor and some well wrought ice forms—no steam on Suki's breath, though—and the frozen corpse that turns up, the first of a batch of skeletons, is somehow not very scary. Confronted by the Editor, Suki is revealed to be a terrorist, a member of the Freedom Foundation. She aims a gun at the Editor and demands to know who controls Satellite 5. She also accuses him of lying to "the people" and says that the entire system is corrupt. Luckily, before she can go on in this vein, the Editor directs her towards the ceiling where some unseen *thing* lurks. Suki then delivers such a good, terrified, *Doctor Who* scream that one might have considered her for a companion—if she wasn't about to shuffle off this mortal coil.

Elsewhere there's more story unfolding with the Doctor offscreen. The presence of Adam provides the possibility for a bit of companion separation, along with the sort of proliferation of subplot we're familiar with from vintage *Doctor Who* adventures. However, the story strand featuring Adam gradually turns out to be a real asset, much the best thing in this exceptional episode. One of the real strengths in Russell T. Davies's writing is his sense of an earthy, warm, and often comic domestic reality. In his *Doctor Who* scripts, this provides a tremendously effective contrast to the aliens, time travel, and general science fiction mayhem. Rose's mother is a prime example, and Davies's notion of providing Rose with a mobile phone (especially doctored by the Doctor) so Rose can ring her from anywhere in time or space is a clever and useful detail.

In "The Long Game," Rose generously lends the phone to Adam and thereby sets in motion his subplot. Adam tries his parents' house back in twenty-first century England, but gets the answer phone. The sound of his voice on the machine summons the family dog in through the dog flap, to sit worshipfully wagging its tail, and listening as Adam's message records. He then hangs up and turns to more serious matters.

Being a computer expert, Adam is taking a natural interest in the computers on Satellite 5. He interrogates a screen and gets a potted history of technological developments since the twenty-first century. Then he hits on the notion of making notes on these advances and innovations by ringing his parents answer phone and relaying what he sees on the screen. It's immediately apparent that he's doing this less

in a spirit of altruistic learning than as a potential cash-in. He's like a
man who's learned the names of next year's sweepstakes winners.

This is already a nice idea, but it develops some interesting complications when Adam discovers that the screen keeps crashing. He goes
in search of technical support and finds himself talking to the Nurse
(played by Tamsin Grieg who, like Simon Pegg, is well known in Britain for her work in offbeat sitcoms such as *Black Books*). The reason
a Nurse is talking to him about hardware problems is that in this particular future people have chips installed in their brain that allow them
to interface directly with computers. What's more, the Doctor has
thoughtfully provided Adam with some spending money to keep him
out of mischief. It transpires that it's enough money to pay for the
installation of the chip and get Adam really deep into mischief.

Although we've already been introduced to the main plot of this
episode, about a huge sinister alien who has taken control of Satellite
5 and is subverting it to its own ends, killing people along the way,
our interest in this is swiftly subordinated to the story of the chip in
Adam's head. We share the inordinate suspense of whether or not he
should have his brain operated on because, strangely, it's a kind of
down-to-earth story that we can feel empathy with. As he sits ner-
vously in a chair waiting for the operation it reminds us of being at the
dentist.

Elsewhere, the Doctor is determined to find out what's going on
on Floor 500, and this involves messing around with the wiring in the
walls of the space station. In this scene, Eccleston really seems to be
hitting his stride. Holding a fistful of cables he's accidentally sliced
apart, he comes across pleasantly like Tom Baker—competent and in-
competent in often equal measure, otherworldly and charming.

Ever since they've arrived on the space station Rose has been complaining about how uncomfortably warm it is, and as the Doctor studies the plans of the cooling system he concludes that it's only the lower
levels of the station that are hot. Floor 500 is freezing cold, and that's
a plot point.

By now the Nurse has completed the (swift and painless) operation
on Adam's head, and she proudly demonstrates the results. He can
open a circular hole in his forehead at will. When Adam sees this aperture sprout above his eyes he, quite naturally, pukes with shock—only
to find a small, neat cube of ice in his mouth. The Nurse chirps about
a special offer and explains that she's thrown in some nano termites

that freeze vomit as it comes up. She takes the vomit cube from him and puts it, tinkling, into a metal bowl.

These small, colourful details are a delight and are considerably more engrossing than the main plot. They also cause the audience to warm to Adam. We can sympathise with this character's plight.

The Doctor and Rose get to Floor 500 where they meet the Editor and find that Suki is still working, despite being dead—zombie style. The Doctor observes that they've all got chips in their heads, and the chips keep them going after life has departed. This explanatory speech highlights what has been perhaps the most appealing aspect of the Doctor's character, for over forty years. In scary situations, he is the one who knows what is going on and (more often than not) knows what to do about it. He is our guide through the darkness.

Now we get to meet the monster on the ceiling, the Mighty Jagrafess of the Holy Hadrojassic Maxarodenfoe, the sort of name that makes one grateful for the cut and paste function. Or, as the Editor understandably prefers to call him, Max. Maxarodenfoe is an extended blob stuck to about half a hectare of ceiling, with some hardly noticeable eyes back in the shadows and, much more noticeably, a mouthful of very sharp fangs. It's the sort of monster that would never have been reliably achievable before the days of CGI. The effects work here is skilful and we accept Maxarodenfoe, all spiky teeth and slimy skin.

The Doctor inspects the giant creature, ponders its immense life span, and concludes that its metabolism is generating all the excess heat they've experienced. Satellite 5 is a life support system devoted to looking after you know who.

The design in this episode is well realized and of a high standard. When Cathica gets into an elevator and opens a keypad, this piece of machinery is suitably grubby and worn, just like a real piece of technology. It's just a small touch, but it shows that the lessons of *Blade Runner* (where Harrison Ford calls Sean Young on a public video phone with a screen streaked with graffiti) have been absorbed and assimilated into the mainstream.

While the Doctor and Rose have been taken prisoner by the Editor and Max, Adam is busy with his own subplot. He is using the brand new hole in his head as a high-speed link to the computers on the space station, simultaneously using the doctored mobile phone to relay this priceless information to his parents' answering machine. In their suburban sitting room, the phone starts to glow with an unearthly blue aura and the dog starts to bark excitedly. It's now clear why the dog is there. It would be a pretty dull scene with just the empty room and the unattended phone. In these small details, we begin to discern Davies's genius with scripts.

With Adam thus occupied and Rose and the Doctor held captive, it is left to a guest character, Cathica, to save the day. She arrives on Floor 500 while the Editor is interrogating the Doctor and Rose. He is getting nowhere with this questioning, but in a nice plot twist he eavesdrops on the communications link to Adam's brain, thereby sucking up all the information he wants. He learns that the Doctor is a Time Lord, and he learns about the Tardis. The Editor decides that the Tardis is a device he'd like to have for his own purposes. The Doctor refuses to help, saying he'll die instead.

This doesn't bother the Editor. He doesn't need the Doctor. He's got the Tardis key, lifted from Adam's pocket . . .

Cathica saves the day. She has her own reasons for wanting to put paid to the Editor and Maxarodenfoe. She resents her lack of promotion, and she doesn't hesitate to tell them so, as she uses her own brain chip to blow the whistle on the conspiracy. Maxarodenfoe begins to overheat and the Editor, realising the game is up, makes a dash for freedom. The zombie Suki still retains a vestige of free will and she seizes his ankle, tripping him up and keeping him there just long enough to be wiped out in the explosion of Maxarodenfoe's huge carcass.

With the main plot out of the way, we're left with Adam's subplot to wrap up. The Doctor is admirably grim as he takes Adam to task for the grief he's caused, and there's a neat shot as they step into the Tardis on Satellite 5, and straight into Adam's parents' suburban living room. The Doctor knows exactly what Adam has been up to with the answer phone. He says that this futuristic information could have caused catastrophic change in the world. He blows up the phone by a judicious application of his sonic screwdriver, wiping out the taped message forever.

Adam is contrite, then verging on desperation as he realises that the Doctor intends to take Rose into the Tardis and go, abandoning Adam to his mundane earthbound existence. Before they leave, the Doctor and Rose have a bit of fun at Adam's expense. The hole in his forehead opens and closes at a specific signal, and the default is the snapping of your fingers. They take turns mischievously snapping their fingers and watching the ghoulish aperture open and close and then, having mocked Adam enough, they leave.

The Tardis is just disappearing as Adam's mum returns home, coming in through the front door. Again it's a marvellous juxtaposition of the utterly alien and the comfortingly mundane. Adam's mum (Judy Holt) hurries in as the familiar Jurassic bellowing of the Tardis peaks and fades, asking what the noise was.

Then she enters the sitting room and finds her son Adam unexpectedly returned (from America, she thinks). She is delighted to see him, and reflects on how quickly time goes by.

To emphasise her point, she snaps her fingers.

The final shot of her stunned expression is priceless.

"The Long Game" is a top episode. The Doctor is ineffectual and it's left to a minor character to save the world, while the subsidiary companion is tied up in a separate strand of narrative. That just doesn't matter. The central plot of "The Long Game" is almost an excuse for the delightful incidentals. These incidentals, including Adam's story, are so good that they make the episode a minor classic.

"The Empty Child" by Stephen Moffat

In some interesting ways, the new series of "Doctor Who" seems to be a return to very roots of the show. For example, in the early Hartnell era the stories themselves didn't have titles, only the individual episodes. Similarly, the two-part stories in the latest season come with individual episode designations but no overall title. Stephen Moffat's two-parter (which began transmission on 21 May 2005) was called "The Empty Child" and "The Doctor Dances." For convenience sake, we'll stick with "The Empty Child" in referring to both episodes. Oddly, it is only the second story in *Doctor Who*'s long history to explore World War II as a period setting (the first was Ian Briggs's "The Curse of Fenric").

The story begins perhaps rather too breathlessly with a chase through space, as the Tardis pursues another alien vessel. Some comic dialogue about the colour mauve being the galactic emergency sign gets lost in the frantic action as the mystery vessel jumps through time to land on the Earth, in 1941 (although the exact period will emerge as a surprise, at least for the Doctor).

The Doctor and Rose step out of the Tardis into a nicely achieved period street. Billie Piper as Rose looks alluring with tousled hair and a Union Jack T-shirt. Moffat's skill with dialogue is immediately apparent, though the Doctor seems a little slow in working out just what the period is, given the abundance of World War II uniforms in the cellar nightclub he stumbles into.

Meanwhile Rose has wandered off. She is drawn to a little boy in a gas mask (Albert Valentine) who stands on a roof calling forlornly for his mother. The child in the gas mask is a great triple bluff. In the first shots, we think this is some kind of inhuman creature, a *Doctor Who* monster. Then we realise it's just a young human being wearing this odd mask to protect him from a much anticipated Nazi gas attack. *Then* we realise, later in the story, that it's an inhuman *Doctor Who* monster after all.

The question here, though, is why Rose seems so determined to go to the aid of the child in the gas mask, standing high above her on a roof. Although this diminutive creature will prove to have all kinds of powers, a siren-like allure is apparently not among them. Certainly, Rose seems unaccountably determined to join the child on the roof-top, just as Sylvester McCoy once mysteriously climbed out on an ice face in *Dragonfire* and ended up dangling by his umbrella.

Rose, in her turn, grabs hold of a handy rope to allow her to scale the building in pursuit of the kid. Wonderfully, the dangling rope turns out to be attached to a drifting barrage balloon that comes loose from London's air defences. Suddenly Rose finds herself floating above London at night.

She dangles there as German bombers sweep over the ravaged city. This is where computer effects really come into their own, rendering the familiar in a new and fantastic way. As the menacing bombers swoop towards her, with that English flag emblazoned on her chest, Rose gets a great line about perhaps having chosen the wrong T-shirt for the occasion.

On the ground, we see a London family scurry into their air raid shelter and then a young woman, Nancy (Florence Hoath), a street-wise opportunist, leads some hungry homeless urchins to invade the house and devour the uneaten dinner that is getting cold on the table. It's oddly reminiscent of "Goldilocks and the Three Bears" or, as the Doctor says when he sits down to join them, a kind of combination of direct Marxist action and a heart-warming musical. Nancy is prag-matically stealing food to feed the hungry.

Meanwhile Rose is still drifting high over London as the German bombs rip the city apart. St. Paul's Cathedral is painted with flames, and the Thames is a long winding black lane below (on moonlit nights the German planes would follow the moon's reflection along the river to strike at the heart of the city). Finally, Rose's grip gives out. She falls.

However, she has been spotted by a futuristic rogue called Captain Jack Harkness (John Barrowman) who is passing as an American volunteer serving as an RAF officer. He has a pair of alien binoculars with which he has zoomed in on the haplessly dangling girl. He has been cheekily admiring Rose's ass (difficult to achieve given the unflattering jeans Billie Piper has been lumbered with). Luckily, it turns out that Captain Jack has a spaceship. It is invisible, and it is tethered to Big Ben's clock tower. He uses an instrument in the spaceship, something that *Star Trek* fan Rose might understand as a kind of tractor beam, to safely catch Rose and retrieve her. (In a nice touch, he tells her to switch off her cell phone because it might interfere with the device.)

The (increasingly sinister) gas-masked kid turns up again, interrupting Nancy's gang's supper at the house. Nancy hints to the Doctor that the boy is no longer human, indeed an empty child. Nancy and the children flee, warning the Doctor not to let the empty child touch him.

In Captain Jack's invisible spaceship, a swarm of golden nanobots are repairing the damage to Rose's hands caused by clinging onto that rope for dear life, high above the war torn city. Billie Piper as Rose is as engaging as ever, seductive, vulnerable, and amusing by turns. She is given some great wisecracks in a story notable for the quality of its dialogue. Captain Jack is a seductive smoothie (indeed, that's sort of his raison d'être). Soon, in a memorable scene, he has Rose out on the wing of his spaceship high above the streets of London, and they drink champagne as the air raid continues. Next, he is playing her Glenn Miller and dancing with her, on the wing.

It's a wonderful scene though anyone who actually survived the sledgehammer slaughter of the Blitz—my mother, for instance—might take issue with the German incendiaries being presented as little more than picturesque pyrotechnics to accompany a smoochie moment. Fortunately, Nancy is soon revealing that her little brother, who is now the gas-masked creature, was killed in just such an air raid, reminding us it wasn't all Glenn Miller and champagne.

The mystery space vessel we saw at the beginning is revealed by Captain Jack to be a colossal McGuffin. It fell to Earth in London a month earlier (time travel being what it is) and is being treated as a German mystery weapon, guarded by the military while it awaits investigation (like the Martian spaceship in *Quatermass and the Pit*). It transpires that Captain Jack is a galactic conman. He has mistaken the Doctor and Rose for "time agents," the gullible marks to whom he intended to sell the mystery vessel.

The Doctor enters a desolate hospital, searching for an explanation to the gas-masked child. Here he finds beds full of zombie adults, all wearing similar gas masks. It turns out that the masks are in fact bonded to their faces, part of their flesh and bone. We meet Doctor Constantine (Richard Wilson) who, in a story marked by high calibre dialogue, gets some great lines. He tells us that he is ill and would be dying if only he could find the time. He explains to the Doctor about the rapid spread of this strange affliction—the zombies with gas mask faces—that is sweeping London. Then he succumbs to the infection himself, CGI effects causing a gas mask to sprout on his face.

Rose turns up with Captain Jack in tow to rejoin the Doctor (the separation of the Doctor and the companion in this story have thrown up such interesting plots that it hardly registers as a device). Rose has led Captain Jack to believe that she and the Doctor are indeed time agents, and has mischievously told him that the Doctor's name is Spock. Our heroes are reunited just in time for a hospital full of gas mask faced zombies to close in on them, one and all clamouring for their mothers. Despite being adults, they all have reverted to lost, abandoned children. However, their touch is deadly and they *are* closing in.

In a brilliant ruse, the Doctor stops them by ordering them to go to their rooms. And, like children, the gas-masked zombies respond. Of course, our heroes could always have resorted to Captain Jack's fifty-first century sonic blaster. In fact, that's what they'll have to do when the zombie nuisance recurs.

Meanwhile, Nancy has made the mistake of returning to the house where she and her gang stole supper. This time, again like Goldilocks, she is caught by the master of the house (Damian Samuels). He bullies Nancy and castigates her for robbing the food that he put on the table, by the sweat on his brow as he puts it. Nancy neatly turns the tables on him, exposing him and then blackmailing him as a black-market profiteer. The man is thoroughly intimidated, and Nancy has a brilliant line about how she can now *see* the sweat on his brow.

The Doctor is busy coping with the mystery of the gas mask zombies and also with the somewhat annoying presence of Captain Jack. His reaction to the interloper is rather like that of the Jon Pertwee

Doctor to the charismatic Professor Jones when he swept Jo off her
feet in "The Green Death."

We learn that Captain Jack is an ex-time agent himself with a grudge
against his former employers. The mystery vessel he used to lure the
Tardis here was, he believed, a harmless piece of space junk. A burnt
out medical vessel. Yet the Doctor is certain it's the cause of the gas
mask affliction.

Stephen Moffat's script is not merely strong on dialogue, there is
also a good solid science fiction plot here. We discover that medical
nanobots have escaped from the crashed vessel and have been blunder-
ingly attempting to do their job. They encountered the body of the
little boy in the gas mask—who was introduced to us as Nancy's
brother—and tried to repair it. They ended up creating a semi-human
revenant with gas mask blended seamlessly to its face, endlessly bleat-
ing for its mother. Having done this, the nanobots set about similarly
"repairing" the DNA of everyone else they come into contact with.
Hence, the weird plague afflicting London.

It's a neat SF plot, but it really takes on greater dramatic weight
when Nancy reveals that the little boy was not her brother but her
son, the result of a scandalous teenage pregnancy that had to be disguised at all costs. This powerful emotional twist increases the stature
of the story, and also paves the way to a happy ending.

When Nancy embraces the gas-masked boy, the golden nano med-
ics swarm around them, and using her DNA, correct their errors.
They repair the little boy properly. Suddenly the gas mask comes off
his face and he is back to life and back to normality. So are all the
other zombies. The Doctor is jubilant. For once, it's a happy ending,
a story with a virtually nonexistent body count (except for all those
unseen casualties of the war, continuing as usual in the background).
By now, Eccleston has settled into the role beautifully—witty, exul-
tant, and full of (pardon the expression) humanity.

For a grand finale, Captain Jack rides a German bomb, in the manner of Slim Pickens in *Dr. Strangelove*, though unlike Pickens he is
preventing the bomb from landing and exploding right on top of the
alien medical vessel, where everyone is standing.

Having nobly rescued everyone else, Captain Jack is now himself in
danger of getting blown up by the German bomb. He is trapped with
it on his spaceship, and (of course) it is going to explode in two minutes. Captain Jack characteristically decides to spend his last moments

casually sipping a martini. However, the Tardis arrives, and he is rescued. In fact, he is taken on board the Tardis, invited to join the party.

And it *is* like a party. Not to be outdone by Captain Jack's Glenn Miller moves, the Doctor is dancing with Rose—to the boogie-woogie.

The Tardis has never seemed so hip.

Appendix One

Recommended Viewing: A (very) short list

For someone who has never seen any *Doctor Who* but would like to dip into the highlights, the following may be a useful guide. Annotations indicate that I don't think a story is worth watching in its entirety or that a certain variant version should be favoured. Where no comments are offered, I feel the whole story is worth watching, in its standard form.

- "Unearthly Child," episode one. The rest of the story is routine caveman stuff, but the very first episode, introducing the Doctor and the Tardis, is exceptional, visionary drama.
- "The Dalek Invasion of Earth." Worth sampling rather than watching in its entirety. The first episode is worth watching for its grim Orwellian evocation of a dystopian future London and the surprise arrival of a Dalek from the Thames like some perverted Excalibur. The scenes later with the Daleks prowling the empty streets of London while Barbara helps the Resistance leader to flee in his wheelchair are also unforgettable.
- "The War Games." The first four, or maybe even five, episodes before its narrative freezes into a holding pattern.
- "Spearhead from Space." Although watchable in its entirety, largely thanks to being shot on film, this first Auton adventure does go on a bit. The special effects are also a bit ropy and then there's that annoying poacher. So perhaps a judicious use of the fast forward button is called for.
- "Inferno."
- "The Talons of Weng-Chiang."
- "The Curse of Fenric." Worth watching despite dodgy monsters. But only in the expanded special edition that is available on the

DVD release. The standard version, as transmitted, has been ru-
ined by editing that increased pace at the cost of depth, mood,
and coherence.
- "Ghost Light."
- "The Unquiet Dead."

Appendix Two
The Do-It-Yourself *Doctor Who* Plot

(for a traditional, golden age *Doctor Who* story)

- The Tardis malfunctions
(optional)
- The Tardis lands on a planet/back in history
- The Doctor and his companion/s discuss the new environment
(repeat as necessary)
- Introduce villain
- Introduce McGuffin
(optional)
(repeat as necessary)
- The Doctor and/or companion leave the Tardis
- Doctor and companion are separated
- Doctor and companion reunited
- Doctor and companion taken prisoner
(repeat above four as necessary)
- Doctor and companion/s face execution
(optional)
- Doctor and/or companion finds McGuffin
(optional)
- Doctor and/or companion loses McGuffin
(optional)
(repeat above seven as necessary)
- Doctor defeats villain
- Doctor and companion/s return to Tardis
- Tardis dematerialises
The End

Bibliography

Aldiss, Brian W., and David Wingrove. *Trillion Year Spree: The History of Science Fiction*. London: Gollancz, 1986. Invaluable and highly readable introduction to science fiction literature. Makes a strong case for Mary Shelley's *Frankenstein* being the first true science fiction novel.

Barron, Neil. *Anatomy of Wonder: Science Fiction. Critical Guide to Science Fiction Literature*. New York: Bowker, 1976. Very useful overview and reading lists.

Baxter, John. *Science Fiction in the Cinema*. London/AS Barnes, New York: Tantivy Press, 1970.

Benton, Mike. *Science Fiction Comics: the Illustrated History*. Dallas: Tayor, 1992.

Cartmel, Andrew. *Script Doctor: the Inside Story of Doctor Who 1986–89*. Surrey: Reynolds and Hearn, 2005. The current author's memoirs, based on diaries I kept at the time of working on *Doctor Who*.

Cornell, Paul, Martin Day, and Keith Topping. *The Avengers Dossier: The Definitive Unauthorised Guide*. London: Virgin, 1998.

Heitland, John. *The Man from UNCLE*. London: Titan, 1988.

Howe, David J., and Stephen James Walker. *The Television Companion: The Unofficial and Unauthorised Guide to Doctor Who*. Surrey: Telos, 2003. A definitive and exhaustive guide to the show. Invaluable.

Howe, David J., Mark Stammers, and Stephen James Walker. *Doctor Who: The Sixties*. London: Virgin, 1992.

Howe, David J., Mark Stammers, and Stephen James Walker. *Doctor Who: The Seventies*. London: Virgin, 1994.

Howe, David J., Mark Stammers, and Stephen James Walker. *Doctor Who: The Eighties*. London: Virgin, 1996.

These three volumes have the advantage of being generously illustrated throughout. They're rather less definitive and up to date, and also less wieldy, than the one-volume *Television Companion* but arguably more of an easy read.

King, Geoff, and Tanya Krzywinska. *Science Fiction Cinema*. London: Wallflower, 2000.

Nicholls, Peter. *The Encyclopedia of Science Fiction*. London: Granada, 1979.

O'Brien, Daniel. *SF: UK*. Surrey: Reynolds and Hearn, 2000.

Pickard, Roy. *Science Fiction in the Movies, an A-Z*. London: Frederick Muller, n.d.

Rigby, Jonathan. *English Gothic: A Century of Horror Cinema*. Surrey: Reynolds and Hearn, 2000.

Rogers, Dave. *The Avengers*. London: ITV Books & Michael Joseph, 1983.

Schow, David J., and Jeffrey Frentzen. *The Outer Limits: The Official Companion*. New York: Ace, 1986.

White, Matthew, and Jaffer Ali. *The Official Prisoner Companion*. London: Sidgwick & Jackson, 1988.

Wingrove, David. *Science Fiction Film Source Book*. Harlow: Longman, 1985.

Index